A FIELD GUIDE TO
FOSSILS
OF TEXAS

FIELD GUIDE SERIES
Gulf
Publishing
FIELD GUIDE SERIES

A FIELD GUIDE TO
FOSSILS

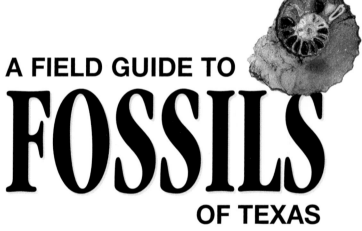

OF TEXAS
CHARLES E. FINSLEY

GULF PUBLISHING

Lanham • New York • Oxford

GULF PUBLISHING FIELD GUIDE SERIES:

A FIELD GUIDE TO
FOSSILS
OF TEXAS

Published by Gulf Publishing
An Imprint of the Rowman & Littlefield Publishing Group
4501 Forbes Blvd, Suite 200
Lanham, Maryland 20706

Distributed by National Book Network

Library of Congress Cataloging-in-Publication Data

Finsley, Charles, 1938–
    A field guide to fossils of Texas / by Charles Finsley.
        p.   cm. — (Gulf Publishing field guides)
    Previously published : 2nd ed. Houston, Tex. : Gulf Pub., c1996.
    Includes bibliographical references and index.
    ISBN 0-89123-044-0 (alk. paper)
    1. Fossils—Texas. I. Title. II. Series.
    [QE747.T4F56   1999]
    560'.9764—dc21   99-18248
                                                   CIP

Contents

Acknowledgments

I owe an initial debt of gratitude to Dr. Glen Dennis Campbell, who urged me to write a few fossil articles for his former publication, *Texas Natural History Magazine*. As a result of those writings, the field guide staff of Texas Monthly Press asked me to attempt this project, now in its second edition published by Gulf Publishing Company.

I continue to receive help and suggestions from virtually every college, university, and museum in Texas. Baylor University's Strecker Museum remains a major source of my photos and advice. Dr. Chris Durden, curator of the collections at the Texas Memorial Museum, University of Texas at Austin, made available a wealth of material, including many invertebrate-type specimens. Over many years, Dr. Joan Echols of East Texas State University has made material from her fine collections available.

Dr. Earnest Lundelius, Jr., and Dr. Wann Langston of the Balcones Vertebrate Paleontology Lab at the J. J. Pickle Campus of the University of Texas at Austin have long been mentors to many of my fossil projects. Dr. Rosalie Maddocks shared her expertise in the former edition regarding the Claibourne Eocene shell beds of southeast Texas. Southern Methodist University continues to be a close resource in Dallas. Dr. David Rohr still holds forth in Alpine, Texas, at Sul Ross University where he originally helped me get photos of Texas graptolites.

This is a book built also around the outstanding work of Texas' private collectors. The Dallas Paleontological Society, the Austin Paleo Society, and the Central Texas Paleontological Society all have members who have helped with this book. To the original help of Mr. William "Bill" Lowe and Mr. Ken Smith has been added the great field work of Mr. Gary Byrd. Gary has contributed several fish, mosasaurs, and even dinosaurs to science in the last two years. He has become the modern counterpart of the late Robert "Bob" Price, who for so many years was my eyes on new Dallas area finds. Then there is always Don and Hollis O'Neill of Pflugerville who mold a lot of the Texas amateur fossil scene. Don says he has built and parted with several entire collections.

So many good friends and contributors! These include Mr. John Moody, Sr., Mr. John Moody, Jr., Mr. Doshier, and Mr. Taylor—all of the Sherman-Denison area. I am sorry to report that between editions, Mr. C. D. Homan of Oglesby, Texas, passed away, as did Mr. Frank Crane of Dallas. Texas lost two great collectors and yet their collections still grace this book. Without access to the vast collection of Frank, Mary, and Stephen Crane, which now resides at the Dallas Museum of Natural History, this book would never have been considered.

When I put the original edition together, I wondered if anyone had great Texas crinoids. Mr. Louis Todd and Mr. Ken Craddock of Denton helped a lot with their collections, and still do. Mr. and Mrs. William Watkins, Mr. Jack H. McLellan, and Mr. Mike Murphy contributed greatly to the first edition. David Bradbury of Los Angeles was my major advisor on trilobites. Mrs. Arlene Pike, an employee and friend over the years, did much of the dirty work on the first edition. Her personal collecting has produced some new species.

A new work on shark teeth by Dr. Bruce Welton and Roger Farish has greatly sharpened our view of that field and has caused me to change a few names. Over the years, a very dedicated small group of individuals in the Paleo Section of the Houston Gem and Mineral Society has produced the finest publications possible on several groups of Texas fossils. No paleontology library is complete without their works on bivalves, brachiopods, echinoids, ammonites, and others. I am in their debt, especially to Mr. and Mrs. T. J. Akers of Spring, Texas.

Artists Doris Tischler and Kathy Roemer still have their fine artwork in the new edition, and Kathy's maps have finally made this second edition. All photos are the author's unless otherwise credited.

My own family, Rosa and Greg, again deserve credit for putting up with the years of work required for both editions.

Naturally, I take all responsibility for using these collections and sources. Any inaccuracy is my doing, as are perhaps a few good choices. In such a changing field as fossil study, one often simply does the best one can between modern study results and old tested conventions, and puts out a new edition once in a while. In such a complex and changing subject as *all* of Texas paleontology, an effort like this must grow slowly edition by edition.

Charles E. Finsley

Introduction

This book is intended for three kinds of readers: those who collect fossils and need a guide for the identification of what they find; those who are not active collectors but would like to know something about the beauty and variety of Texas fossils; and teachers and students who need a resource book on Texas fossils and geology.

No one knows how many different kinds of Texas fossils there are. This is because scientists are still debating just where to draw the line between certain similar kinds of fossils, and also because the number of Texas fossils is so large that even estimating it is difficult. All the forms of life that have occupied Texas during 600 million years of geologic history would need to be included. Roughly, the number of species of Texas fossils – from microscopic creatures to giant dinosaurs – is certainly over a half million.

Of course, that many descriptions or photos of fossils would fill several volumes. The first problem, then, was how to choose which species would be included in a guide such as this one. The decisions were made in several ways. First, every collector would quickly agree that some well-known species of fossils should be included, primarily because they are encountered so often. For that reason, the most frequently collected fossils have been included. Second, many publications (and many unpublished graduate theses and dissertations) deal with one aspect or another of Texas paleontology. Any fossil species that appeared prominently in such publications was considered a candidate for inclusion. Third, as one travels and looks at different fossil collections, a number of very unusual or beautiful specimens of less common fossils are found. Some of these have been included because of their unique qualities. In sum, the reader of this book should find here representatives of Texas's most common, most important, and most noteworthy fossil finds.

One additional goal was to find the best, biggest, or most complete fossil of each kind ever collected in Texas. As a result, many of the fossils illustrated here will serve as a standard against which individuals can judge their own collections. No doubt better specimens will exist in readers' collections than are shown here. That fact should make anyone who possesses such a specimen even more aware of its high quality.

The scope of this book is broad. I first envisioned a representative selection of common fossils from microfossils to vertebrates. Naturally, specialists in the fields involved might be disturbed by the audacity of such a project. Nevertheless, a volume that attempted less would omit some very interesting material and would be less useful to teachers and students who wished a broader survey of the field of Texas fossils. I originally decided that several hundred photographs would be used in the book, but the inclusion of several species in some of those photos made the total number of species illustrated much higher.

Certainly, the final work includes enough material that if it were the holdings of any one collector, it would be a broadly representative Texas collection. As such, it should be an inspiration for people who aspire to collect such material. At the same time, it should serve well the desire of those who are not active collectors to see what Texas contains in the way of fossil treasures. These pages survey the best of many excellent collections.

As research for the book progressed, it became obvious that some compromises had to be made if something useful were to be publishable in a reasonable period of time. I therefore decided to deemphasize microfossils and ostracodes. However, the section on fossil preparation contains some material on them, and there is still much here for someone interested in such tiny fossil forms.

A few other areas undoubtedly lack species of interest to individual collectors. Some names used here will almost certainly have been superseded by newer names among the thousands of publications about fossils. In a sense, this book is offered as a catalyst for an open discussion among fossil enthusiasts about what should have been in it. The fruits of such a discussion should make possible an eventual revision of it that will be a finer book yet.

Who would attempt to write such a book? Certainly many excellent geologists have deferred such a task over the years. The author is, and must be, a generalist, someone who has a broad interest in all fields of fossil study and who has been in a position to observe a panorama of Texas fossil material for many years. I have worked for many years with the fossil collections of the

Dallas Museum of Natural History, and I have attempted to make those collections very wide in scope, not exclusively vertebrate or invertebrate. The main goal of that museum's fossil work is to tell the story of Texas in all its aspects.

This book has also generated an opportunity for a great amount of fieldwork, which has included excavating mammoths, mosasaurs, and giant sea turtles as well as collecting crinoids, trilobites, and many Cretaceous molluscs. I have also been able to work with a great variety of other collections at the museum: mammals, birds, insects, sea shells, rocks, minerals, reptiles, and plants. All of this work has been in done in an environment that emphasizes the interconnections between the many forms of nature. I believe that this has been a unique and helpful background for embarking on the difficult task of this book. If I approach the great variety of fossil forms to be dealt with here with any confidence, it is because I can appreciate them all, even if I can not master them all.

I have taken courses in geology at the University of North Texas, Southern Methodist University, and the University of Texas at Dallas. These have been helpful, but my greatest friends and teachers have been the hundreds of so-called amateur collectors who have educated me by their frequent and wonderful finds. The impetus to write this book is to be found largely in my conviction that it is now time to draw these observations together into something that makes sense out of all the individual discoveries that are housed in so many scattered collections.

1. What Is a Fossil?

The existence of fossils, the remains or traces of ancient things, was once a new idea. As with most new ideas, there was confusion about what was going to be called a fossil. From the modern viewpoint, it might seem that the definition could have gone only one way—the way it did. But that is not the case. Originally, anything "dug up" was called a fossil. Buried historical objects and archaeological objects were then considered to be fossils.

The definition, as scientists eventually framed it, could have continued to include such materials, but it did not. Instead, we now have several sciences concerned with things that are "dug up." The one that this book deals with is paleontology—the study of the remains or traces of once-living things from the past. We favor today a very precise definition: *Fossils are the remains or traces of some part of the anatomy of once-living things that are older than our recent geological experience.* This definition is worth looking at part by part, because it can tell us much about fossils.

Fossils are called *remains or traces* because one might find either a preserved actual part of the original creature or merely a mark or trace in the rock. Both are fossils. Since one creature can leave several marks in the rock, one creature might create several fossils — a point not always realized. A dinosaur, for instance, might leave many tracks.

Some part of the anatomy is included in the definition because mere acts of nature (wave marks, sand formations, or interesting rock forms) are not considered to be fossils. Similarly, items manufactured by prehistoric peoples are excluded — they are not part of the maker's anatomy — and are considered instead to be archaeological artifacts rather than fossils.

Fossils are said to be derived from *once-living things*. It is important to note that this includes all living forms, plant or animal, simple or complex, whether very large or quite microscopic.

Everyone knows that fossils must be old; just how old is harder to say. For sake of having some standard to go by, most scientists would agree that *older than recent* times is required in a definition of a fossil. Sometimes materials that just barely fail the age test by being slightly too recent are called *subfossils*. Note that by our definition some human remains, especially from the Old World, are old enough to be considered fossils — hence, the field of archeopaleontology or paleoarcheology.

Notice that neither "turning to stone" nor any other phrase referring to change in the material is mentioned in the definition. There are many ways in which fossils are preserved, but none of them is specifically required in the definition of a fossil. The only real requirement for remains or traces of living things to become fossils is that they should simply somehow last. The number of ways fossils are preserved is as vast as all the varied functionings of nature.

Ways In Which Fossils Are Preserved

In general, either something durable about the material itself (hard parts, etc.) or something particularly protective about the environment that surrounds it (ice, tree sap, etc.) is necessary for any material to have a chance at preservation. However, soft-bodied creatures are occasionally preserved, and illustrations of several are included in this book (for example, Jellyfish, Color Photo 8).

Molds and casts are among the most common ways creatures become fossils. After the creature is covered with sediment, the entire form decays or dissolves away, leaving behind, as a hole in the sediment, a mold of its surface. Such a mold will usually have imbedded in it the creature's exterior texture; it is called an *exterior mold*. If the original buried creature was in any way hollow (a clam shell, say) then sediment might have filled the creature's interior. After the creature has dissolved away, this interior filling is called an *interior mold*. Interior molds contain only sediment; German geologists named these stone replicas of shell interiors *Steinkerne* – "stone kernels." Many Texas fossil clams and snails are known only as steinkerns.

If an exterior mold later fills with sediment, which will take on the texture of the original's exterior from the mold's inside surface, then a cast is created. Much confusion over whether a fossil is a mold or a cast can be avoided if one remembers that casts must be formed in molds.

Another very common way for fossils to be preserved involves "turning to stone." This can happen in two ways. What we normally call *petrifaction* occurs when mineral-laden groundwater seeps through porous wood or bone and leaves a mineral deposit in all the porous spaces; whether or not the original material remains for long, the structure is retained by the mineral matter that filled it. In longer periods of exposure to mineral-laden water, it very often happens that a less durable and more soluble mineral in the original creature will slowly trade places with a mineral in the surrounding oil or groundwater. Fossilization occurs by replacement of the original mineral content.

Another method of fossilization is carbonization. Plants, especially, contain a large amount of dark carbon, which can form a fossil plant as either a thin, dark stain or a mass of soft carbon coal after other less stable portions of the original plant decay. Trace fossils are yet another variation on how fossils are formed. Traces such as footprints or tail drag marks were never part of the actual creature, hence they only need protection to survive. A rapid burial by sediment is all that is required.

Sometimes the original material of a creature is preserved without any change. Frozen mammoth remains in the far north

are well-known examples. Some shells and many teeth are hard
enough simply to last unchanged for millions of years.

The Matrix In Which Fossils Are Found

Since rapid burial or covering is important to most ways of
preserving fossils, most fossils are embedded in some surrounding material. Geologists call this material *matrix.*

Such rapid burial can protect the fossil-to-be from being eaten
or scattered by predators; seal it off from damaging air, weather,
or running water; provide the minerals needed for petrifaction or
replacement; or encase it to form a mold of its shape.

In order to understand the matrix in which fossils are found,
it helps to understand types of rock in general.

There are three broad classes of rock: *igneous* rock, which has
a hot, molten history – like granite, basalt, lava, and ash falls;
sedimentary rock, which accumulates as beds of lime, mud, or
sand either underwater or by wind action; and *metamorphic*
rock, which starts out as either igneous or sedimentary rock and
is changed by heat or pressure (often deep in the earth) into a new
class of rock.

Since igneous and metamorphic rocks involve heat and pressure in their formation, they are generally not the best rocks in
which to find well-preserved fossils, although they do occasionally contain some fossils.

Sedimentary rocks, however, are the major source of fossils.
Important sedimentary rocks for fossil finding are limestone,
shale, sandstone, chert (flint), and loose sediments like gravel
and sand or cave debris.

Limestone is basically a creamy white rock, but it can have
many darker colors, depending on impurities contained in it. It
is primarily composed of the mineral calcite, often in the form
of microscopic tests (shells) of single-celled fossil creatures. Calcite is a rather soft mineral (number 3 on Moh's Scale of Hard-
ness). *Chalk* is the name often applied to especially soft
limestones that powder easily. The common test for limestone is
a drop of weak acid; even the acetic acid in vinegar will do.
Upon the touch of the acid drop, the limestone will bubble and
fizz (called *effervescence*) and give off the harmless gas carbon
dioxide. One must remember, however, that if a small amount
of calcite is present in a shale or a sandstone, it might also react

similarly. Go by overall characteristics rather than just one test. *Shale* is best identified by the fact that it is composed of very fine clay particles. Hence, it is smooth and rather soft to the touch. It generally forms thinner beds than the other sedimentary rocks. Its color can vary from light to dark; dark shales generally contain more organic material and more fossils.

Sandstone is just what the name implies, a gritty rock composed of sand-sized particles, often silica (quartz). Sandstone is seldom formed in ocean depths. Because of that, it is the most likely of the rocks to contain the fossils of land-dwelling creatures. Dinosaur hunters are particularly fond of sandstone. Ocean edges, freshwater streams, or desert dunes may represent the environment of deposition of the sandstone, or the kind of place and things that were happening when a creature died and was placed by circumstances in a sediment.

Chert or *flint* is a quartz sediment usually deposited as a lump, nodule, or vein in other sedimentary rock. Its special fossil content is often limited to microorganisms that are very difficult to remove from such hard, insoluble rock.

Loose sediments are generally the result of younger fossil-bearing deposits along streams, in cave debris, or in the muddy beds of temporary lakes. They consist of sand, gravel, rockfalls, and mud. Most of these are less than three million years old and therefore from the last geologic epoch before the present – the Pleistocene. In order to interpret the past, one must especially note the particle size involved in these sediments. The presence of large particles, as in gravel, implies a rather violent environment of deposition (a fast-running stream, for instance). The best fossil preservation will be found in quieter, less damaging circumstances of deposit. Mammoths and mastodons, horses and bison are common fossils found in the Pleistocene stream deposits of Texas.

Sedimentary rocks are usually deposited in layers, which are often called *beds* or *strata*. These originally were laid down horizontally, even though later earth movement can tip them or bend them in strange ways. Because the changes in beds of sedimentary rock from their horizontal position is good evidence of large movements in the crust of the earth, this idea has come to be called the *principle of original horizontality*.

Since each bed of rock is laid down upon earlier beds, the

youngest rock beds are at the top of a pile of layers and the oldest is at the bottom, assuming they have not been disturbed by earth movements. Think of it as the pile of old newspapers in your garage. The paper you threw away last will be atop the pile, and the oldest paper should be at the bottom of the pile. In geology this is called the *principle of superposition.* It can help you distinguish the older and younger fossils in a certain cliff.

Understandably, the type of sedimentary rock being deposited at one given time in the same ocean will differ with depth, distance from shore, and many other factors. Yet all of these different types of rock are of the same age and are simply different looks or "faces" of the same geologic story. Geologists recognize the different "faces" that such contemporaneous rock can have by calling them *facies changes.* By much the same reasoning, it is understandable that some areas will pile up much more rock while other areas may, at the same time, be piling up less or none at all. So no two cliffs or outcrops should look exactly alike. Matching different rock layers involves not only comparison of the kind and color of the rock but also matching the fossils found in different layers, a much more reliable procedure. Thus a thin blue layer of limestone containing Fossil A can be matched to a thick white layer in another location by the presence there also of Fossil A. Naturally, in practice this demands much more detective work, but the overall principle of matching rock layers by rock characteristics and by fossils is called *correlation.* It can be especially helpful in determining how rocks have shifted on each side of a crack in the earth's rock layers, in geology called a *fault.*

When we look at a cliff with varying sedimentary rock layers, we are looking at a record of past events. Each change, which may be observed as a different kind or color or fossil content of a bed, is a record of changes in the ancient world at that place. If things seem to have proceeded smoothly between beds or formations of rock, we say they are *conformable.* Obvious changes between layers are called *unconformities.* Often only a subtle change in the fossil content of the beds can mark an otherwise invisible unconformity.

All of this is to point out that paleontologists must study rock layers and their fossils in many different locations to put together a complete picture of life and environmental changes in the past. Yet this complete patchwork of rock layers has been put together for most areas of the world for most periods of time. Taken together, when the principle of superposition (youngest on top, oldest on the bottom) is applied to this pasted-together column of rock and fossils, we can see the large picture of fossil changes down through time and discover many things about life in the past that we would otherwise not know.

There is one other principle that is important to understanding the fossil past. It is the guess that basic conditions on the earth have remained essentially the same through time, and that what we see happening in the living world today, as plants and animals adapt to their environments, is similar to what creatures have done in the past. Thus if a fossil creature has fins or paddlelike legs, we assume that it lived in the water as similarly built creatures do today. Some authors phrase the principle as "the present is the key to the past." Officially it is called the *principle of uniformitarianism.* This principle has been useful, but it has also led to some incorrect assumptions, especially when information has been incomplete.

2. The Texas Geological Map

To fossil collectors, the main attractions of Texas geology are its variety and the fact that its rocks, from virtually all periods of geologic time, are accessible. Collectors can find, preserved in the rocks, fossil representatives of all forms of life.

Geologic maps, such as the one shown in Text Illustration 1 and the detailed maps in the Appendix, help illustrate the state's variety. You may purchase the excellent "Geological Highway Map of Texas," which is published by the American Association of Petroleum Geologists as Map No. 7 of the United States Geological Highway Map Series in cooperation with the United States Geological Survey. The ultimate in detail is provided by the *Geologic Atlas of Texas,* printed as individual sheets for certain areas by the Bureau of Economic Geology in Austin.

A first glance at such a map reveals the many shadings and textures, representing rocks from many different periods of time. Close examination reveals several larger patterns representing the major events in Texas's geologic past.

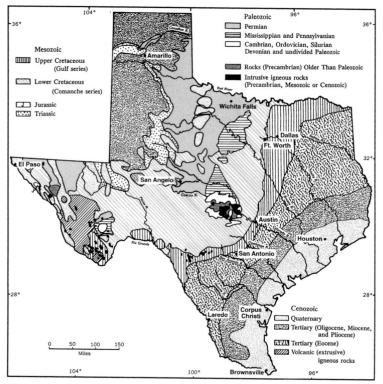

Text illustration 1: Texas geological map.

Perhaps most obvious, is the way several rock layers seem to repeat the curve and shape of the Gulf coast. Even though far inland today, they are just what they seem to be — old beaches and seafloors of a larger Gulf of Mexico that once extended over much of Texas.

One of the great facts of Texas geology is that Texas was covered by an enlarged Gulf of Mexico during the Cretaceous period 80 to 100 million years ago, toward the end of the Age of Dinosaurs, and that the retreating Gulf, since the Age of Dinosaurs, has laid down successive beaches and seafloors across East Texas. The plentiful fossil shells of the Lower Cretaceous limestones of Central Texas, the fossil bones of huge sea reptiles (mosasaurs and plesiosaurs) in North Texas Upper Cretaceous shales, perfectly preserved fossil shells of East Texas Eocene deposits, and the "Texas State Stone," East Texas salicified palmwood, are all part of the fossil legacy left behind by the retreating Gulf of Mexico.

What forces can cause such an overrunning of the continent by the sea? Perhaps movements in the molten rock of the earth's mantle beneath the edge of the continent sucked the Gulf coast downward. Perhaps a general melting of glaciers and polar ice caps increased the liquid volume of the sea. Quite likely, increased activity of molten rock rising to the seafloor through cracks in the middle of the oceans displaced a great volume of seawater to spread across the low areas of the continent such as the Gulf coast. Probably a combination of all these factors helped produce the great shallow seas that covered Texas and left behind their legacy of old Gulf seafloors and shorelines across East Texas.

Returning to our examination of the geologic map, one notices an abrupt change in the map textures running on a line approximately through the cities of Dallas, Waco, Austin, San Antonio, and Uvalde. This is the line of a feature known today as the Balcones Fault Zone. It is much more than a texture change on the map. In the vicinity of Austin and San Antonio, the feature is a quite obvious change in elevation and topography. One can stand to the east of those cities and notice that there is a definite highland to the west. To understand the very complicated and ancient history of this prominent Texas feature, one must view it as the location of the ancient edge of Texas and the North American continent. One must also accept the current geologic theory that continents drift slowly across the planet and occasionally collide with other continents. Some 300 million years ago, all the major continents of the world were joined together to form one large landmass called Pangaea. In that way, the present region of the Balcones Fault Zone was the ancient edge of Texas as Texas joined to South America and the other continents. As South America crashed slowly into Texas, rocks thrust one over the other to form a giant mountain range, the Ouachita overthrust, along the same line where today stand several important Texas cities. In case you find this hard to believe, scientists also have concluded that this is exactly the way India collided with Asia to produce our planet's highest mountains, the Himalayas.

Later, along this same line that bisects Texas, South America broke slowly away and began opening up the Gulf of Mexico.

The mountains eventually eroded away; but since they had made East Texas a highland, rivers flowed westward into a great Permian Basin in west central Texas. This Permian Basin accumulated sediment and dead organisms to form great oil and gas deposits. In Triassic times, these westward-flowing streams meandered more slowly through the base of the Panhandle to provide a stream edge environment for giant amphibians and strange reptiles, whose remains are plentiful in Texas Triassic rocks today. There were then no Rocky Mountains to the west to hinder such streams.

By the Cretaceous period of the Age of Dinosaurs, the mountains were long eroded away and the Gulf of Mexico moved inland across Texas to begin piling great beds of limestone, shale, and sandstone on top of this ancient continental edge. Under Dallas today, the Ouachita mountain roots are buried beneath 3,000 feet of Gulf bottom sediments. The once mountainous area was covered completely by great flatbeds of marine sediment.

But the story of the actual Balcones Fault Zone was just beginning. A zone of weakness remained beneath the great load of sediment. Finally, during early Tertiary times, the rocks cracked along the fault zone to create the famous Balcones Fault Zone. Rock layers on the Gulf side of the fault slipped thousands of feet lower than their counterparts west of the fault. It must have been a violent earthquake zone for millions of years. Today it is fairly stable and quiet.

The elevated position of the Lower Cretaceous limestones west of the fault zone causes the underground water in them to form many springs and caverns along the zone. The caverns sheltered many Pleistocene animals such as mammoths and saber-toothed cats. As a result, these caves today are often productive fossil hunting sites, and many interesting and important finds have been made in them.

One of the most prominent features of the Texas geologic map is the circular area of various textures at the center of the state, just west of the city of Austin. Called the Central Mineral Region or the Llano Uplift, it consists of very ancient Precambrian period rocks — far too old themselves to contain any very recognizable fossils. Nonetheless, this feature has created one of the most interesting fossil outcrops in Texas. When the older, deeper Precambrian rocks were uplifted by geologic factors still poorly known, they also bent upwards, in a circle around them, a series of fossil-bearing strata of much greater age than usually found on the surface in Texas.

The phenomenon was much like a bullet piercing several layers of material. Because of this, as one approaches the uplift area, one passes from Cretaceous to Pennsylvanian to early Paleozoic rock layers, such as the Cambrian period. Since many fossils of great interest to collectors (such as trilobites) have many interesting species limited to the early Paleozoic era, this uplift creates a very desirable fossil-collecting opportunity.

Straight west of the Llano Uplift in the Big Bend area of the Texas geologic map occurs another, smaller, circular area of rock of early Paleozoic age – the Marathon Basin. Similarly, fossils of the Cambrian, Ordovician, and Devonian periods occur there as well, making the Marathon area a mecca for collectors.

Immediately west of the Marathon Basin's ancient Paleozoic rocks occurs a large area of volcanic ashes and lavas. These are of great interest to mineral collectors, but because they were too hot while forming, they contain few if any fossils. They are the result of forces released after the Age of Dinosaurs (the Mesozoic era) by the newly formed Rocky Mountains, which shoved and cracked the rocks of the Big Bend region, releasing volcanic lavas and ashes from below.

At a glance one can see that the northern extension of Texas, the Panhandle, is marked by some interesting changes in texture on the geologic map. Most of the western edge of the Panhandle is of one uniform texture that marks the elevated, flat plains country of the southern High Plains of North America. For reasons that still elude historians, the Spaniards called this area the Llano Estacado, which has been translated as the Staked Plains. Composed of rather recent sediments washed down from the Rocky Mountains during the last ten to fifteen million years, the Staked Plains is geologically much younger than the rest of the state. It is an excellent area in which to find fossils of the great herds of grazing animals such as horses, camels, and prehistoric elephants that occupied these plains just before modern times. Temporary pools of water, some miles in extent, have formed on the flat, poorly drained Llano Estacado for millions of years. Today they are called playa lakes. Their very unreliable source of water provided both a place and a reason for many animals to die there and be buried and fossilized.

The center of the Texas Panhandle on the geologic map has a prominent line running north and south separating the flat plains of the western and northern Panhandle from the Permian sediments to the east. This line is a prominent difference in elevatión as well, where the eroded edge of the Rocky Mountain outwash stands in places several hundred feet above the land to the east. The limey soils of the plains have formed a calcified soil called *caliche,* which resists further erosion of the cliff face and gives the feature its popular name, the Caprock.

At the base of the Caprock a very important layer of fossil rock from the Triassic period is exposed. On the geologic map the Triassic outcrop parallels the north-south line of the Caprock and expands several counties wide at the base of the Panhandle. It is important because it represents dry land deposits from the Age of Dinosaurs, unlike the plentiful sea-bottom Cretaceous rocks from later in the same era. The Triassic, therefore, offers the chance to find remains of large land reptiles or dinosaurs that were not sea dwellers. Although not extensive, these Triassic beds yield very interesting fossil material.

Just below the eastern Panhandle, and to the east of the Triassic rock layers, is a large outcrop of Permian period rock. Since many of the Permian beds are quite reddish due to iron content, this area is often called the Permian Redbeds. These represent the last part of the Paleozoic era. Trilobites were just facing extinction, and on land the fin-backed Dimetrodon reptile heralded the great reptiles yet to come in the next era, the Mesozoic. Many relatively large predinosaur age reptiles were excavated in the Permian Redbeds during the late 1800s and the early 1900s. Similar to the Triassic rocks, the Permian rocks are mainly land deposits. For millions of years this part of Texas was on the western side of the mountains that were thrust up by continental collisions along the line occupied today by the Balcones Fault. Ancient rivers running westward across these Permian and later Triassic areas provided the best places for fossils to have formed.

Those are the most obvious aspects of Texas geology as revealed by the geologic map. Such variety should provide fossil collectors with many good clues as to where to begin a fossil hunt. Remember, although it merely looks like textures on a map, all that land is under ownership. Always get permission.

3. Collecting Fossils

The most important thing to remember when collecting a fossil is that it has waited for you to come along for perhaps millions of years, with all its clues about itself intact. When you collect it, you take on responsibility for those clues — which even the most professional collector must disturb somewhat when plucking a fossil from its surroundings. Keep records. Be observant.

A good collector will have a field notebook for recording the exact rock situation, layer, and formation in which the fossil was laying. Naturally, the location will be noted. Excellent collectors will use their powers of observation to make a few comments about just how the fossil was embedded and other surrounding features of interest, such as what other common fossils were in the same layer. Science is built on observations, not on a pile of fossils alone.

Just as important, good collectors will have materials with them to protect the fossil from damage until it gets home. The most inexpensive wrap is old newspaper, although some delicate and small specimens require little boxes or bottles. It is a good idea to wrap a number or name with the fossil that will relate it to the notebook notation.

At home or in the lab it will be necessary to clean or to repair each specimen. The best and simplest way to do that is to soak the specimen in water and gently brush or pick the remaining matrix (the clinging rock) from it. That will not always be enough. Detergents may help, mild or strong depending on the severity of the problem. Additional soaking time is usually preferable to resorting to harsher methods.

Small sonic (sound wave) cleaners are on the market and provide a next step toward loosening stubborn matrix. These accomplish wonders with a minimum of time or damage. Even harder matrix will require either aggressive work with a dental pick or even hammer and chisel work to remove it. When it comes to chisel work, a very small ball-peen hammer and a chisel with a rather small, sharp but rounded-corner tip is controllable by most workers. Such hand chisel work can be an art in the proper, patient hands.

The more mechanized ways of doing this cleaning usually involve either a pen-sized air hammer, such as the Airscribe sold by Chicago Pneumatic, Inc., or a small "abrasive blasting" machine much like a little sand-blaster in a cabinet. Most of the commercial models of such machines come equipped with too large a nozzle for fossil cleaning. They can be adapted to handle the sort of small nozzle offered by painter's airbrush companies. All of these machines are expensive enough to be of interest only to very serious fossil collectors. They will, however, remove even the hardest material from the fossil. The small vibrating scribes used to mark identification numbers on possessions are cheap, useful substitutes for such work.

All of these methods are good for either vertebrate or invertebrate fossils. At the beginning of the section on microfossils, a special description of that cleaning process is given.

One of the most common problems encountered in collecting or repairing fossils is how to make soft or crumbling fossils harder. This is often called *stabilizing,* and it should be done right in the ground on very fragile material. Basically, hardening involves impregnating the fossil with a dissolved material which upon drying will stick everything together from inside each tiny porous space. Larger cracks still need to be glued. Since the idea is to penetrate deep into the fossil, first applications of the hardener (which can be plastic, varnish, shellac, or various glues, such as Elmer's) must be thinned down severely. Each hardening material should be thinned with the proper thinner. Some thinners are chemical, some are petroleum products or alcohol, and some are just water. Generally, fast evaporation and quick hardening are preferable. Water-soluble hardeners are less smelly or messy and are easily removed later, but they dry and harden very slowly. Hardening may be especially appropriate when the fossil is in a wet place and cannot be moved.

After a particular hardener and thinner are chosen, a solution is prepared containing only one part hardener to six or eight parts thinner. This should penetrate very readily. When it has dried, another application is prepared using twice the amount of hardener as before. With each application the specimen should be very thoroughly soaked with the solution. Try several applications, increasing the thickness of the solution each time. It is probably best to stop when a dry specimen just begins to show a sheen of the hardener on its surface. The heavily varnished look is not thought attractive by most collectors.

Large breaks in fossils should be repaired with glue. For quick temporary repairs in the field or lab, various quick-drying "airplane cement" glues like Duco can be used. It will not last well over many years, however, and should be replaced with more permanent glue later. Epoxy is best for very strong, long-lasting repairs. The slower-setting epoxies are considered to be more permanent, but five-minute epoxy is necessary when many pieces must be repaired one after the other. It is sufficiently durable for most purposes.

Elmer's glue is slow drying and subject to softening in water or heat. It is probably best used in an already wet specimen in the field and replaced if possible later. Super glues (cyanoacrylates) are expensive and offer only super drying time with limited strength. Consider if the speed is absolutely needed before using them.

Common molding plaster is very useful for filling in small holes in fossils, and it should be made a familiar companion of a fossil preparator. On the following pages the steps necessary for making a plaster field jacket for fragile fossils is shown in detail. It is a good field technique even when its use is only to keep various parts of a fossil in the same relative position during transport to home or lab. Rare finds should always be jacketed with all the surrounding matrix possible. That allows careful and often witnessed removal of the rare find so that later questions about every detail can be answered. In such cases one never knows what questions will be asked by people more knowledgeable than oneself. It may be that a rare find should be prepared only by an expert. If you collect it along with copious matrix in a plaster field cast, it can then be turned over to an expert with the least regrets.

Making a Plaster Field Cast

(Text Illustration 2) The fossil to be encased in a plaster jacket is excavated around until it sits atop an earth pedestal with slightly undercut sides.

(Text Illustration 3) Exposed parts of the fossil are covered with wet tissue paper to prevent their being stuck in the later plaster. All undercuts are filled in with the paper.

(Text Illustration 4) Wet burlap cloth strips are soaked in plaster and bandaged over the pedestal in an overlapping manner.

(Text Illustration 5) In an hour, when the plaster has set, the pedestal is carefully dug loose underneath and turned over to provide a sort of plaster cradle for the fossil.

(Text Illustration 6) Later the fossil will be carefully excavated from the jacket. This allows each fragment to be handled carefully in the better working conditions of a laboratory.

At some point after cleaning and repair, a permanent number should be placed on the specimen. That is part of cataloging. Every serious collector will have a permanent notebook or card file where every fossil that becomes a part of the collection will have an entry that lists such things as the best identification possible and a brief note about the source location and why the identification was selected; data about who collected it and exactly where and when; and extra observations made when it was collected or interesting details gained later about it, for instance by visitors to your collection who have special knowledge. This notebook or file is your catalog. The catalog can be just a numerical list, or certain cross-indexed special files can be made. The most common special file is made by keeping duplicate cards of your numerical catalog refiled in either an alphabetical order by genus names or refiled in a special scientific order (phylogenetic order) that keeps related items close together. This phylogenetic order is the order used in many fossil identification guides and can simply be arranged by letting one such book be your "bible" for that order. If your collection contains a wide variety of items, you may need several specialized "bibles."

The point of these arrangements is twofold. When at some future time you stand with one of your numbered fossils in hand and want to know what you decided its identification was many years ago, you can go to your numerical catalog and look it up by number. When you are asked if your collection has a certain kind of fossil in it, you can go to your alphabetical or phylogenetic catalog and look it up by name. It is not necessary to have both an alphabetical and phylogenetic catalog, and the phylogenetic ("what's related to what") file is the better choice in that it will let you find all closely related species close together in the file.

Text illustration 2: Fossil excavated to sit atop dirt pedestal.

Text illustration 3: Top of dirt pedestal and fossil being covered with wet tissue.

Text illustration 4: Sides and top of pedestal are covered with strips of burlap cloth soaked in wet plaster.

Text illustration 5: After plaster hardens, pedestal is cut loose as a unit.

Text illustration 6: Inverted plaster field cast supports fossil for transport.

In today's computerized world it is advisable to consider putting all these catalogs on computer diskettes (with many duplicate diskettes for protection from computer errors). The simplest and cheapest computers will handle thousands of catalog entries and cross-index them quickly for you. Such a task is not technically difficult, and one needs to know very little more about computers than what the salesperson in a good store can teach you in an hour. Such computer programs are called *database programs,* and fossil catalogs require only the simplest of them.

The storage of a fossil collection can be done in cabinets or boxes to individual taste, but one thing is necessary: The catalog entries should allow you to find where specimens are stored.

Collections that are well prepared and well cataloged can become quite valuable, not only to science but also as tax-deductible donations to museums. The greater value in either case lies in the carefully recorded information, even more than in the specimens themselves.

Special Thoughts About Fossil Collecting

Several suggestions can be made about maximizing one's pleasure and success in fossil collecting. A beginner's first worry is always where to find fossils. As experience and interest begin to grow, the collector should gain access to one of the fine geological libraries in the major universities of Texas. These libraries contain the vast number of geological publications of the University of Texas's Bureau of Economic Geology. The publications abound in fossil site locations. It is from these that the more experienced collectors find long-forgotten productive sites. The publication that lists the site will probably also have some lists of what fossils have been found there, making identification somewhat easier. Asking other collectors for their sites is something one should do only with very good acquaintances, and then sparingly. Libraries also contain field trip guidebooks put out by the various geological societies across the state. These are excellent sources of information.

Most collectors quickly tire of collecting just a broad range of common fossils and specialize in one kind. This is a very useful process, because it deepens one's knowledge on a particular subject. If the specialty is not a common one, a person could rather quickly become a much-sought-after expert in one fossil group.

Trying to collect all the Texas representatives of even a small fossil specialty can pose a real challenge and be especially rewarding. Professional paleontologists are more likely to help nonprofessionals if they show some knowledge of a specialty. For one thing, specialization will raise one's knowledge to the point where a collector can recognize truly new and unusual specimens — perhaps even new species. That helps one's entry into the world of serious and professional paleontology, where genuine scientific progress is made.

Finally, a word about ethics. Most of Texas is owned by private individuals. It takes only a little courtesy to obtain the support and friendship of landowners where one wishes to hunt. On the other hand, nothing does more harm to amateur and professional fossil collecting than a collector who is found illegally on private land. It makes absolutely no difference whether or not you are doing any harm or going very far into someone's land. If it is private, get permission!

State parks are off-limits in Texas and do not allow collecting.

Eventually most collectors reach a point where sheer possession of specimens means less to them than the fascinating story of earth history that fossils represent. An experienced collector will actually collect fewer specimens, but they will be items that have greater meaning to his collection. The aim of this book is to cultivate collectors of that caliber. I am not at all sure that students should "collect" fossils. I suggest that students mark the site of their finds with flags, make plaster replicas of their finds, and then return them to nature. Remember, removing a fossil from its natural environment means breaking the chain of information about its past — a chain that has been undisturbed for millions of years.

4. How To Use This Book for Fossil Identification

As a museum curator, I am asked to identify things brought into the museum every day. What goes through the mind of a collector beginning the identification of a fossil?

First he or she reaches for an important tool—the hand magnifier lens, or loupe. Professional standards call for ten-power magnification, but anything over five-power will work. (Stronger powers should be avoided because strong magnification reduces the observable area and usually distorts the clarity.) In using a lens, place the lens close to the eye and move the specimen back and forth to focus. Many misidentifications are made for lack of close-up inspection. Don't trust your eyes.

How do you identify a fossil using this book? To begin, you must answer the questions in this section about the fossil you wish to identify, proceeding in an orderly fashion:

1. Choose a possible type of fossil from the shapes and texture descriptions.

2. Thumb through the photo section where pictures of such fossils are shown.

3. Note carefully the rock formation in which each pictured fossil was found. (It need not be exactly the same as where you found your fossil, but it should at least be of the same geologic period.)

4. Pick out a picture that matches most closely the one you are identifying.

5. Look up the description and see if it sounds like what you have. Perhaps a similar but unpictured genus or species will be mentioned that sounds closer to your fossil than the one shown. Sometimes suggestions are made about similar species from other formations than the one mentioned in the photo.

6. Finally, if you feel a little uncertain after reading the description, look over the photos again for a better match. Always remember that it is more scientific to be careful about taking the first identification to come along; keep your decision somewhat general until you learn more. No true scientist would fault you for healthy skepticism. One other principle keeps rash identifications to a minimum: "The unusual very rarely ever happens!" So before proclaiming to the world a very rare find, take a second look.

The most complete identification refines an identification all the way to a species. That is foolish and unnecessary for any but the most experienced collector or a person who has specialized in that type of fossil. Great experience is required for species identification. Only if the photo matches perfectly and the geologic formation and location are very close to where your fossil was found should you trust a species name. Back off a little until you have more experience; use instead the larger name, the genus.

The genus is the first part of the scientific name and is always capitalized. Many species make up one genus. A genus name can be followed in a written identification with the abbreviation *sp.*, meaning "some species of," if you want to be careful. If you are quite sure you are close to the right species, then say "probably" such-and-such a species; if you are less sure, say "possibly." The abbreviation *aff.* means it bears a "resemblance to," while *cf.* means it "compares well to" some species.

On a label might be written, *Texigryphea sp. cf. navia* or *Neithea sp. aff. irregularis.* The perfect collector will find room to note on the record card or in the collecting notebook just why or why not the identification seems good; for example, whose book was used for comparison and just what about the description is comparable and what is not. Later, when talking with other collectors, you will know why you chose the identification you did. Few collectors will do all that, but the scientific value of the collection leaps a hundredfold with such simple notes!

The Questions To Ask

Question number one should be: "Is the object a fossil or simply a rock?" Never trust what the overall shape resembles. Always look for small details to make your decision sure. Does the object possess some regular pattern, such as equal parts spreading (radiating) out from a center (radial symmetry)? Otherwise, does the object have an exactly matched left and right side (bilateral symmetry)? Is there a surface texture that repeats itself in some small detail? If the answer is yes to any of these, it probably is connected to past life and is a fossil. Objects that are not fossils but do resemble parts of once-living things are called pseudo-fossils.

Question number two: What are the rock layer and other fossils in it like, and, if possible, what geologic period of time does it represent? If possible look up the formation's geologic period on a geologic map.

This can set your thinking along the right lines. If the rest of the rock layer was full of seashells, then one should think of sea and not land creatures. If the rock layer is from after the Mesozoic era (the Age of Reptiles), then dinosaurs, ammonites, trilobites, and many other things would be highly unlikely. This book will suggest periods of time appropriate to each kind of fossil. If you are far from that suggested period, think three times before leaping to an identification. You can always simply say that your fossil is "much like" the one shown and be honest about it.

Question number three: Does the object show a certain shape or texture that is usually characteristic of a particular fossil group? Characteristic shapes and textures include:

Curved shape
  Gastropods (snails). Usually an even and unbroken curve
    or coil.
  Cephalopods (nautilus and ammonites). Curve marked by
    dividing lines (suture patterns).
  Teeth. Shiny enamel coating (tan, brown, or black). Meat-
    eating (carnivore) teeth – fish, amphibian, reptile, or
    mammal – are often slightly curved. Roots of other (her-
    bivore) teeth are often slightly curved.
Tube-shaped
  Scaphopods (tusk shells). Small, thin-walled, slightly
    curved and tapered.
  Straight cephalopods. Small to medium, tapered but not
    curved. May have surface ridges.
  Crinoid stem fragments. Stacked buttons, no taper.
  Worm tubes. Irregular twisting masses.
Horn-shaped
  Corals (solitary). Sides have fine lines (septa) radiating up
    the fossil.
  Unusual bivalves. One valve large, the other valve a small
    cap. No septa.
  Loosely curved cephalopods. Surface with ornament of
    ribbing. May show suture lines dividing septa.
Two-shelled
  Bivalves (clams and oysters). Either irregular-shaped or
    each valve a mirror image of the other valve.
  Brachiopods (lamp shells). Each half of each valve a mir-
    ror image of the other half of the same valve. A few are
    irregular.
Branching
  Sponges. Irregularly branched if at all. Pores very irregu-
    lar in size.
  Bryozoans. Surface with fine, regular tiny holes (zoecia).
  Corals. Sides often with fine lines. Top with radiating parti-
    tions dividing pie-shaped septa.
  Plant stems. Bark or irregular pore pattern on surface.
    Dark color.
Round shape
  Sea urchins (regular echinoids). Five-part centered pattern
    of pores or tubercles.

Algal spore bodies (Porocystis). Has porous surface. Off-round.

Heart shape

Heart urchins (irregular echinoids). Five-part pattern of pores but pattern parts not of equal length.

Bivalves (clams) when both valves are viewed edge-on.

Porous-textured

Sponges. Pores and shape irregular. May also be connected spheres.

Bryozoans. May be twiglike, lacy, or matlike. Pores neatly regular.

Algal spore bodies (*Porocystis*). Round.

Algal "stems." Very irregular in texture and shape. A "cop-out" category. Often resorted to when uncertain.

Three-parted

Trilobites. Three long ridges make up body. Also head, thorax, and tail.

Shark teeth. Some have three ridges. Some have three points (cusps).

Brachiopods (lamp shells). A middle fold (sulcus) can form three areas of the shell. No definite head.

Many-armed

Starfish. Star-shaped. Five-armed.

Brittle starfish. Long five-armed. Small central disk.

Crinoid crowns. Many-segmented arms above a cup of five-sided plates.

Segmented

Crustaceans (crabs, shrimp). Often interestingly tubercled.

Plant stems. Regular divisions. Dark color.

Insect legs. Thin and often spined.

Crinoid arms and stems. Segmented calcite plates or buttons. Often show cleavage where abraded.

Enameled

Tooth enamel. May be tan, brown or black. Very shiny even when unpolished.

Bone-like texture

Bone. May be fish, amphibian, reptile, bird, or mammal. Tertiary bone will be yellow or light tan when clean.

Cretaceous and older bone will usually be dark brown,
grey, or black. *Identify bone by surface texture, not overall shape. Shape is often a trick of nature caused by
natural rock concretions.*

Now that you have an idea of what general kind of fossil you
may have, turn to the photos and descriptions of that general
group of fossils to see if some illustration very closely resembles yours.

Following is a metric system conversion chart to assist you in
determining the sizes of fossils described in this book.

	Metric	**U.S.**
Millimeter (mm)	0.001 m	0.03937 in.
Centimeter (cm)	0.01 m	0.3937 in.
Decimeter (dm)	0.1 m	3.937 in.
Meter (m)	1.0 m	39.37 in.
Kilometer (km)	1,000.0 m	0.6213 mi.
Fathom (fm)	1.829 m	6.0 ft.

5. Fossil Descriptions

At the outset, a few words of explanation are in order. The photographs referenced in the fossil descriptions can be found in the color and black and white photograph sections (plates) of this book. Terms that may be unfamiliar to the reader are defined in the glossary at the end of the book. Measurements given in the photo captions are approximate and are intended only to give some idea of size. Unless otherwise specified, they usually represent the longest dimension of the subject. If there are several fossils, the longest measure of the largest specimen is given. In some cases, a specific measurement is taken and its location is stated. For the reader's convenience, a metric conversion table is provided at the end of Chapter 4.

Although relying greatly on the identifications provided by the collector, in some cases the author has taken the liberty of changing a scientific name. In all cases, the author accepts full responsibility for the identifications printed here. In the event of

mistakes, please assume that the named collector is not at fault.
Some abbreviations may need explanation: fm. = formation;
gr. = group; Co. = county; mm. = millimeters; sp. = some
species of; cf. = compares favorably to; Cret. = Cretaceous;
Penn. = Pennsylvanian. All towns listed are in Texas, since this
is a book about Texas fossils.

Microfossils

The fascinating study of microscopic fossils, which are plentiful in Texas, is too often neglected by students and collectors because of unfamiliarity with how to collect and prepare them and
a mistaken notion that very powerful magnification is needed to
see them. Many are fairly easily prepared, and most are subjects
of great interest and beauty to those who dare.

What are microfossils? They are obviously very small,
although some are quite visible to the naked eye. They include
pieces of larger creatures, juvenile or reproductive stages of
otherwise larger life forms, and truly microscopic animals and
plants. They are especially convenient to collect, since a small
piece of rock can contain thousands of specimens; and they are
convenient to store and transport, since a large collection can be
housed in a small cabinet. They are often good *index fossils,*
which means they are quite plentiful and distributed over a wide
geographic area and through many rock layers; certain species
are characteristic of certain time periods and environmental conditions.

Since many collectors are unfamiliar with microfossil preparation, I will describe the process. In Text Illustration 7 several
pieces of microfossil preparation equipment are shown: (A) is a
binocular microscope of 15 to 40 power; (B) is a bottle with a
good water-tight lid for decanting microfossils from matrix; (C)
is a fine sieve for straining microfossils from a matrix and fossil
solution; (D) is a sonic cleaner, a tool that is faster than decanting
for separating microfossils and matrix; (E) is a group of
microfossil slides for storing the washed fossils. The exact use
of these tools is explained in the following section.

The basic idea is that there is more very small fossilized
material embedded in most rock layers than there are larger
forms. These microfossils can be preserved for many millions of
years.

Text illustration 7: Sieves, special slides, sonic cleaner, and microscope for microfossil preparation.

Step one in microfossil preparation involves collecting a small specimen of rock thought to contain micro material. Precautions must be taken to avoid microscopic dust already in the collecting bag or particles of rock that might have fallen from other rock layers than the one desired or residue on a used digging tool. A very small trowel full is sufficient.

Step two is to break down the rock containing the specimens. This can be started by gentle physical crushing by hand or with a hammer. After the material is gently crushed, soaking in water is often enough to break it down to micro material and mud. Certain rocks require more drastic solvents. The use of those should be under professional advice. Much work can be done with limestones and shales that dissolve in water. The action of the water can be enhanced by the addition of water softeners or hydrogen peroxide in small quantity. Often a few days of soaking will aid in dissolving the matrix of the rock.

Step three is to wash away the "muddy" parts of the solution to clean and free the micro material. This is done professionally by the use of sonic cleaning devices, the cheaper of which are available to amateurs. In such, sound waves remove the last mud from the fossils while they are still in the watery solution. After sonic cleaning the solution is poured through very fine screens to hold back the small fossils and let the "mud" wash on through and down the drain. A standard size for the final sieve is often 200 meshes to the inch, as sold by scientific supply houses. A very acceptable alternative (and cheaper) method of washing away the mud is called "decanting." Decanting involves placing the dissolved rock in a large bottle with a tight lid and simply shaking up the whole thing. Then allow the slightly heavier fossil material to settle to the bottom, and carefully pour off the muddy water without pouring out the fossils. Refill the bottle with clean water and repeat the process many times. Eventually, the fossils alone will remain in the bottle. The use of hot water and perhaps a nonsudsing detergent in the decanting can help. Many imaginative methods have been invented by micropaleontologists to free micro material from surrounding rock.

After such washing, simply dry the remaining pile of material. It will contain interesting undissolved mineral grains as well as fossils.

Step four is to examine, mount and store the small specimens. At least 20-power magnification is needed to see the specimens. One hundred power is needed for detailed identification. The microscope must use reflected light (light from above the specimens), since they are too dense to allow light from below to pass through without silhouetting. Common binocular scopes are fine. The amateur can obtain or borrow less expensive models of such scopes. Again, only 20 to 30 power is enough to begin.

A very fine red sable brush, moistened with the tongue, will serve well to pick up individual specimens under the scope. Paper, metal, and glass slides are sold by scientific supply companies specifically to hold microfossils. Specimens can be placed on them in a "strew" of many fossils or in individual, numbered squares one by one. If one desires to keep a specimen in a square, diluted white glue can be smeared thinly on the slide and allowed to dry before specimens are mounted. The brush moisture will loosen the glue under a specimen as it is touched down. Moisture will allow repositioning for study at any time. Such slides can easily be cataloged and require little storage room.

Even an inexpensive experience in microfossil collecting can become a fascinating interest. The field is very important geologically as an excellent key to strata identification and the study of past environments. For many it has been a lucrative occupation, especially in the oil industry. Much research continues into the information possible from microfossils.

For example, several common Texas microfossils are illustrated:

Text Illustration 8 shows material washed from the Taylor group, Upper Cretaceous, of Dallas County.

Text Illustration 9 shows one of Texas's largest "microfossils," *Orbitolina texana* (Roemer), width 4 mm., which forms an important index layer in the Glen Rose formation, Lower Cretaceous. Shown also in Text Illustration 9 is a microfossil slide containing typically minute microfossils from Jasper County.

In rocks of the Pennsylvanian period, tiny but visible "wheatgrain"-shaped microfossils called *fusilinids* occur, Text Illustration 10 and Color Photo 3.

The majority of microfossils (all of those shown here) are Foraminifera. Called "forams" for short, these fossils are the small shells (tests) built by single-celled organisms. The name *foram* refers to very microscopic openings in these tests through which the protoplasm of the animal stretches for feeding on tiny organisms. Text Illustration 11 shows a fine scanning electron microscopic photo of the foraminifer, *Heterohelix,* a very common genus in Upper Cretaceous rocks.

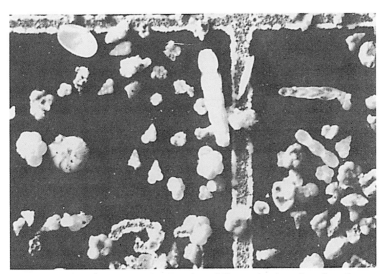

Text illustration 8: Typical microfossils—*foraminifera* and *ostracodes*—from the Taylor gr., Upper Cretaceous Period, Dallas Co.

36 *Fossils of Texas*

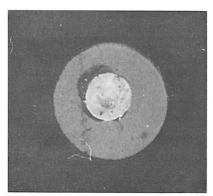 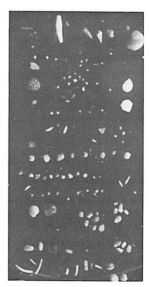

Text illustration 9: *Orbitolina texana,* Glen Rose fm., an *index fossil* (left), and a typical microfossil slide (right).

Text illustration 10: Wheat grain-shaped microfossils called *fusilinids.*

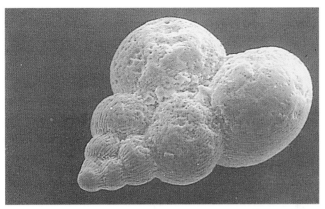

Text illustration 11: A common Upper Cretaceous foraminifera called *Heterohelix*.

The sand and gravel in streambeds that drain areas having a large amount and variety of fossil material, e.g., the Sulphur River in Northeast Texas, are very productive to sift for microfossils of all kinds. Color Photos 1 and 2 show a variety of such micro material, from single-celled to vertebrate.

Paleobotany — Fossil Plants

Stromatolites (Photo 1)
Precambrian through Paleozoic in abundance. Some forms persist today. These represent mounds of algal growth, and they often exhibit a layered structure. Some are quite large. As fossils, most are rather vague and formless except for layering and swirling patterns in the rock that are otherwise hard to explain.

Porocystis globularis Giebel (Photo 2)
Lower Cretaceous, especially Glen Rose formation. A somewhat flat-ended ball with a regular porous texture. One end has a small, round, roughened attachment point as if it were once connected to a stem. These are generally considered algal in origin. "Seaweed" reproductive bodies.

Lepidodendron (a form genus, "lepidodendrid") (Photo 3)
Pennsylvanian period. Trees growing to thirty meters tall. Leaves formed along trunk and branches in a spiral pattern. That

pattern is visible in the angled rows of diamond-shaped leaf scars
on fossil remnants of the trunk or branches. Such plants
reproduce by alternation of generations. Asexual spores formed
in cones drop into a necessarily watery environment and produce
small aquatic plants that in turn produce eggs and sperm. The
sperm must be in water to reach the eggs and produce the larger,
cone-bearing plants; the cycle then repeats. This is reason to believe that such plants must have lived in swampy places. One of
the scale trees, *Lepidodendropsis corrugata* (Dawson), is a common species. (See also *Sigillaria*.)

Stigmaria (Photos 4, 5)
A catch-all name given to all root-like fossils found especially
in connection with *Lepidodendron*. *Stigmaria* gets its name from
small rounded pits ("stigmaria") that are usually less regular than
the scars on lycopod trunks. The species *Stigmaria Ficoides*
(Sternberg) is common.

Sigillaria (Photo 6)
Pennsylvanian period. A tree nearly as tall as *Lepidodendron*
but with square to rounded leaf scars arranged in vertical rows
up an unbranched trunk. A common species is *Sigillaria
ichthyolepis* (Presl), which exhibits leaf cushions on the bark of
this scale tree.

Calamites (a form genus, a "calamitid" or "equisetopsid" — horsetail) (Photos 7, 8, 9)
Pennsylvanian period. A tree growing to fifteen meters; relat-
ed to modern-day *Equisetum*, horsetail rush (a much smaller
plant). The trunk has regularly spaced nodes that appear on fossils as a sunken line across the trunk at intervals with close-
spaced, vertical ribs between them. Has sexual alternation of
generations (see *Lepidodendron* above). *Asterophyllites* is a common genus applied to the whorled leaves of a calamitid. The
scientific class is called *Equisetopsida* — the horsetails. The
leaves are moderately narrow and of slightly irregular length
when compared to other whorled leaves such as *Annularia* or
Sphenophyllum.

Annularia (Photos 10, 11)
Permian period. Very orderly, small, narrow leaves in a regularly whorled pattern. Leaves may enlarge slightly near tips. Plant may be branched.

Sphenophyllum (Photo 12)
Pennsylvanian period. Whorled leaves that enlarge evenly to a rather wide, truncated tip, vaguely resembling a cloverleaf pattern. Leaves are wider than most *Annularia* and wider and fewer in number than most *Calamites* whorls.

Pecopteris (a form genus, "pecopterid") (Photos 8, 27)
Pennsylvanian period. A true, spore-producing fern, still needing an alternation of generations to reproduce, as did many plants of this period (see *Lepidodendron*). Short leaflets, about 2.5 times as long as wide. Sides of leaflets are smooth and nearly parallel with blunt, rounded tips. Leaflets are closely attached to stalk along most of their base. Formed trees to 15 meters tall; hence called *tree ferns*. *Asterotheca lamuriana* (Heer) is a common Texas genus under the pecopterid form genus.

Neuropteris (a form genus, a "neuropterid") (Photos 13, 14)
Pennsylvanian period. Called *seed ferns* because they developed seeds fertilized by wind-blown pollen and escaped reliance on a moist environment as needed in an alternation-of-generations arrangement (see *Lepidodendron*). Seed ferns may be direct ancestors of flowering plants. *Neuropteris* leaflets have delicately arching veins and lobed bases attached to the stalk at only one point. *Neuropteris ovata* Hoffman is a common Texas species that fits the general description well.

Also see photographs of *Linopteris,* Photo 15; *Alethopteris,* Photo 16; *Megalopteris,* Photo 17; *Lescuropteris,* Photo 18 and Color Photo 5; *Callipteris,* Photo 19; *Gigantopteris,* Photos 20, 21; *Danaceites,* Photo 22; *Delnortea,* Photo 23; and *Phagophytichnus,* Photo 24, all of which are seed ferns.

Linopteris obliqua (Bunbury) (Photo 15)
Pennsylvanian period. A net-vein pinnule of a seed fern that

is a good indicator of the early Desmoinesean, Pennsylvanian period.

Alethopteris ambigua Lesquereux (Photo 16)
Pennsylvanian period. Leaflets have expanded bases that join together along the leaf rachis (stem). Leaflets are at less than a right angle to the stem and seem to lean toward the pinnule tip.

Megalopteris dawsoni (Hartt) (Photo 17)
Pennsylvanian period. A seed fern with feather-like pinnules, showing a typically neuropterid fine-veined look.

Lescuropteris moori Lesquereux (Photo 18; Color Photo 5)
Permian period. A seed fern with delicate pinnules and deeply cut wavy edges. This gives a frilly look to the frond.

Callipteris conferta (Sternberg) (Photo 19)
Permian period. A seed fern indicator of the earliest Permian.

Gigantopteris americana White (Photos 20, 21)
Permian period. Fronds often forked. Leaflets large, with veins running at angles to veins of adjoining leaflets, resembling file teeth.

Danaeites emersoni Lesquereux (Photo 22)
Permian period. Seed fern with a long frond with long secondary pinnules extending at a sharp angle. The secondary pinnules are edged by yet smaller pinnules (doubly pinnate). The smaller pinnules almost overlap those of adjacent secondary pinnules.

Delnortea abbottii (Photo 23)
Permian period, Leonardian series. Rare evidence of West Texas Permian land fossil deposits, hence the youngest known Texas Permian plant. A very large frond coming to a sharp point, doubly pinnate. A highlight of the collection of Sul Ross State University.

Rhacophyllum (Photo 25)
Permian period. Exact relationships are difficult to place.

Leaves broad and spreading, edges irregular, lettuce-like. Very common in Harperville formation.

Tainiopteris (a form genus, a "tainopterid") (Photo 26)
Permian period. Strap-like leaves with veins at nearly a right angle to the stem. Alike on each leaflet. *Tainiopteris newberryana* Fontaine and White is one typical Texas species.

Cordaites (a form genus, "cordaitean") (Photo 27)
Pennsylvanian and Permian periods. Probably an early relative of the conifers of today (which began in the Pennsylvanian period). Has strap-like, long leaves, often just seen in part as a long, parallel-sided strip of dark color with faint parallel veins. *Artisia* is a genus based on a trunk with regular cross-partitions. *Cordaites borassifolius* (Sternberg) is a common example of the leaves.

Walchia (Lebachia) (Photos 28, 29)
A common genus of fossil conifers. Several species are found in the Texas Permian period rocks.

Paleotaxites praecursor White (Photo 30)
Permian period. A conifer very much like a small cordaitean. The leaves are long and strap-like but much smaller than *Cordaites*.

Trichopitys (Photo 31)
Pennsylvanian period. A sparse-foliaged, evergreen spray of thin leaves. A ginkgophyte.

Frenelopsis (Photo 32)
Lower Cretaceous, Glen Rose Formation. Indistinct branching plant imprints, suggestive of coniferous scaly patterns.

Cycad Leaves (Photo 33)
Cycad leaves from Upper Cretaceous, Brewster County. Indicative of swampy environment along a large embayment of the Rio Grande River area as part of an enlarged Gulf of Mexico during the late Cretaceous period.

Cretaceous Broadleaf Trees (Photos 34, 35)
Upper Cretaceous. By the end of the Mesozoic era, the Age
of Dinosaurs, broadleaf trees and flowering plants had appeared.
Texas's Upper Cretaceous rocks, especially the Woodbine formation, contain many such fossils. The presence of such fossils
usually indicates a land environment or at least an area near
shore. Carbonized trunks and twigs occur in many Upper Cretaceous formations, especially in the lower Eagle Ford group.

Euonymus glanduliferus Ball (Photo 36)
Paleocene epoch. A broad triangular leaf, related to the
modern Wahoo tree. Very modern-appearing leaves occur plenti-
fully in the early Cenozoic era, Tertiary period; especially in the
Eocene epoch. The University of Texas at Austin has the finest
collection of Tertiary leaves.

"Petrified" Palm Wood (Color Photo 6)
Tertiary period. Scattered through the sands of East Texas,
which were retreating beaches of the Gulf of Mexico during the
last 50 million years, are logs and stumps of palm trees replaced
by silica. Fossil palm wood is the official state stone of Texas.
It is distinguished from other fossil wood of the East Texas area
by its small, dot-like tubes that run through the middle of the
wood. Broadleaf and conifer wood show rings of vessels instead.

Quercus (Color Photo 4)
Pleistocene epoch. Broadleafed shrub or tree. Leaf often deeply lobed on margin (edge). Often found in the layered sediments
of playa (temporary) lakes in the flat, poorly drained Texas high
plains in the Panhandle. Many other amazing plant and animal
remains occur in those thin-bedded sediments. See especially
tufted seed, Photo 37; also Photos 439 (fish) and 314, 315, and
316 (insects) from same deposits.

Phylum Porifera — Sponges
Sponges are very simple and mostly soft-bodied animals. Their
structure consists of only two layers of cells, separated by a jelly-
like mass that contains a reinforcement of needlelike, mineral-
ized spicules and fibrous, organic spongin. Spicules are

siliceous, calcareous, or spongin. The spicules of some sponges scatter after the death of the sponge and form a part of the microfossil material. Only sponges whose spicules form a rigid framework endure as whole fossils. In Texas, fossil sponges occur primarily in late Paleozoic strata but are also found in the Lower Cretaceous. *Girtyocoelia,* a Pennsylvanian period genus, is the sponge most found in Texas collections.

Talpaspongia clavata King (Photo 38)
Permian period, Clyde formation, Talpa limestone. Sponge is a club-shaped mass with porous exterior and round cross-section.

Heliospongia (Photo 39)
Pennsylvanian period. A massive sponge, more or less shapeless but generally elongate. Surface pores are small enough to make one look closely. *H. excavata* King is generally solitary with irregular constrictions. *H. ramosa* Girty is similar but more likely to show branching structure.

Girtyocoelia (Heterocoelia) (Photo 40)
Pennsylvanian period. Like a string of connected small balls, each nearly separate. Definite tube through the middle of the string. A few pores on ball surfaces. May branch. Much like *Girtycoelia.*

Girtycoelia (Photo 40)
Pennsylvanian period. Like *Girtyocoelia,* but balls are less separate and there is no central tube. Pores are larger than *Girtyocoelia.*

Amblysiphonella prosseri Clarke (Photo 41)
Pennsylvanian period. This sponge is a stack of fat, irregular cells with an internal wide tube connecting them into a straight or curved mass. The undulations of each bulging cell show through a surface of fine and fairly regular pores. Rather closely resembles an encrustation of bryozoan.

Wewokella (Photo 42)
Pennsylvanian period. Roughly cylindrical masses of sponge, cylinders often joined side by side. Surface can show a fine

porosity, but usually much of the surface is a coarse stringiness somewhat resembling rough tree bark.

Maeandrostia kansasensis Girty (Photo 43)
Pennsylvanian period. Stemlike, otherwise rather flowing featureless shape. Surface shows small irregular openings, but larger openings than *Heliospongia* (quite visible). Walls thick.

Fissispongia jacksboroensis King (Photo 44)
Pennsylvanian period. Thin, stalky sponges with some simple branching. Surface exhibits a fine, irregular porosity. This species is somewhat thicker than a pencil and has few and very small tubercles at random places. *F. spinosa* King has a smaller diameter, less branching, and more and larger spinous tubercles.

Phylum Cnidaria — Jellyfish and Corals

Jellyfish are unlikely to produce fossils, being entirely soft-bodied. Yet there is at least one fairly common occurrence of jellyfish fossils in the Texas Cretaceous. Conularia are difficult to place in classification schemes, but they are often found in Texas late Paleozoic rocks and are considered by many paleontologists to be related to jellyfish and corals.

The class Anthozoa, which contains mostly the corals in terms of fossils, also embraces the largest number of fossil forms in this phylum. A polyp, a single coral animal, secretes a calcareous cup in which to live. The cup is divided by partitions that radiate outward from its center and are called *septa*. A polyp builds one cup on top another, living in the uppermost which is called the *calyx*. The whole structure of one coral animal is called a *corallite*. Such corals that live unconnected to other corals are called *solitary corals* (or *horn corals*).

Like floors in a building, tabulae form horizontal divisions of the corallite and appear as growth lines on the outside of the coral. Microscopic growth lines on some Texas corals have been found to show daily growth within larger annual growth lines.

Since corals from farther back in time show more daily growth lines per year than the 365 shown by modern corals, it is estimated that the Earth rotated faster on its axis in the past, making the year for a Texas Pennsylvanian period coral more than 400 days long, each day being shorter than our present days. The gravitational drag of the moon is thought to be responsible. In theory, the Earth will continue to slow its spin in the future. Many coral animals live together in colonies in which the individual corallites join together to form a corallum. Such corals are called *colonial corals.*

In Texas, fossil corals occur in Paleozoic, Mesozoic, and Cenozoic deposits but are only greatly abundant in rocks of the Texas Pennsylvanian period.

Kirklandia texana Caster (Color Photo 8)
Upper Cretaceous period, especially Woodbine formation. Imprints of soft polyps of jellyfish are found in what may have been ancient beach sands. This is an especially good example of a fine fossil left by a very soft-bodied creature. Similar fossils occur in the Lower Cretaceous Washita division.

Conularia (Photo 45)
Upper Cambrian through Permian. A small, four-sided pyramid with closely and evenly spaced cross-ribbed ornamentation. Several divisions or lines run the length of the shell. Complete specimens may show a small attachment swelling at the pointed end of the shell. The fossil surface may have a tooth-enamel-like luster due to its composition of chitinophosphate.

Tollina trapezoidalis Flower — a chain coral (Photo 46)
Ordovician period. The calyxes of this coral are linked together in a somewhat wide chain. Calyxes are staggered along the chain. Chain corals are exclusively early Paleozoic era forms.

Cumminsia aplanata (Cummins) (Photo 47)
Pennsylvanian Bend group, Smithwick shale. A small, squat, round, thickly built solitary coral with calyx of four well-developed fossulae and a tapering base that leads to an attachment point.

Lophophyllidium (Photos 48, 49)
Pennsylvanian through Permian. Small, solitary horn corals, several times as long as wide. Sides marked by many longitudi-

nal furrows. Center of calyx often has a tall column that may
stick up above calyx rim in broken specimens. Thirty to fifty septa of alternating length. *L. proliferum* (McChesney) has a fairly
smooth exterior, while *L. spinosum* Jeffords has many small external tubercles.

Caninia torquia (Owen) (Photo 50)
Pennsylvanian period. Large, solitary horn coral; can reach
nine inches in length and up to two inches wide. Many specimens
are bent at right angles. Calyx is deep. Very common in the
Texas Pennsylvanian period rocks.

Cladophyllia furcifera Roemer (Photo 51)
Lower Cretaceous, Fredericksburg division. A branching
coral with cylindrical stems four to six millimeters in diameter.
No central column. Only primary septa reaching center of calyx.
Outside of coral has fairly regular wrinkled banding, giving a
crude "crinoid stem" look.

Adkinsella edwardensis Wells (Photo 52)
Lower Cretaceous, Edwards formation. A large coral of the
Edwards formation reef associations. Calyx large, septa sharp
and not touching in center. Septa alternate long and short. Generally embedded in a reef of rudistid bivalves, etc. A solitary coral.

Favia texana (Photo 53)
Upper Cretaceous, Austin group. A colonial coral with many
round or oval corallites, each with a raised rim. Overall corallum
usually domed. This species inhabited the area around the Cretaceous volcanoes, such as Pilot Knob near Austin. The warm volcanic waters were very favorable to this coral, allowing fast
growth.

Montastrea (Photo 54)
Lower Cretaceous, Fredericksburg division. Massive, shapeless corallums composed of circular calyxes between which the
radiating septa interfinger. *M. travisensis* (Wells) has smaller
calyxes that are more irregularly crowded together. *M. roemeriana* (Wells) has larger, more evenly spaced calyxes.

Septastrea keroides (Photo 55)
Paleocene, Midway group. Dome-shaped corallum composed
of many closely spaced calyxes. Septa well developed, meeting
in calyx center to form a united area. The genus *Septastrea* also
occurs in the Lower Cretaceous Edwards formation in a more irregularly shaped corallum.

Siderastrea tuckerae Wells (Photo 56)
Lower Cretaceous period. Medium-sized domed-shaped corallum composed of many small, raised, circular calyxes. Bottom
shows layered growth rings.

Astrocoenia guadalupae Roemer (Photo 57)
Lower Cretaceous, Edwards formation. A colonial coral of
massive growth habit encrusting slabs. Calyxes all connected by
their adjacent walls. Their individual shapes are polygonal.
Twenty-four septa of which twelve reach the columella in the
center.

Blothrocyathus harrisi Wells (Photo 58)
Lower Cretaceous, Trinity division. Corallite is a large (20-30
mm. wide) solitary shaft of irregularly stacked calyxes, which
may grow many inches tall. Thin septa, primary ones reaching
calyx center.

Turbinolia (Photo 59)
Eocene epoch. An extremely small, cone-shaped solitary coral
with septa forming ribs down outside of corallite. Calyx circular
with raised central cone formed from ends of several septa.

Paracyathus (Photo 60)
Paleocene epoch. Small, solitary corals with numerous septae.
Exterior marked by fine upright lines. Tall cone-shaped corallite.

Parasmilia (Photo 61)
Lower Cretaceous. Small (twenty- to twenty-five millimeter-
long) solitary coral; tapered to flattened attachment point at base.
Many septa, most reaching center of calyx. Septa granular and

extending as regular longitudinal lines down sides of coral. *P. austinensis* Roemer (Fredericksburg division) has an evenly flared base for a larger attachment area. *P. bullardi* Wells is found in the Trinity division and has thinner septa near center of calyx and less regular longitudinal lines on the exterior.

Flabellum (Photo 62)
Paleocene to recent. Small solitary coral with sides compressed to make calyx longer than wide. Septa meet to form a slightly raised partition lengthwise in the calyx. Septa do not extend outside rim of calyx, although the outside of the coral has longitudinal ridges and concentric growth lines. Base of coral narrows to a small stemlike point.

Endopachys maclurii (Lea) (Photo 63)
Eocene epoch. Much like flabellum in pinch-sided look to make calyx longer than wide, but septa extend partway down exterior of coral, and base of coral is swollen.

Balanophyllia (Photo 64)
Eocene epoch. Small, solitary corals, usually with a scar at base from attachment. Cross-section of coral is elliptical. Septa and fine external striations both numerous, fine, and somewhat branching. Slender, curved, hornlike species is *B. irrorata* of Texas Eocene strata. *B. desmophyllum* is a larger, less slender species of the same strata. *B. ponderosa* is a larger species of the Midway group, Paleocene Epoch in Texas.

Archohelia (Photo 65)
Eocene Epoch. A pencil-shaped colonial coral with small calyxes scattered along the sticklike colony.

Chaetetes milleporaceous Edwards and Haime (Photo 66)
Pennsylvanian period. Traditionally viewed as a colonial coral, but corallum composed of long, slender (0.5 mm. wide) tubes that often share common walls. The tubes have irregularly spaced tabulae in them. Calyxes divide by growing cross walls and have varying shapes.

Phylum Bryozoa — Moss Animals, Sea Mats

The individual bryozoan animal, a small creature with a tentacle-fringed mouth, lives in a small pit called a *zooecium* in a calcified colonial structure called a *zoarium,* which can be massive, spiral, branching, lacy, or latticelike. The profusion of small pits, arranged rather irregularly and lacking the radiating septa of most corals, help identify a specimen as a bryozoan. Bryozoans often encrust other fossils or rocks. They are most abundant in the Texas Pennsylvanian period but are found in the Mesozoic and Cenozoic as well.

Polypora submarginata (Meek) (Photos 67, 68)
Pennsylvanian period. Zoarium has the appearance of a lacy mat with ladderlike openings resembling irregular ovals. Ten to twelve zooecia directly border each large opening in the mat; other zooecia cover the mat arms in very irregular rows. The arms of the mat have no longitudinal keels separating zooecia. A ridge or keel between the rows of zooecia is indicative of the similar genera *Fenestella* and *Fenestrellina.* The dissepiments are smaller than the arms, are thin, and do not bear zooecia. A common lacy bryozoan of the Lower Cretaceous, Edwards formation is shown on Photo 70.

Rhombopora lepidodendroidea (Meek) (Photo 69)
Pennsylvanian period. Slender branches with zooecia arranged in regular, angled rows. Very plentiful in some Pennsylvanian formations in Texas.

Phylum Brachiopoda — The Brachiopods

Brachiopods resemble clams and oysters in many ways, and it is important in fossil identification to be able to separate the two groups. Geologically, brachiopods appear in the rocks somewhat earlier than the other bivalves. Brachiopods have their greatest profusion in Paleozoic strata and have diminished in abundance since then. Clams and oysters share the Paleozoic with the brachiopods but have reached greater numbers in Mesozoic and Cenozoic time. At present they greatly outnumber brachiopods.

It adds to the confusion that the two shell halves of both brachiopods and clams are called *valves*. The larger valve of a brachiopod will usually show a beak-like underturn with a small opening from which, in life, emerged a fleshy stem (a *pedicle*) that attached the brachiopod to the ocean bottom. It is called the *pedicle valve*. The smaller valve is called the *brachial valve* because it "brachiates" or hinges open to allow water into the brachiopod shell. Both valves on a brachiopod are usually bilaterally symmetrical.

Clams and oysters may have a beak to the valves, but never an opening for a pedicle. Most important, only a few clams even come close to bilateral symmetry of each valve itself. Clams can be bilaterally symmetrical only when both valves are viewed from the side or end together. Brachiopods rarely show such symmetry viewed edge on since the larger valve will "beak over" the hinge line asymmetrically.

Brachiopod fossils are most often found with both valves still together, while clams and oysters generally separate at death. This is caused by the rubbery ligament that springs clam and oyster shells open whenever the muscles relax. Brachiopods have no such springy ligament; hence in death their shells generally remain closed and together.

Brachiopods are scientifically divided into two groups, the inarticulate brachiopods, without well-defined, toothed hinge lines connecting the valves, and articulate brachiopods, with well-defined hinge lines. The inarticulate brachiopods are those most often found in Texas's oldest Paleozoic rocks. Articulate brachiopods are most common in late Paleozoic rocks. One genus, *Kingena,* is common in Texas Lower Cretaceous strata. Some brachiopods are found in the Cenozoic as well. Strangely, Texas's most recent sediments contain inarticulate brachiopods, just as do Texas's oldest fossil strata, showing the durability of such primitive brachiopods.

Inarticulate (Hingeless) Brachiopods
Linguella similis Walcot (Photo 71)
Upper Cambrian period. Tear-drop-shaped shell with one valve slightly smaller than the other. Bluntly pointed beak grooved for attachment of fleshy stalk (pedicle). Often abundant in Cambrian "coquina" assemblages.

Lingula (Photo 72)
Silurian to Recent. A pointed-fingernail-shaped shell with two
nearly equal valves, often a polished surface with faint concentric growth lines. *L. carbonaria* Shumard and Swallow is found
in the Pennsylvanian period. *L. subspatulata* Hall and Meek is
recorded from the Upper Cretaceous Woodbine, and Navarro
formations. One of the oldest continuously existing genera, *Lingula*, are still around after four hundred million years!
Trigonoglossa sp. are similar but quite triangular in outline with
strong concentric growth marks. *Trigonoglossa* is a
Pennsylvanian-Mississippian period genus in Texas.

Articulate (Hinged) Brachiopods

Billingsella coloradoensis (Shumard) (Photo 73)
Upper Cambrian period, Wilberns formation. A wide shell
with small wings. Ornament of rays and concentric ridges intersecting. Slight sulcus.

Finkelnburgia obesa Cloud (Photo 74)
Ordovician period, Ellenburger-Tanyard formations. Fragile,
delicate valves. An index fossil to the Texas Ordovician.

Leptaena analoga (Phillips) (Photo 75)
Mississippian period. A concave-convex brachiopod, but with
wide, flattened shell and characterized as a genus by strong concentric wrinkles on valves.

Rhipidomella carbonaria (Shumard and Swallow) (See Photo 76, Derbyia)
Pennsylvanian period. A flattened or somewhat convex shell,
a little longer than wide, with a small projecting beak area. Sides
almost parallel. Ornament of very fine-branching, radiating lines
and concentric growth marks, some of them quite coarse. *Derbyia crassa* (Meek and Hayden) is very similar but has a straighter hinge line, a little more thickness, and is slightly wider than
long. *D. bennetti* Hall and Clarke is similar but has an irregular,
pointy beak area. *D. cymbula* Hall and Clarke is a very large (up
to 75 mm. width) and very wide species found in the Upper
Pennsylvanian and Lower Permian periods. *Orthotetes kaska-
skiensis* McChesney is a Mississippian species that is similar to

Derbyia but flatter and slightly more rounded rectangular in outline.

Chonetes granulifer Owen (Photo 77)
Pennsylvanian period. Small- to medium-sized shell with semicircular outline; wide, almost straight hinge with ten small spines each side of beak. One valve convex; one valve concave. Ornament of very fine even ridges. Tips of shell make small wings. Only slight fold or sulcus at most.

Chonetina Flemingi (Norwood and Pratten) (Photo 78)
Pennsylvanian period. Like *Chonetes* but with a deep, narrow sulcus and strong fold. Ornament of fine radiating ridges. *Chonetinella* ssp. are similar but the surface of the shell covered with small spines. It is a Lower Permian period species.

Lissochonetes geinitzianus (Waagen) (See Photo 77, Chonetes)
Pennsylvanian period. Much like *Chonetes* but with a smooth exterior and a broad fold and sulcus, which can vary from deep to none (Gries 1970). Faint growth lines may be present. Widespread throughout U.S.

Mesolobus mesolobus Norwood and Pratten (Photo 79)
Pennsylvanian period. Shaped much like *Chonetes* sp. but with a broad sulcus with a middle fold on the ventral valve, and a low fold with a middle sulcus on the dorsal valve. Ornament of tiny scattered spine bases over both valves. May also have smooth or fine ribbed surface. *M. inflexus* (Girty), Photo 79, has a very small, narrow middle fold and middle sulcus. It is an indicator of the Mid-Pennsylvanian.

Juresania symmetrica (McChesney) (Color Photo 9, Photo 80)
Pennsylvanian period. A medium to large shell, with a high arched ventral valve and a flat or slightly concave dorsal valve. Broad arched beak. Hinge straight but much less wide than the total shell. Little if any sulcus. Slanted or erect spines on both valves. Ornament of concentric lines crowded with tiny bumps for spine bases.

Marginifera muricatina (Dunbar and Condra) (Photo 81; see also Photo 82)

Pennsylvanian period. Easily mistaken for a small *Juresania*. This species is wider for its height, has a very concave dorsal (flatter) valve, and has spines only on the larger, curved ventral valve. The hinge line is almost as wide as the whole shell. *M. lasallensis* (Worthen), Photo 82, is similar but has slightly larger surface ridges and has concentric overlying layering on the half of the larger valve nearest the beak.

Echinaris and Liosotella (Photos 83, 84, 85)

Permian period. These are both brachiopods of the Word formation in the Glass Mountains near Marathon, Texas. Dr. G. Arthur Cooper of the National Museum of Natural History, Smithsonian Institution, etched something more than fifty tons of limestone rock from this area in various acids. It is a dangerous procedure because of possible acid spills and burns. The etching removes the limey rock yet does not affect the fossils because they are replaced by silica (quartz), which does not dissolve in most acids. Such work is only for trained specialists, but it yields very delicate fossil structures unobtainable by normal cleaning.

Collemataria (Lyttonia) (Leptodus) nobilis americanus (Girty) (Photo 86)

Permian period. West Texas. Skeletal, ribcagelike pattern as shell conforms to internal structure. Specimens shown are naturally rain-etched from the Glass Mountains near Marathon, Texas.

Prorichthofenia (Richthofenia) permiana Shumard (Photo 87)

Permian period, West Texas. A horn-coral-like shape but lacking any coral central structures. Actually a brachiopod equivalent of the aberrant growth habit of some oysters, where one valve becomes a cone and the other a mere cap. Glass Mountains material.

Reticulatia americanus (Dunbar and Condra) (Photos 88, 89)

Pennsylvanian period. Much like *Juresania* but with longer

hinge line approaching the width of the shell. Flatter (dorsal) valve has no spines, and both valves have a characteristic reticulated pattern, where fine lines in two directions cross each other. Width greater than length, dorsal (flatter) valve only mildly concave. *R. portlockianus* (Norwood and Pratten) is similar, somewhat smaller (maximum size usually less than 40 mm.), length and width about equal, dorsal (flatter) valve quite concave in middle. *R. bassi* (McKee) is a very large Permian species of West Texas. It has arched ears at sides. An older name for this genus is *Dictyoclostus*.

Echinoconchus knighti Dunbar and Condra (Photo 90)
Pennsylvanian period. A large brachiopod with the larger valve domed with almost vertical sides. Hinge line less than maximum shell width and most species slightly longer than wide. Ornament of wide, rounded concentric bands on both valves, occasionally still bearing spines. Exterior usually has pearly luster.

Linoproductus prattenianus (Norwood and Pratten) (Photo 91)
Pennsylvanian period. A large, unequal-valved brachiopod, like *Juresania* and *Reticulatia*. Also resembles them in having one valve domed over in a fat curve. Differing from them in having a wide scattering of very large spine bases appearing like widely spaced warts across its surface. It has a surface marked with fine wavy lines but lacks the cross-patterned reticulation of *Reticulatia*.

Composita subtilita (Sheppard) (Photos 92, 93)
Pennsylvanian period. A very common oil-lamp-shaped shell with a circular pedicle opening, a surface of only faint growth lines, and a deep fold and sulcus. Thin, small specimens have been called *C. ovata* Mather, while larger more robust specimens have been called *C. subtilita* (Sheppard). Study (Gries 1970) indicates a likelihood that these are merely differences of habitat and maturity. Gries retreats to the more general species *C. wasatchensis* (White). A tiny look-alike for the genus *Composita* is *Cleiothyridina* (Photo 94). It differs in the straightness of the profile of the valves as they approach the beak. This puts the beak at the point of a sharp right angle.

Neospirifer cameratus (Morton) (Photos 95, 96)

Pennsylvanian period. A large "winged" shell, the wings making the shell length only about two-thirds the width. Ornamented with many rounded, radiating ridges, which are larger and more rounded on the sulcus and fold. Called popularly by some North Texas ranchers "fossil butterflies" because of the wings. *N. dunbari* (King) is also large and winged, but has sharp radiating ridges. It also has several broad radiating folds, which are more pronounced than on *N. cameratus*. *Spirifer rockymontanus* Marcou is very similar but has length only slightly less than the width and ridges more uniform over entire shell surface. *Neospirifer texanus* (Meek) is similar but slightly longer than wide, with no wings. *N. condor* (Orbigny) is a large Permian-period species. *N. alatus* Dunbar and Condra (Photo 96), is a very wide, winged Pennsylvanian species.

Punctospirifer kentuckiensis (Shumard) (Photo 97)

Pennsylvanian period. Like a small winged *Neospirifer* but with tips slightly more pointed on good specimens. Length of valve about half the width. Ornament of large deep ridges each widening and subdividing away from the beak. Gap between valves, under beak, is large for shell's size, causing the beak to be somewhat high, isolated, and hook-like. *P. transversa* (McChesney) is very similar, with tips on good specimens quite pointed and ridges only moderately large.

Phricodothyris perplexa (McChesney) (Photos 98, 99)

Pennsylvanian period. Medium-sized shells with both valves very convex. Beak (ventral) valve thicker than the dorsal valve, and in all the "thyrises" the beak is thick and massively curved. Dorsal valve a wide oval in outline. Where well-preserved, low magnification shows concentric rows of double spines. *Crurithyris planoconvexa* (Shumard) (Photo 99) is similar but with nearly flat dorsal valve of more circular outline. *Ambocoelia planoconvexa* (Shumard) is probably the same species as *Crurithyris planoconvexa*, as explained by Gries 1970. *Brachythyris chouteauensis* (Weller) is a slightly larger Mississippian period shell, convex on both valves and ornamented by eight to ten large, rounded ridges that widen away from the beak and are especially wide and flaring on the fold of the shell. The general "thyris" shape sets apart these small brachiopods.

Hustedia mormoni (Marcou) (Photo 100)

Pennsylvanian period. A small, flattened, drop-shaped shell with many fine radiating ridges, some dividing into two. Pedicle opening round and visible. *H. miseri* Mather is similar but with more convex valves. *H. hessensis* King of the West Texas Permian period has valves so convex as to make the shell almost spherical, and only about seven large rounded ribs. Its beak area is quite narrowed.

Kingena wacoensis (Roemer) (Photo 101)

Lower Cretaceous. Medium-sized, smoothly contoured brachiopod of typical ancient-oil-lamp shape. Brachiopods are often called "lamp shells." Profile of this shell can be oval or circular. Both valves are rounded convex. It has a well-defined beak and foramen (opening). It is the only common brachiopod in the Texas Lower Cretaceous.

Phylum Mollusca – The Mollusks

Mollusks are a very important, large, and diverse group that includes the sea, land, and freshwater snails, sea and freshwater bivalves (clams and oysters), living and extinct cephalopods (squids, octopuses, nautiluses, and ammonites), and the less well-known scaphopods and chitons. In Mesozoic and Cenozoic sediments they virtually dominate the fossil record. They are present in the Paleozoic all the way back to the Cambrian.

Class Gastropoda – The Snails

The gastropods have a one-piece shell consisting of a cone coiled either as a flat coil or rising into a spired coil. Each full turn of the shell is called a *whorl*. The shell opening is called the *aperture*. In life the aperture is protected by a horny covering called the *operculum,* but it rarely fossilizes. The aperture may show various slits for water intake and expulsion.

Euphemites nodocarinatus (Hall) (Photo 102)

Pennsylvanian period. A small snail coiled into a symmetrical ball. Many small sharp ridges follow the direction of the coil, none much more prominent than the others. On some species a weak keel develops.

Pharkidonotus tricarinatus (Shumard) (Photo 103)

Pennsylvanian period. A moderately small snail, coiled in the broad-apertured, symmetrical fashion that marks all members of this superfamily. The coil is followed around by three knobby ridges, the knobs of which are joined in weak cross ridges. *P. pericarinatus* (Conrad) is similar, but with the central ridge dominant and with overall weaker knobs.

Bellerophon crassus (Meek and Worthen) (Photo 104)

Pennsylvanian period. Small to medium-sized snail. Broad-apertured symmetrical coil. Marked by fine cross ridges and one central smooth ridge in the direction of the coiling. Aperture has broad notch in upper aperture lip. *B. heucoensis* of the Texas Permian period has an aperture much wider than it is high and a narrow, prominent notch in the upper lip of the aperture.

Straparollus (Photo 105)

Pennsylvanian and Permian periods. Small to medium-sized snails, coiled flatly. Divided into several subgenera. Several old genera are now treated as subgenera. In the old genus *Straparollus* the whorls are in contact, and each whorl is rounded in cross section. The old genus *Serpulospira* has most whorls open and out of contact with each other. The old genus *Euomphalus* has a sharp-angled cross-section to the whorl that results in a raised shoulder around the whorl. The old genus *Amphiscapha* has a rough, horny surface to the whorls, above and below.

Trepospira discoidalis Newell (Photo 106)

Pennsylvanian period. Medium-sized snails coiled with a low spire, somewhat flattened at peak. Top surface marked by a spiral of small, even bumps. Specimens with a slightly raised spire and slightly lowered aperture lip (making the shell altogether taller) are placed under *T. sphaerulata* (Conrad).

Glabrocinculum grayvillense (Norwood and Pratten) (Photo 107)

Pennsylvanian period. Small snail with only low to moderate spire. Top of each whorl sloping, with no straight vertical drops from whorl to whorl as in *Worthenia*. Ornamentation in two directions, causing a bumpy pattern where they cross.

Worthenia tabulata (Conrad) (Photo 108)
Pennsylvanian period. Medium-sized snail with moderately high spire. Sides of each whorl straight up and down or even angled slightly inward, forming a sharp angle with a row of nodes at the outer edge of each whorl. Ornamentation in two directions crossing at places to form bumpy pattern.

Goniasma lasalllensis (Worthen) (Photo 109)
Pennsylvanian period. A medium-sized, high-spired snail with relatively little siphon tube below. Best characterized by sharp-edged whorls (much like a very stretched-out *Worthenia*). *Meekospira,* Photo 110, is similar but with simple straight-sided whorls. A plain little high-spired snail.

Strobeus (Photo 111)
Pennsylvanian period. Fat little snails with usually a short spire and a short, broad siphon tube coming off each end of a rounded middle. *S. littonanus* (Hall) is the shortest-spired of the genus. *S. primogenius* (Conrad) has a modest spire. *S. regularis* (Cox) has a spire as long as the last whorl. The older genera, *Soleniscus, Macrocheilus, Macrochilina,* and *Sphaerodoma,* have often been used for what are best called *Strobeus.*

Architectonica alveata (Conrad) (Photos 113 and 130)
Eocene epoch, Claiborne group. A small to medium-sized snail with shell a low, flat spiraled cone. Outer edge usually sharp-angled. Umbilicus is deep and in this species edged with triangular indentations. *A. scrobiculata* (Conrad), Photo 113, is lower and ornamented with spiral beaded lines top and bottom. *A. phoenicea* Gardner is similar but found in the Midway group of the Paleocene epoch.

Cerithium bosquense Shumard (Photo 114 and Color Photo 12)
Lower Cretaceous period, Comanche Peak and Walnut formations. A large, long-spired snail with flattened whorls that show some weak undulating ornamentation, appearing as weak nodes along the suture of each whorl with the whorl before it. A complete specimen shows twelve to fifteen whorls. A characteristic of this genus is the way each whorl narrows at its base to seem-

ingly slip into the whorl below it. *Macrocerithium,* described by
Stephenson, is a medium-sized genus in the Woodbine formation.

Mesalia (Turritella) seriatim-granulata (Roemer) (Photo 115)

Lower Cretaceous period. A moderately large, slender snail
once in the genus *Turritella,* but differing from it in having a
slightly less steeply pointed spire and a small anterior canal notch
at the base of the aperture. This species is named for its five alternating knobby spiral lines of ornament, well separated by plain
lines.

Mesalia claibornensis Harris (Photo 116)

Eocene epoch, Claiborne group. A moderately small snail,
elongate and sharp-pointed. Sides of whorls make an even taper
from base to point. Basal width about one-third to one-fourth the
height.

Mesalia alabamensis (Photo 140)

Paleocene epoch, Midway group. A moderately large, tall-
spired snail. Basal width broad for this genus; ornament of well-
marked close-spaced lines revolving with the whorls.

"Turritella" Limestone (Color Photo 11)

Lower Cretaceous. Many snails resembling *Turritella* create a
layer in this limestone found near Gatesville, Texas. It is cut and
polished for lapidary purposes.

Turritella vertebroides Morton

Upper Cretaceous, Navarro group. A long, pointed snail with
sutures between whorls slightly indented. Ornament is of four to
six plain raised spiral ridges with lesser ridges between. *T. trilira*
Conrad, also from the Navarro group, has three or four slightly
more prominent ridges.

Turritella mortoni Conrad (Photos 117 and 118)

Paleocene and Eocene epochs. A long, pointed snail with side
of each whorl sharp-angled and slightly concave between angles.
Some minor spiraled lines between angles. *T. humerosa* Conrad
is in same layers and is very elongate, with sides of whorls

almost flat between raised spiral ridge near suture between whorls. *T. hilli,* Photo 118, is a very long, thin Paleocene, Midway group species. *T. aldrichi,* Photo 118, in the same epoch has convex sides between whorl lines and a very swollen final whorl.

Anchura (Photos 119 and 120)
Lower Cretaceous period. A moderately large snail with a moderately high spire and with base drawn out into a long thin canal. Lip of aperture flared into a wide extension, which is usually broken off from specimens.

Calytraphorus popenoe Gardner (Photo 131)
Paleocene epoch, Midway group. A medium-sized snail with a rounded middle and long high spire. Body whorl blankets exterior of shell, hiding inner whorls and making exterior somewhat drop shaped. Siphon moderately long and thin.

Gyrodes (Sohlella) spillmani (Gabb) (Photo 121)
Upper Cretaceous period, Navarro group. A small snail with low, almost flat spire and enlarged outer whorl. Aperture large. Other similarly shaped members of this genus occur throughout the Cretaceous and Tertiary periods. *Gilbertina texana* Gardner is a similar low-spired, fat snail with an enveloping outer whorl; it is Paleocene epoch, Midway group. *Polinices,* Photos 122 and 141, has a similarly enlarged outer whorl, but has a slightly more elevated spire. It is Upper Cretaceous and early Tertiary. A common species is *P. harrisii* Gardner, Paleocene, Midway group.

Cypraea (Photos 130 and 131)
Paleocene epoch. A small snail with outer whorl completely dominating the shell. Outer whorl wrapped around like a tightly closed fist. *Cypraea* and *Cylichnina* in the Paleocene, Midway group are similar. *Cylichnina* differs in being wider on the umbilical end of the shell; the others are wider on the spire end. *Volvulina* is a large cast with a similarly all-enveloping outer whorl, mostly from the Lower Cretaceous, Glen Rose formation.

Epitonium (Photo 123)
Paleocene epoch. A very distinctive small snail with moderate width and moderately long spire. Surface is marked by close-

spaced varices (old aperture lips) like vertical bars on each whorl. Whorls are rounded without angular shoulders. *E. cookei* occurs in the Paleocene, Midway group.

Amaurellina alabamensis (Photo 123)
Paleocene epoch, Midway group. Small snail with enlarged outer whorl and modest spire. Narrow umbilicus.

Sinum bilix (Conrad) (Photo 124)
Eocene epoch, Claiborne group. A small snail with rounded modest spire and large aperture. *S. declive* (Conrad), Photo 124, is a similar, slightly more rotund species also in the Claiborne group.

Leptomaria austenensis (Shumard) (Photo 126)
Lower Cretaceous period. A large, flat snail with a very depressed (low) spire of four slanted-topped, steplike whorls. *Pleurotomaria glenrosensis* Whitney in the Lower Cretaceous Glen Rose formation is a smaller but similar snail. Each whorl has a keel at its outside edge often composed of small bumps.

Tylostoma tumidum Shumard (Photo 127)
Lower Cretaceous period. A moderately fat snail but still with an elevated spire, about one-half the total shell height. Top of whorls rounded. Umbilicus present. Usually only preserved as a cast. Aperture ovate with thickened outer lip. *T. elevatum* Shumard, if a valid species, has spire longer than the body whorl. It is also Lower Cretaceous. *T. hilli* Whitney from the Buda formation is a very large species, shell somewhat compressed and spire only one-half the height of body whorl. *T. pedenalis* (Roemer) from the Walnut and Comanche Peak formations is another very large species (116 mm. height), which is distinguished from *Lunatia* by *Tylostoma*'s squarer-shouldered whorls. The Paleocene, Midway group has a snail shaped similarly to *Tylostoma* in *Lacunaria lithae* Gardner.

Lunatia pedernalis (Hill) (Compare to Photo 127, Tylostoma)
Lower Cretaceous period. A very large snail with low spire and an open umbilicus. Whorls overlapping and rounded to a thin upper edge. Whole shell may be flattened side-to-side.

Levifusus mortoniopsis (Gabb) (Photos 128 and 129)

Eocene epoch, Claiborne group. Small snail with broad spire about as high as wide, and siphon tube about twice as long. Ornament of moderately spaced, pronounced wavy lines over rather sharp regular bumps. *L. pagoda,* Photo 129, and *L. lithae* Gardner are Paleocene epoch, Midway group species. *Pleurotomella whitfieldi,* Photo 141, is similar but with less-wavy lines and a longer siphonal canal. *Latirus stephensoni* Gardner (also Midway group) is similar but with more pronounced and rounded regular bumps and almost no siphon tube at base of shell.

Mangelia schotti Gardner (Photo 132)

Paleocene epoch. A small snail with a moderately high spire (when intact). The outer whorl is graceful and vase-shaped, with a rotund shoulder and tapering siphon below. Ornament is of strong ridges lengthwise on the shell, with numerous fine lines crossing the ridges. *Lyria wilcoxiana,* Photo 129, is similar but lacks the fine cross lines. This graceful "draped funereal urn" shape is characteristic of "lyre" shells in whatever genus or period including the Recent.

Distorsio septemdentata Gabb (Photo 133)

Eocene epoch, Claiborne group. A moderately small snail with quite a broad body whorl (the width just about half the height, give or take). Ridges and lines running in two directions make an ornament of bumps where they cross. The whorls are not of uniform width even in the same whorl. Whorls overlap irregularly, hence the name *distorsio.* Aperture lip moderately thick, with many ridges entering the aperture like teeth on its inner surface. Siphon short, small, and slightly twisted. A more twisted siphon on a short, broad shell with many bumplike projections is the Tertiary genus *Murex,* very similar to *Distorsio.*

Falsifusus ludovicianus (Johnson) (Photo 134)

Eocene epoch. Small snail with moderate spire and moderately elongate siphon. Whorls have minute spiraling wavy lines over regular rounded bumps.

Volutocorbis texana Gardner (Photo 135)

Paleocene epoch, Midway group. A medium-sized snail with

a modest spire and an enveloping body whorl. Ornament of spiral and vertical lines crossing each other in a cancellate pattern. *V. rugatus* (Conrad) is slimmer and with wider-spaced vertical lines and a taller spire making up one-third of the shell.

Athleta petrosus (Conrad) (Photo 136 and Color Photo 10)

Eocene epoch, Claiborne group. A small to medium-sized snail. Spire moderate (about one-third height of shell), broadly tapering body whorl. Aperture wide but long; lip thin. Columella has two or three small ridges entering aperture. Tops of first two whorls from the lip have sharp spines. *A. lisbonensis* (Plumber) is similar but has more rounded shoulder on body whorl and smaller spines on the large whorls.

Lapparia crassa Stenzel and Turner (Photos 137 and 138)

Eocene epoch, Claiborne group. Medium-sized snail. Spire and siphon almost equidistant from a broad width at midshell. Spire prickled with widely spaced large spines. Aperture moderately long with large spiral ridges on the columella leading into the aperture. *L. mooreana* (Gabb), Photo 138, similar but with spire and shell more slender.

Olivella (Compare to Photos 139, 140, and 141, Pseudoliva)

Eocene epoch, Claiborne group. Small snail. Body whorl covers most of shell; spire is variable but is generally rather low. Spiral notch above suture between whorls. Band on base of body whorl. Aperture has small notch at upper end and broadens toward base, with ridges on inner lip. *Pseudoliva* is similar but with obviously more spire height.

Pseudoliva vetusta Conrad (Photos 139, 140, 141, and Color Photo 10)

Eocene epoch, Claiborne group. A small snail with a low-to-modest spire and a large rounded body whorl, which inflates the middle of the shell, hence "olive-shaped." Body whorl has a spiral line on its lower one-third. Lip of aperture very thin. Aperture widest near middle, no ridges on inner lip. *P. scalina*, Photo 140, in the Paleocene, Midway group, has faint vertical folds ending in teeth at the top of each whorl. *P. ostrarupsis*, Photo 141, is a small "olive" shell with a rather long spire; also Paleocene. Also see *Olivella*.

Cochlespira engonata Conrad (Photo 142)
Eocene epoch, Claiborne group. Small snail. Tall spire and moderately long canal formed by long aperture. Whorls are slanted and form a sharp, pronounced spiral ridge down the shell. No other ornament.

Coronia genitiva (Casey) (Photo 131)
Eocene epoch, Claiborne group. Small snails with very high spires making up two-thirds of shell. Spire is ornamented with large and small spiral rows of beads near tip. As ornament proceeds downward, small beaded line becomes one or more spiral lines. Large beaded line becomes more a row of vertical ridges. Siphon tube long. *C. mediavia*, Photo 131, is a Paleocene epoch, Midway formation species of similar shape.

Conus sauridens Conrad (Photo 143 and Color Photo 10)
Eocene epoch, Claiborne group. A medium-to-large snail. Broad, even-tapered, cone-shaped, with low spire. Aperture is a long slit down the length of the shell. Aperture lip thin.

Orthosurcula (Photo 144)
Paleocene epoch, Midway and Kincaid groups. Small to medium-sized snails with high spires and long, graceful siphons. Broadest point on shell about middle. *O. longispersa* Gardener is quite thin, with ornament of spiral lines; *O. adeona* (Whitfield) is the broadest of the group and has small bumps as well as lines on the whorls; *O. francescae* Gardner has moderate width with line ornament lower and small vertical ridges near point. The outside of each whorl is somewhat sharp-angled. *O. phoenicea* Gardner has spiral lines and wavy vertical ridges for ornament. *Exilia pergracilis* Conrad is similarly graceful and high-spired, but is quite thin and has rounded whorls with fine vertical ridges crossing fine spiral lines.

Protosurcula gabbii (Conrad) (Photo 145)
Eocene epoch, Claiborne group. Medium-sized snail with

long, graceful shape caused by high spire ornamented with fine spiral lines. Siphon long and slender, about equaling spire in height.

Olivellites plummeri Fenton and Fenton *(Photo 112)*
Pennsylvanian period. Traces of snail burrows. Such burrowing patterns are common in sedimentary rocks.

Class Rostroconchia — A Primitive Step toward Bivalves

Conocardium, a "rostroconch" (Photo 146)
Pennsylvanian period. A small bivalvelike shell with lots of gape to the valves, which in fact do not function. The shell's wide gape is edged with small toothlike projections. This type of fossil was once thought to be a bivalve, but now is thought to be an earlier prototype of bivalve development. Its two "valves" grow from one valve in the juvenile (larval) stage. It is a fine novelty to seek for a collection.

Class Bivalvia — Oysters, Clams, etc.

Animals covered by a shell usually consisting of two parts called *valves*. The valves are considered left and right, while the opening side of the shells is the bottom of the bivalve. One or two muscles close the shell halves and often leave distinctive scars inside the shell. The shells are opened by an elastic ligament. Upon death the muscles relax and the ligament may spring the shells apart. Bivalves are often found as fossils with separated valves. The beaklike projections on the rear of the shell are called *umbones*. In front of the umbones is a flattened area along the hinge line called the *lunule*. If bivalves are ever bilaterally symmetrical, it is on each side of the hinge line.

Nucula (Photo 147)
Silurian to Present. A small clam with equal valves. Rear of each valve truncated (shortened), other end only moderately long. Interior of valves show small teeth in hinge and toothlike grooves all along lower margin. *N. ciboloensis* Stephenson is a relatively large member of this genus, 9 to 35 or 40 mm. in length. Found in the Kemp Clay, Navarro group, Upper Creta-

ceous. *N. Bybeei* Whitney is quite small, with oval shape and very tiny low beaks (Glen Rose formation, Lower Cretaceous). *N. wenoensis* Adkins is a medium-sized species from the Washita group, Lower Cretaceous. *Nucula (Nuculopsis) croneisi* Schenck is a small, triangular, rather thick, faintly concentrically marked species from the Paleozoic, Pennsylvanian period. *Nucula (Nuculopsis) girtyi* (Schenck) is another Pennsylvanian species. These are small, triangular, mildly elongate clams with usually a slight gape between valves.

Nuculana (Compare to Photo 147, Nucula, and Photo 149, Yoldia)

Pennsylvanian and Permian periods to Present. Small clams with equal valves but very much more elongated from the beaks forward than *Nucula*. Forward end often coming to a point. *N. bellistriata* (Stevens) is a Pennsylvanian-Permian species with strong concentric ridged ornamentation. *N. longifrons* Conrad is one of a number of Navarro group, Upper Cretaceous species. *Solyma* Stephenson is similar to *Nuculana* in the Navarro group, Upper Cretaceous, but is slightly enlarged and rounded in the extension in front of the beaks. *Yoldia,* Photo 149, of the Cretaceous to Recent, is similar but with less-pointed posteriors, less-raised beaks, and a slight gape at each end.

Astartella concentrica (Conrad) (Photo 148)

Pennsylvanian period. Small clams with fine, sharp concentric surface marking. Beaks prominently raised and slightly slanted backward. End away from beaks may be truncated.

Allorisma terminale Hall (Photo 150)

Permian period. A large bivalve, elongate in shape, with rounded concentric ridges most prominent near the beaks. Valves gape somewhat at far end. On smaller species in this genus the upper margin of the shell has an upward flare.

Arca simondsi Whitney (Photo 151)

Lower Cretaceous, Trinity group. Large steinkerns 75 mm. in length or more. Shoe-shaped with wide-spread, raised beaks. Ridge on steinkern shows the original division of the valves. On the upper posterior, the ridge is marked by a large muscle scar on both sides.

Cucullaea terminalis Conrad (Compare with Photo 152, *C. kaufmanensis*)

Lower Cretaceous, Trinity division. A large common steinkern of the Glen Rose formation. Beaks are strongly curved and are nearly terminal at the anterior end of the shell. *C. recedens* Cragin occurs in the Fredericksburg division of the Lower Cretaceous. Its beaks are slightly less terminal. *C. kaufmanensis,* Photo 152, from the Paleocene, Midway formation, has beaks that are definitely not terminal, but still strongly incurved.

Brachidontes pedernalis (Roemer) (Compare to Photo 153, *B. filiscuptus, and Photo 154, Modiolus.*)

Lower Cretaceous. A long "muscle" shell with a strong diagonal ridge from the beaks, which are extremely anterior, to the far lower margin. Ornament is numerous branching ribs lengthwise on the shell. *B. filisculptus* (Cragin) in the Upper Cretaceous, Woodbine formation, is similar, but with very delicate ribs. *Inoperna concentricecostellata* (Roemer) is a similar shape and is Lower Cretaceous, Glen Rose formation, and has concentric ridged ornamentation primarily on the upper half of the shell. *Modiolus,* Photo 154, has a similar shape with concentric growth marks overall. It has many Lower Cretaceous species, many (like probably the one illustrated) undescribed.

Pinna comancheana Cragin (Photo 155)

Lower Cretaceous. Large flattened bivalves with one end pointed and the other wide (wedge-shaped). Usually broken when found. Closely related to the pen shells of the Texas coast today. Shell thin with a filling of limestone. Very similar species found in the Washita division are more likely to be *P. guadalupe* Bose.

Myalina subquadrata Shumard (Photos 157 and 156)

Pennsylvanian period. A medium-sized flat bivalve, oblong in shape with a short, very straight hinge line ending in a sharp, side-pointing beak. Valves slightly unequal. *M. copei* Whitfield, Photo 156, is a Lower Permian species with a longer straight hinge line, pronounced concentric growth lines, and a somewhat triangular shell shape with margin deeply indented by a deep sulcus. *Pteria* in the Lower Cretaceous, is like a fat cast with a long angular wing off a straight hinge line, much like Myalina shape, but having no biological relationship.

Inoceramus labiatus Schlotheim (Photo 158; also compare to Photo 160, I. comancheanus, and Fossil Pearls, Photo 159 and Color Photo 18)

Upper Cretaceous. Especially Eagle Ford group or its equivalents. Very plentiful and often very large flat oyster. Somewhat oblong with prominent beaks bent to one side. Ornament of concentric raised lines with smaller growth lines between them. Frequently preserved as imprints filled with a thin layer of shell. *I. fragilis* Hall and Meek is a similar Eagle Ford species with fainter, less regularly concentric lines. A large form in the Austin group, *I. subquadratus* Schluter, has a width as great as its length. *I. undulatoplicatus* (Roemer), also in the Austin group, has a wrinkled exterior with folds radiating toward the shell edge from a central ridge. *I. comancheanus* Cragin, Photo 160, is a Lower Cretaceous species of medium size with fifteen to twenty well-defined concentric ridges. Do not confuse this species with Upper Cretaceous forms.

Neithea texana Roemer (Photo 161; also compare to Photos 162 and 170)

Lower Cretaceous, Washita division. Shell shaped much like a modern scallop. Beak bent under at top of shell; from the beak, six large ribs radiate evenly toward lower edge of shell. One valve (the left) almost flat, the other valve convex. Smaller ribs are between the six larger ones; all are crossed by fine concentric lines. All ribs, raised or lower, are of equal width. Under the beak are small side ears. The valve's lower edge is not strongly scalloped. *N. georgetownensis* Kniker, Photo 162, has its main ribs split lengthwise by narrow furrows. *N. subalpina* Boese, Photo 163, is a slightly smaller, narrower species with pronounced ribs and deep furrows between them. The difference between tall and low ribs is great, and the valve lower edge is scalloped. *N. irregularis* (Boese), Photo 164, is similar to the above but has additional thin ribs between the larger ones; this occurs irregularly. *N. wrighti* (Shumard), Photo 165, in the Georgetown formation has only four or five very large radiating ribs, which give an angular toothy look to the lower edge of the valve. *N. whitneyi* Kniker, in the Buda formation, is similarly angular with deeper, narrower, less flat-bottomed furrows than the somewhat milder folder *N. wrighti. N. roemeri* Hill, Photo 166, in the Buda formation, is large with large ears containing radiating lines. Broad, gentle folds on the valves have wider ribs than the depressions between. *N. duplicicosta* (Roemer), Photo 167, in the Edwards formation is similar but with no lines on the ears and fairly equal-sized ribs throughout. *N. casteeli* Kniker, Photo 168, has twenty-six ribs, every fifth of which is taller; occurs in the Upper Cretaceous, Austin group. *Radiopecten mississippiensis* Conrad is a large-eared species in the Upper Cretaceous, Navarro group. *Chlamys stantoni* (Hill) is very similar but is found in the Glen Rose formation, Lower Cretaceous and has large rough ears and many radiating double ribs. The Pennsylvanian and Permian strata contain various large-eared shells that resemble *Neithea.* They are *Aviculupecten,* Photo 170, if they possess low, rounded radiating ridges (often of two sizes); or *Acanthopecten* when possessing sharp radiating ridges and noticeable concentric growth lines. *Pecten venustus* Morton in the Upper Cretaceous, Navarro group, is similar, but both valves are convex as in true pectens. *Neithea* species have a flat left valve.

Plicatula subgurgitis Bose *(Photo 171; also compare to Photos 172 and 173)*

Lower Cretaceous. Plicatulas are called "cat's paw" clams because of their paw shape, having one valve convex and one valve flat. Ornament is of coarse, radiating ribs with small spines, which near the lower edge of the shell resemble cat claws. Size rather small. *P. dentonensis* Cragin, Photo 172, in the Denton formation, has finer radiating ribs and fairly regular concentric ridges. *P. mullicaensis* Weller of the Upper Cretaceous, Navarro group, has many slender spines. *P. filimentosa* Conrad, Photo 173, is a common species in the Eocene epoch, especially Cook Mountain formation. A similarly shaped shell, but moderately large, is *Spondylus,* Photo 174. It has a tear-drop shape with large spinelike bumps in staggered rows.

Lima wacoensis Roemer *(Photo 175)*

Lower Cretaceous period. Small to medium-sized clams with

about twenty radiating ribs coming asymmetrically from the upper corner of the shell, *not* from a central beak as in a *Neithea*. Ribs sharp-topped with wide, evenly sloped interspaces. In *L. wacoensis* top and bottom shell margins are nearly parallel. *L. mexicana* is a more West Texas species with a wider shell and more prominent ribs. *L. pecosensis* Stanton, Photo 176, is found in the Lower Cretaceous of Central and West Texas. It has sixty radiating ribs and flares wider at the posterior end. Stephenson (1941) has described several species of *Lima* from the Upper Cretaceous, Navarro group. One huge species, *L. sayrei* Stephenson, is 95 mm. high and 33 mm. thick.

Pycnodonte mutabilis Morton (Photo 178)

Upper Cretaceous period, Taylor and Navarro groups. Massive dome-shaped oyster with small beak and exterior roughened by concentric growth marks. Often a radial fold separates a winglike portion of the shell from the rest. *P. vesicularis* (Lemarck) is an older name used for *P. mutabilis,* especially in the Escodido formation in South Texas. *P. wardi* (Hill and Vaughan), in the Lower Cretaceous, Glen Rose formation, is small with a large attachment scar on its exterior. *P. aucella* (Roemer) in the Upper Cretaceous, Austin group, is similar, but with a slight posterior flare to the shell. Right valve of all species is flat, fitting inside the curving, convex left valve. *P. newberryi* (Stanton), Photo 177, is an Upper Cretaceous, Anacacho formation species. All pycnodonts look like "unimaginative" *Texigryphea* — less roll, less flare, less interesting.

Texigryphea mucronata (Gabb) (Photo 179; compare to Photos 180-184)

Lower Cretaceous, Fredericksburg division. Left valve larger than the right and greatly arched, with a beak curved fairly straight under. Surface growth bands of only moderate roughness. Rather elongate and narrow for this genus, with deep fold (sulcus) running length of shell. *T. marcoui* (Hill and Vaughan), Photo 180, is considered a variation of *T. mucronata. T. roemeri* (Marcou), see Photo 181, is similar, but larger and coarser with a less curled, slightly slanted beak and a wider basal flare. This species has also been called *T. graysonana* Stanton, Photo 181. It occurs in the Washita division of the Lower Cretaceous, Grayson, Del Rio, and Buda formations. *T. navia* (Hall), Photo 182, in the Lower Cretaceous, Fredericksburg division, Kiamichi formation, is characterized by its flattened appearance with the beak slanted to the side. On the side of the shell opposite the radial fold is a slightly raised keel running the length of the shell. *T. washitaensis* (Hill), Photo 183, in the Lower Cretaceous, Washita division, has hardly any radial fold and has the most flared base of any Texas member of this genus. Its surface is relatively smooth. *T. gibberosa* (Cragin), Photo 184, has an elongate, arched-shape shell from the Duck Creek formation, Lower Cretaceous. *T. newberryi* (Stanton) is a typically "gryphea" hooked shape but with rather plain markings, found in the Upper Cretaceous, Anacacho formation. It has now been placed in *Pycnodonte newberryi,* Photo 177.

Exogyra ponderosa Roemer (Color Photo 19; also see Pearl, Photo 185; compare to Photos 186-188)

Upper Cretaceous period, Upper Austin and Taylor groups. Very large and heavy shell with beak curled in same plane as width of the shell. Ornament of coarse concentric growth lines, or in some rather smooth. Only minor radial lines, if any. *E. laeviuscula* Roemer, Photo 186, in the Austin group, Dessau formation, is very similar but has a very well-developed beak curl, often more than once around. Also in the Dessau formation, Austin group, is *E. tigrina* Stephenson, which has radial ridges that fork frequently near the curled beak. Brown color bands, which give the shell its name, are often preserved. Presence of pronounced radial ridges (costae) mark *E. costata* Say, Photo 187, of the Navarro group. *E. cancellata* Stephenson has both radial ridges and concentric growth lines, which form raised bumps at their intersections. It is restricted to the Neylandville Marl formation, Navarro group, although ancestral forms relating it to *E. ponderosa* occur in slightly lower (earlier) beds. Stephenson (1941) suggests a similar evolution of *E. costata* from *E. ponderosa* passing through two varieties, *E. ponderosa* var. *erraticostata,* Photo 188, and *E. costata* var. *spinifera,* as the radial ridges (costae) developed. *E. whitneyi* Boese is a large, rather smooth species with a broad, incurved beak, from the Central and West Texas Lower Cretaceous, Buda formation.

Amphidonte walkeri (White) (Photo 189)
Lower Cretaceous, Washita division, Duck Creek and Fort
Worth formations. A very large flat oyster with a flattened spiral
beak that has practically become part of the shell. Undulating
surface of concentric growth lines, somewhat rough. Right valve
smaller and flat or concave. Considered the same species as *Exogyra americana* (Marcou).

Ceratostreon texanum (Roemer) (Photo 190)
Lower Cretaceous, Fredericksburg division, especially Walnut
and Comanche Peak formations. Flat crescent shape, much like
a smaller *Amphidonte* but with a rough central keel from which
radiate irregular ridges. Formerly called *Exogyra texana* Roemer. The lower Fredericksburg and the Trinity division, Glen
Rose formation, has a smaller, less-ridged species, *C. weatherfordense* (Cragin), Photo 191.

Ilymatogyra arietina (Roemer) (Photo 192 and Color Photo 16)
Lower Cretaceous period, Washita division, Del Rio, Grayson, and Main Street formations. A small corkscrew-shaped oyster. Larger left valve is an irregular open spiral. Right valve is
very flat and small. Formerly called *Exogyra arietina* Roemer.

Gyrostrea cartledgei (Boese) (Photo 193)
Lower Cretaceous, Washita division. This species looks like a
cross between the rugged ridged shell of an "ostrea" type of oyster, with the slightly hooked beak of a *Texigryphea*. The smaller
valve is very "gryphea"-like. Its name is almost a mixture of the
two.

Crassostrea soleniscus (Meek) (Photo 194)
Upper Cretaceous, Woodbine formation. An elongate oyster
with generally a curved beak. Surface of rough concentric markings. Few, if any, long ridges.

Ostrea perversa Cragin (Compare to Photo 197)
Lower Cretaceous period, Washita division, Del Rio, Grayson, and Fort Worth formations. A large, thin-shelled, oval oyster with smooth to slightly ridged exterior, irregular beaks on

both valves. A very similar species is *O. franklini* Coquand in the Trinity division, Glen Rose and Bluffdale formations. *O. crenulimarginata,* Photo 197, in the Paleocene, Midway group, is typical of the flat, undulating shape of most "ostrea" oysters.

Lopha quadriplicata (Shumard) (Photo 195)

Lower Cretaceous period, Washita division, Denton, Weno, Pawpaw, and Main Street formations. A small crescent-shaped oyster with four main radiating folds splaying out its lower margin. *Ostrea crenulimargo* Roemer is very similar, but has up to eight radiating folds and is in the Fredericksburg and Trinity divisions, Lower Cretaceous. *Agerostrea falcata* (Morton), Photo 196, is also similar, but has less flare to the shell edge and is in the Upper Cretaceous, Taylor and Navarro groups.

Lopha bellaplicata (Shumard) (Compare to Photo 198)

Upper Cretaceous period, Eagle Ford group or equivalents. Medium-sized shell, irregularly ovate in outline and somewhat thick. Ornament of radiating folds crossing concentric growth lines. A similar, even thicker species in the Lower Cretaceous is *L. subovata* (Shumard), Photo 198.

Lopha travisana (Stephenson) (Photo 199)

Upper Cretaceous period, Austin group. A large oyster, oblong with a slight curve. Both valves nearly equal in thickness. Ornament is a central ridge with rather regular radiating ridges from it to the shell edge. Line between valves is zigzag.

Chondrodonta (Photo 200)

Lower Cretaceous, Edwards formation. A rather flat oyster with fine-branching, ridged ornamentation. A component of Edwards reef material, where many genera are cemented together.

Rastellum (Arctostrea) carinatum (Lamarck) (Color Photo 17)

Lower Cretaceous, Washita and Fredericksburg divisions. A medium to large, narrow, curved oyster with a strong central ridge flanked by very regular radiating, short side ridges. The wide ridges form a very toothy closure between the two equal valves. In short, the shell looks like a small set of false teeth!

Trigonia clavigera (Cragin) (Photo 201)
Lower Cretaceous, Washita division. Shell with valves of
equal size. Shaped like a section from an orange; pointed at each
end, concave at top, and convex on bottom edge of shell. Surface
ribbed. Fifteen to twenty bumps (once spines) on each rib. One
end of shell (rear) slightly higher than the other. A similar small
fossil with fewer than twenty-five ribs per valve is *Ptereotrigonia
guadalupae* (Boese), Photo 202. It is in both the Fredericksburg
and Washita divisions.

Venericardia (Photos 203, 204, 205, 206)
Cretaceous to Recent. Medium-sized cocklelike clam with
equal valves that look quite heart-shaped when viewed from end.
Ornament of prominent radiating ribs. Bottom edge of shell
wavy (crenulated) inside. *V. planicosta densata* (Conrad), Photo
204, is very common in the Eocene. *V. smithi* Aldrich, Photo
205, is similar in the Paleocene, Kincaid formation, but with
wider ribs. *V. mediaplata,* Photo 206, is very similar in the
Paleocene, Midway formation. It has slightly fewer and wider
ribs than *V. smithii Magicardium,* Photo 207, is a Paleocene,
Midway group genus that resembles a *Venericardia* but is slightly
elongate in width.

Some small *Protocardia* occur in the Paleocene, Midway
group; they have fine radial ribbing and large beaks less slanted
than the beaks of *Venericardia. Callocardia,* Photos 208, 209,
and 210, has a similar internal mold, having a thick, heart-
shaped mold viewed on end, but lacks the crenulations along the
bottom margin. Its exterior is without ribs and with numerous
concentric growth lines. *Callocardia haetofi* Gardner, Photo
209, is a Paleocene epoch, Midway group species, with strong
beaks and shell wider than tall. *C. pteleina* Gardner, Photo 210,
is similar but with weak beaks; *C. kempae* Gardner, Photo 208,
has strong beaks, but it is as tall as it is wide. *Corbula,* Photos
220 and 201, is similar in shape and concentric ornament but is
elongate on one end and often ridged or flattened out along that
elongate end.

Crassatella antestricta Gabb (Photo 211)
Eocene epoch, Claiborne group. Small to medium-sized,
slightly elongate, cockle-shaped clam with a smooth exterior

with some faint concentric growth marks. *C. texalta* Harris in the same strate is much larger and thicker. *C. gabbi* (Safford), Photo 212, is a Paleocene, Kincaid formation species. Its intenal mold shows bottom crenulations but has a flared bump on the upper rear margin indicative of the more horizontally elongate shell that these two genera have than *Venericardia*.

Protocardia texana (Conrad) (Photo 213 and Color Photo 13)

Lower Cretaceous, Washita and Fredericksburg divisions. A moderately large clam with equal valves. Thick and well-rounded in appearance. Ornament of fine lines, radiating downward on one end and concentric on the bulk of the shell. *P. multistriata* Shumard is a small species, with the "protocardia" shape and two-directional ornamentation, found in the Weno formation, Washita division, Lower Cretaceous. Some small Paleocene *Protocardia* are ornamented only with fine radial ribs.

Arctica roemeri (Cragin) (Photo 214)

Lower Cretaceous, Trinity division, Glen Rose formation. A large clam usually found as a steinkern. As high or higher than wide. Definitely less thick than high. Large beaks strongly curved and at midtop of shell. A very obvious posterior muscle scar on each valve. The Glen Rose formation has several other species. *A. medialis* (Conrad), Photo 215, is smaller and as thick as high. *A. texana* (Conrad) has beaks spread widely. *A. gibbosa* (Giebel) has thicker, blunt beaks that are definitely off-center of the shell toward the rear.

Cyprimeria texana (Roemer) (Photo 218)

Lower Cretaceous, Fredericksburg and Trinity divisions. A medium to large, more or less round, fairly flat clam that is thinned to a very sharp edge everywhere but at the hinge-line. Generally a rather featureless steinkern. In the Weno formation of the Lower Cretaceous, Washita division, many species are represented with original shell still attached. *Cyprimeria washitaensis* Adkins, Photo 217, is one good example of the excellent preservation in that formation. The Upper Cretaceous also contains several better-preserved species of this genus. *Dentonia*, Photo 216, is a similar shape but slightly fatter and with more enlarged beaks. It is in the Upper Cretaceous, Woodbine formation.

Tapes (Photo 219)
Upper and Lower Cretaceous. Small oblong clams with small but definite beaks hooked sharply to the anterior (front) end of the shell. Lower Cretaceous species are mostly steinkerns. Upper Cretaceous (especially Eagle Ford group) often retain some shell material.

Panopea henselli (Hill) (Compare to Photo 222, Homomya)
Lower Cretaceous, Trinity division, Glen Rose formation. A medium-sized clam, almost twice as long as high. Beaks form a large central bump. Rear of shell usually appears broken off. Beaks not near shell end. Ornament of sparsely spaced concentric ridges. *P. sellardsi* Whitney is similar but slopes slightly to the rear end and has no slant toward the beaks on the anterior. *Homomya knowltoni* (Hill), also in the Glen Rose formation, is similar, but the bottom line of the shell is more curved, beaks are far to the anterior, and ornamental lines are more irregular than *Panopea. Homomya bravoensis* Bose is close to *H. knowltoni* in shape but with beak virtually terminal; it is a Fredericksburg division species.

Caprina occidentalis Conrad (Photo 223)
Lower Cretaceous, Edwards formation. A curled, "goathorn"-shaped reef-forming bivalve. One valve is a short stub by which it attaches to objects in a reef. The movable valve is curled like a horn and resembles a horn coral or an ammonite.

Sellaea cordata (Roemer) (Photo 224)
Lower Cretaceous, Fredericksburg division, Edwards formation. Attached (right) valve a moderately wide cone attached to the reef by the narrow end. Other valve (left) is like melted ice cream in the cone of the other valve. It is an enlarged cap, overhanging the conical valve.

Eoradiolites davidsoni (Hill) (Photo 225 and Color Photo 14)

Lower Cretaceous, Fredericksburg division, Edwards formation. Right valve a tall, straight-sided cone. Ornament of vertical folds, closely spaced and fairly straight. Cone flares slightly at top. Other valve is a low cap. A slightly broader, more angular species in the Edwards formation is *E. quadratus* Adkins, Color Photo 14. *E. robustus* Palmer is also in the Edwards formation but is a fat cone spread almost as wide as high. The folds are more irregular and fewer.

Durania austinensis (Roemer) (Photo 226 and Color Photo 15)

Upper Cretaceous period, especially Austin group and its equivalents. A medium to large "palm tree trunk"-like structure. Larger valve is tube-shaped with an off-center cavity surrounded by a thick wall composed of cellular texture with veinlike, branching canals radiating from center. Exterior has longitudinal, coarse lines and surrounding growth marks. Oyster shells are often attached, and this genus is colonial and may have several large shells grown thickly together. The smaller valve is coarse, caplike, and seldom found. The author has seen individuals eleven feet in length. *Sauvagesia,* Photo 227, is similar but has a ligamental ridge at the top of the central cavity on one side.

Pholadomya sanctisabae Roemer (Photo 228)

Lower Cretaceous, Fredericksburg and Washita divisions, especially Kiamichi and Goodland formations. A small clam fatter (inflated) on the anterior end and thinned on the posterior, where the valves gape apart slightly. Ornament of ridges radiating from the beaks downward, each broken into small bumps (granulations), which decrease on the somewhat flared posterior of the shell. *P. shattucki* Boese, Photo 229, is a larger (medium-sized) species found in the upper part of the Washita division of the Lower Cretaceous. *P. lincecumi* Shumard, Photo 230, is an elongate species of the Upper Cretaceous, Taylor group. It has prominent radiating ridges. *P. papyracea,* Photo 231, is similar and in similar strata but has fainter, more numerous ridges.

Laternula simondsi Whitney (Photo 232)

Lower Cretaceous, Trinity division, Glen Rose formation. Shell shaped much like *Panopea* or *Homomya* but very thin in

cross-section with ends thinned when viewed from above, and in
this species often showing a small slit across the top of the beaks.
L. texana (Cragin), Photo 233, is similar but larger and found in
the Fredericksburg division, especially the Comanche Peak formation.

Liopistha jurafacies (Cragin) (Photo 234)
Lower Cretaceous, Trinity division, Glen Rose formation.
Large steinkerns, usually with little ornamentation. Posterior end
elongated. *L. banderaensis* Whitney, Photo 235, is a little less
elongate and has a quite straight anterior end. *L. walkeri* Whitney, Photo 236, has quite terminal beaks. *L. solida* (Cragin) has
quite high, narrow beaks. *L. alta* (Roemer) is almost as high as
long, with central beaks. All of these are Glen Rose formation
species. *L. formosa* Stephenson is a small species occurring in
the Upper Cretaceous, Navarro group. It is a small, fat clam with
the rather angular ends typical of the genus and very pronounced
bumpy ridges radiating from the beaks. In the beak area, several
concentric ridges dominate.

Class Scaphopoda — Tusk Shells
Dentalium (Photo 237)
Late Paleozoic to Recent. Small shells, tusklike in shape but
open at both ends. Ornament often of fine ridges down the shell
and even finer growth lines. *D. (Plagioglypta) canna* White occurs in the Texas Permian period and is fairly straight with ornament only of fine encircling growth lines. *D. (Graptacme)
mediaviense* Harris, a larger, thicker-walled species, occurs in
the Paleocene epoch, Midway group. *D. (Graptacme) minutistri-
atum* Gabb and *D. thalloide* Conrad occur in the Eocene,
Claiborne group. The latter (*thalloide*) has ridges of alternating
or unequal length.

Cadulus (Compare to Photo 237, Dentalium)
Cretaceous to Recent. Much like *Dentalium* but with widest
point on shell not at the end, but in the middle. Various species
occur in the Upper Cretaceous, the Paleocene, Eocene, and more
recent sediments.

Class Cephalopoda — The Nautiluses and Ammonites

The nautiluses and ammonites are the most complex of all the mollusks. Their shells can be straight or loosely or tightly coiled. In the nautiluses and ammonites the shell contains many small empty chambers, and at the outer end, one large living chamber. Some fossils are well-enough preserved to show these upon being sliced open. Where each chamber wall meets the main shell, a suture line occurs. These are often visible on the fossil. Their shape is a most useful identification tool for specialists. A tube called a *siphuncle* passes from the living chamber back through all preceding chambers. It may have been for buoyancy regulation.

Generally speaking, nautilus species are somewhat thicker in cross-section than ammonites. Nautiluses have a rather straight or slightly wavy suture pattern, while ammonites have a very lacy, elaborate pattern. As an ammonite suture line curves toward the shell opening (aperture) it is called a *saddle*; as the line curves away from the aperture, it is called a *lobe*. Ammonite sutures come in three forms: goniatites, with a primitive slashing, zig-zag pattern; ceratites, with notches only on the backward-facing lobes and none on saddles; and true ammonites, with divisions in both lobes and saddles.

Michelinoceras (Photo 238)
Pennsylvanian period. Straight-shelled nautiloids with a smooth surface. Siphuncle small and central. Usually small. Living chamber often crushed in. Formerly called *Orthoceras*. *Pseudorthoceras* sp. have a very large siphuncle. *Euloxoceras greeni* Miller, Dunbar, and Chondra has an off-center siphuncle and inclined suture patterns. *Protocycloceras,* Photo 239, is a Pennsylvanian genus that differs from the others by having strong ridges around the shell in parallel layers.

Cooperoceras (Photo 240)
Lower Permian period. A loosely coiled nautiloid with thin spines projecting from the sides. Groove on outside of whorls and ribs on sides of outer whorl.

Paleozoic Era Cephalopods (Photos 241, 242, 243, 244, 245, 246, 247, 248)

Pennsylvanian and Permian periods. These usually small cephalopods are often characterized by less complex and often more angular suture patterns than the elaborate, lacy suture patterns of Mesozoic era ammonites. A zig-zag suture (called *goniatitic*) is often found, as in Photos 243, 244, and 246. A pattern involving simple rounded lobes and very complicated saddles (called *ceratitic,* Photo 247) is also common in the Paleozoic era. These are intermediate steps of development from the simple straight or curved sutures of early nautiloid cephalopods toward the complicated sutures of the later ammonites. Yet the simple sutures of nautiloids still exist in the present, while all other suture patterns have died out. Is simple better?

Paraceltites elegans Girty (Photo 241)
Permian period. Whorls of shell very little overlapping (evolute), sides ribbed, suture a simple deep wavy pattern with two side lobes. Shell thin when viewed edge-on. A similar, perhaps identical species, *P. ornatus* Miller and Furnish, occurs in the Permian, Word formation.

Neoglyphioceras entogonum (Gabb) (Photo 242)
Mississippian period. Coiled shell with a number of well-spaced parallel lines running with the direction of the coil. Shell somewhat compressed when viewed edge-on. About every quarter whorl, a deep groove bands the whorl. Suture very zig-zag (goniatitic) but more so nearer the venter. *Lyrogoniatites* is similar and also Mississippian, but it is fat in cross-section. *Owenoceros* is similar but Pennsylvanian and has closer-spaced rotating lines, and the suture lobes are notched with several teeth (ceratitic pattern).

Gonioloboceras goniolobum (Meek) (Photo 243)
Pennsylvanian period. Coiled shell with smooth exterior and venter. Suture pattern a dramatic zig-zag goniatitic pattern with large angular lobes and saddles.

Schistoceras smithi Boese (Photo 244)
Pennsylvanian period. Coiled shell with smooth exterior,

venter broadly arched, umbilicus large. Suture pattern saddles somewhat like a bottleneck.

Eoasianites (Photo 245)

Pennsylvanian period. A small, globular cephalopod with a wide umbilicus. Suture of eight main lobes and eight main saddles.

Neodimorphoceras texanum (Smith) (Photo 246)

Pennsylvanian period. A rather thin, smooth cephalopod with a small, narrow rounded saddle on the side of the venter, which is followed by a large anular saddle on the side of the shell.

Waagenoceras guadalupensis Girty (Photo 247)

Permian period, primarily in West Texas. A nearly globular (very involute) ammonite with a moderately complex suture pattern. Lobes more divided than the saddles. *Properrinites boesei* Plummer and Scott is simpler in suture pattern and with sides more compressed. *Perrinites hilli* (Smith), Photo 248, is also similar but has still more side compression and with suture lobes divided into long "Christmas trees."

Paracymatoceras texanum (Roemer) (Photo 249)

Lower Cretaceous, Washita division. Coiled very much like modern Chambered Nautilus. Siphuncle slightly closer to inside of whorl. Ornament of very broad S-shaped ribs. *P. hilli* (Shattuck), Photo 250, is similar but with fatter shape and only faint growth marks for ornamentation. It occurs from Lower Cretaceous, Buda formation upwards into the Austin group. A dwarf nautiloid of similar fat, coiled shape, *Adkinsia bosquensis,* Photo 260, is found in the Lower Cretaceous, Del Rio formation.

Eutrephoceras Hyatt (Compare to Photo 251, Cimomia)

Paleocene and Eocene epochs. Roundly coiled with outer whorl covering the others. Aperture wider than high (kidney-shaped). Among the ball-shaped nautiloids it has very straight sutures. *Cimomia vaughani* (Gardner), Photo 251, is similarly shaped but has a wavy suture pattern. *Woodringia splendens* Stenzel is also ball-shaped but shows a slightly more flattened outer whorl and an even wavier suture pattern than *Cimomia*. *Cimomia* occurs in the Upper Cretaceous as well as the Paleocene.

Hercoglossa Conrad (Photo 252)
Paleocene and Eocene epochs. Coiled with height greater than width. Suture pattern deeply wavy. Outer edge of whorls broadly rounded. *Deltoidonautilus elliotti* Stenzel is similar but with a definite pointedness to the outside of the whorls, making the aperture rather triangular. *Deltoidonautilus* also has its siphuncle very near the inside of the whorl, as compared to a more central location for *Hercoglossa*. *Aturia,* Photo 253, shows a large inside siphuncle position, but with the rounded aperture of *Hercoglossa*. *Aturia* species show much more shell height than width viewed from the aperture. *Aturia* also has a sharp suture lobe on each side of the venter.

Idiohamites fremonti Marcou (Photos 254 and 255)
Lower Cretaceous period, Washita division. Curved but not coiled. Ornament of large regular ribs. Often described as "candy cane"-shaped. This genus was formerly called *Hamites*. A similar genus, *Didymoceras*, Photo 256 (also called *Cirroceras*), twists in three dimensions irregularly; *Idiohamites* is curved in only two dimensions.

Sciponoceras gracile (Shumard) (Photo 257)
Upper Cretaceous, Eagle Ford group. Once widely called *Baculites gracilis* Shumard. Small, straight or nearly straight, slender tubelike ammonites. Coiled only in the youngest (and usually missing) part of the shell. Ornament of faint ribs, which are stronger on one edge of the shell than on the other edge. Besides the ribs, there are slight constrictions to the diameter of the tube that are a little more than the diameter of the tube apart. These separate it from the genus *Baculites,* which seems to have evolved from it. *Sciponoceras* forms a zone in the Eagle Ford group. In northeast Texas it is in the mid-Britton formation, and it and other mollusks in that zone usually are still covered with a layer of white nacreous material. The zone is a worldwide marker of the division of two European fossil stages, the Turonian above and the Cenomanian below. It is a marker for the base of

the Turonian. *Baculites ovatus* is a larger, baculite species found in the Upper Cretaceous, Taylor group. Also in the Taylor group, *Baculites taylorensis* Adkins, Photo 258, is characterized by bumpy nodes on its sides. A baculite that often reaches several feet in length and several inches in diameter occurs in the Navarro group.

Plesioturrilites brazoensis (Roemer) (Photo 259)
Lower Cretaceous, Washita division, especially. Shell forms a high snail-like spire. All whorls in contact. Ornament of ribs with four bumps each, the bumps becoming larger on the larger whorls. Many authors use the name *Mariella* for this genus.

Scaphites hippocrepis (DeKay) (Compare to Photo 261; also see Photo 260)
Upper Cretaceous period. Shell forms a tight coil, then grows straight for a distance (perhaps slight) before another lesser coil. Ornament of equally spaced ribs with sharp, dramatic bumps (if at all) on the edges of the venter. *Hoploscaphites* sp. is similar but with many rows of small bumps rotating with the whorls. *Acanthoscaphites nodosus* (Owen) is similar but with two rows of large bumps (nodes), with the largest nearest the venter. *Trachyscaphites springeri* is a very ornamented species, having three rows of sharp nodes. It is Upper Cretaceous, Taylor group. *Scaphites* occurs in Lower Cretaceous, Washita division, with one species a pyritized miniature in the Del Rio formation and other Washita division formations, Photo 260. Scaphitid ammonites occur in two forms within each species; a fatter form with more overlapping coils (involute), and a thinner, slightly more strung-out (evolute) form. Cobban interprets these as clear female (fatter involute) and male (thinner evolute) forms.

Exiteloceras annulatum (Shumard) (Photo 262)
Upper Cretaceous period, Eagle Ford group, especially. Shell an open coil with many evenly spaced ribs (costae), each rib with a pair of tubercles, one on each side of the venter. Usually a small to medium-sized shell. All similar, open-whorled, costate, tubercled ammonites were once in the form genus *Helicoceras*.

Engonoceras pierdenale (Buch) (Photo 263)

Lower Cretaceous, Fredericksburg division; also lower parts of the Upper Cretaceous. Shell a smooth involute coil with wavy traces of three lines of nodes on some specimens. Last whorl thickened near aperture. Venter flat to roundish on last whorl. Suture pattern lobes divided into several stubby fingers, saddles deep and rounded, with some rarely having a midpeak. *Metengonoceras*, Photo 264, is a very similar genus; there is interest in combining the genera. *Metengonoceras* sutures have very slightly divided lobes and plain rounded saddles. Both are Lower Cretaceous genera in Texas, but can appear in the Upper Cretaceous, especially the Eagle Ford group. A miniature, pyritized *Engonoceras* occurs in the Del Rio formation and its time equivalents. To confuse the issue, the Woodbine and Eagle Ford groups of the Upper Cretaceous contain a very compressed, involute, and nearly identical genus, *Epengonoceras,* in the opinion of some authors.

Sphenodiscus pleurisepta (Conrad) (Color Photo 21)

Upper Cretaceous period, Navarro group, especially, and its equivalents. Often quite large, even when found as pieces only. Involutely coiled shell with smooth or slightly bumpy sides, tapering to a narrow, sharp, or sharply rounded venter. Suture pattern with saddles slightly less divided than the lobes, but saddles are always some divided with a bulbous end to the saddle.

Placenticeras meeki Bohm (Photo 265 and Color Photo 23)

Upper Cretaceous period. A medium to large involutely coiled shell with smooth (or somewhat wavy) sides tapering to a flat or nearly flat venter, which may round in the last whorl. Suture pattern with elaborate divisions of both lobes and saddles equally. *P. whitfieldi* Hyatt in the Taylor and Navarro groups is very smooth-sided with a very narrow, flat venter. *P. guadalupe* (Roemer) is similar from Austin group equivalents. *P. placenta* (DeKay) was once used as a name in Texas, but has been placed under *P. meeki.*

Oxytropidoceras, a form genus, "oxytropidocerid" (Photos 266, 267, 268)

Lower Cretaceous period, Fredericksburg, Walnut, and Goodland formations. A disc-shaped, coiled ammonite with many rounded-topped ribs, a high keel, and broadly rounded venter with no prominent shoulders. This genus has been divided into several others in recent years. *Oxytropidoceras* is now limited to the above description. Two genera split from it are *Manuaniceras*, with flat-topped ribs, and *Venezolicera*, with the same high keel and many ribs, but having definite shoulder and side tubercles. *Manuaniceras* extends its time range up into the Washita division of the Lower Cretaceous period. *Adkinsites*, Photo 268, is a similar high-keeled species with rounded shoulders and nodes along the inside of each whorl.

Eopachydiscus marcianus (Shumard) (Photo 269)
Lower Cretaceous Period, Washita division, especially Duck Creek formation. A giant, thick-coiled ammonite with very weak ribs, if any. Often found around Lake Texoma and Lake Whitney. *E. laevicanaliculatum* (Lasswitz), Photo 270, has faint but definite broad ribbing. This genus was formerly placed under Desmoceras, Photo 280, a fat ammonite with S-shaped, widely spaced ribs with finer striation in between.

Mortoniceras sp. (Photos 271, 272, 273, 274)
Lower Cretaceous, Washita division. A moderately large ammonite with nodes or bumps on the shoulder of all whorls. A dominant ammonite of the middle Washita division. Miniature forms occur in the Paw Paw formation, preserved in pyrite.

Schloenbachia leonensis Conrad (Photo 275)
Lower Cretaceous. Medium-sized ammonite with raised keel on venter. Shoulders of venter with prominent tubercles. Sharp ribs on sides of whorl bear many evenly spaced tubercles.

Texanites texanus texanus (Roemer)
Upper Cretaceous period, Austin group. Venter has a low, rounded keel bordered by a shallow depression. There are many ribs, each ornamented with five tubercles. The many-sided tubercles and Upper Cretaceous occurrence should identify this genus.

Parapuzosia
Upper Cretaceous period. A large ammonite with a rather inflated whorl and rounded venter. Fine small ribs are in between larger, less frequent ribs. A large, fat ammonite of the Upper Cretaceous.

Budaiceras (Photo 276)
Lower Cretaceous period, Upper Washita division. These coiled shells have large ribs moderately spaced with a low-keeled venter broken into elongate tubercles free from the ribs. *Stoliczkaia* are similar, but the ribs cross the broadly rounded venter without a keel. Ribs may alternate in length with some at differing angles. Ribs may become fainter on the outer whorl.

Metoicoceras whitei Hyatt (Photo 277)
Upper Cretaceous period, especially Eagle Ford group. An involute coiled ammonite with fairly straight sides and large straight ribs, often alternating long and short. Venter concave between a row of nodes at each side of the venter. No midventer (siphonal) tubercles. Umbilicus small.

Calycoceras (subgenus Conlinoceras) tarrantense (Adkins) (Photos 278, 279, and Color Photo 22)
Upper Cretaceous period, especially Woodbine group. Formerly very widely known as *Acanthoceras wintoni* Adkins; or with stouter individuals (otherwise similar), as *Metacalycoceras tarrantense* Adkins. Cobban finds the two intergrade into each other as one variable species (male-female differences?). Much like *Metoicoceras* but capable of more pronounced side nodes and somewhat thicker cross-section. Ribs may be of two alternating lengths, but continue across the flat or rounded (never concave) venter. The ammonites from the Woodbine group often reveal interesting internal chambers and calcite crystals when cut on a rock saw; they are sold internationally. The subgenus *Con-*

linoceras is named in honor of the late James P. Conlin of Fort Worth, excellent collector of Cretaceous ammonites. If *Acanthoceras* occurs, it would differ in having three rows of tubercles across the venter, or a fusion of such. If these names bother older collectors, perhaps it might help to know that *Calycoceras, Acanthoceras,* and *Metoicoceras* are all in the family Acanthoceratidae, so the differences are slight at most.

Prionocyclus sp. (Photo 281)
Upper Cretaceous period, Eagle Ford group. Small ammonites with whorls rapidly and regularly expanding. Many prominent ribs, close-spaced, S-shaped, and occasionally branching. Often flattened in the bedding plane or as imprints only. Often in groups. Especially abundant in the limey Kamp Ranch member of the Arcadia Park-Britton formation contact.

Subclass Coleoides — All living cephalopods except *Nautilus*
Includes squids and octopi, but is most represented as fossils by the belemnites.

Order Belemnoidea
Belemnitella — The Belemnites (Photo 282)
Upper Cretaceous. "Sharpened pencil"-shaped shell; pointed on one end, fairly straight-sided, long and narrow, slightly narrowed on the end opposite the point (if complete). Structure of shell is thick-walled and of thin radiating crystals. Shows no suture lines, as do nautiluses or ammonites. Not segmented, as is a crinoid stem.

Phylum Annelida — Segmented Worms
Worms would be far too soft-bodied to leave plentiful fossil evidence if it were not for the fact that some of them secrete limey tubes that do preserve well — nicely enough to make several varieties of annelid worm tubes fairly common fossils. They may occur alone or in masses, attached to rocks or other fossils. In Texas, annelid worm fossils can be found in rocks of all ages.

Class Polychaeta

Serpula (Photos 283, 284)

Cretaceous period to Recent, possibly earlier. Long, spaghetti-like tubes twist and turn, usually in masses attached to shell material. Surface of tubes marked only by growth ridges around the tube, not along them in this genus. It is common practice to refer to these fossils as simply "serpulid" worm tubes. *Spirorbis* sp. is much like *Serpula* but tightly coiled and snail-like. *Rotularia* sp. is also coiled but narrows at the open tube end where *Spirorbis* does not. *Spirorbis* goes back into the Paleozoic Era; *Rotularia* is Cretaceous to Recent.

Hamulus (Photo 285)

Cretaceous period. Calcareous tubes, somewhat conical in shape, with three to seven ridges running along the tube. Some of the ridges in some species may be larger than others. Tube also shows growth marks, the edges of which are often slightly bent back. Extinct today.

Thalassinoides sp. Burrows (Photo 286)

Upper Cretaceous, Taylor group. Burrows of sea-bottom worms. Often the explanation for tubelike discolorations on the surface of bedding planes.

Phylum Arthropoda —
Jointed-Legged Animals

Among the arthropods, trilobites, crustaceans, and ostracods are the most important in terms of leaving a plentiful fossil record. Insects and spiders belong to this phylum, but their thin exoskeletons and their greater occurence on land and in the air has reduced the number of fossils that remain of them. Nonetheless, insect fossils can be found in Texas and are of great interest to collectors because of their delicacy and rarity. Through the trilobites this phylum reaches back in time as far as the Cambrian. Although the trilobites became extinct at the end of the

Paleozoic era, the other arthropods have remained among the most successful animals up to the present. They are characterized by segmented bodies; paired, jointed legs; and a chitinous or calcified external skeleton.

Class Trilobita — Trilobites

Elvinia cranidia (Photo 287)
Upper Cambrian period, especially Mason, Burnett, and Llano counties. Found usually as isolated heads or pygidia. Glabella a broad, blunt cone with several cross furrows, one or two complete. Brim in front of glabella is broad with thickened lip or rim. Pygidium is broad and blunt, bullet shaped with rimlike border. *Bolaspidella,* of the Mid-Cambrian period, is similar but has a broad glabella with side furrows seldom completely across. Area in front of glabella broad with downturned front edge. Pygidium small with no distinct rim.

Lygdozoon arkansanum (Van Ingen) (Photo 289)
Cephalon broad and crescent-shaped with a bulbous glabella that reaches the front edge without a border. Eyes large, half-moon-shaped and set near rear of the cephalon.

Griffithidella (Compare to Photos 290, 291, 292, 293, 294, Ditomopyge)
Mississippian period. Known mostly from pygidia, which have a rounded outline with a somewhat pointed central lobe. Pygidium is very low in profile, except for tip of central lobe. Pygidium with weaker segment separations than the thorax. *Thigriffithides roundyi* (Girty) is in similar strata (Chappel Limestone, San Saba County) but has a longer rounded pygidium with a rounder-tipped central lobe and more distinct segments. When one is uncertain about being in either Mississippian or Pennsylvanian rocks, these two Mississippian species can be easily confused with the Pennsylvanian genus *Ditomopyge.* The central lobes of the pygidia on all three are slightly different and usually preserved in viewable condition.

Ditomopyge (Photos 290 to 294)
Pennsylvanian period. A plentiful Pennsylvanian trilobite, characterized from other trilobites of the same time period by

having no flat band in front of the broad glabella, which reaches all the way to the forward edge of the cephalon and bulges very slightly as it does. Thorax with nine segments. Pygidium rounded in outline with center lobe raised slightly and crest often flattened. Tip of central pygidium lobe is squared off when viewed from above. Many of these have been mistakenly identified as *Griffithides,* a Mississippian period genus, which closely resembles it but has never been found in Texas. *Griffithides* has a broader, lower central pygidium lobe and is quite grainy in texture. *Ditomopyge* is definitely Pennsylvanian.

Ameura *(Photos 295, 296)*
Pennsylvanian period. A rather common trilobite with fairly broad glabella, widest at the eyes. Glabella has small flat band in front of it. Pygidium elongate and subtriangular. Thorax with nine segments. Generally devoid of ornamentation. Many specimens of this genus were misidentified as *Phillipsia* sp.

Paladin *(Photo 297 and Color Photo 34)*
Pennsylvanian period. Many specimens of this genus were identified incorrectly as *Griffithides.* Glabella somewhat narrow, not quite reaching the front margin of the head. Pygidium rounded with central lobe not particularly broad and with segments bordered by a smooth edge.

Delaria *(Photo 298)*
Permian period. Much like *Ditomopyge* in having a broad glabella that reaches the front margin of the head without an intervening band. This genus has an even broader front to the glabella than *Ditomopyge,* causing a lightbulb-shaped glabella with small bumps instead of glabellar lobes. Pygidium less strongly marked than *Ditomopyge* and with central lobe somewhat more elongate, causing pygidium to be very slightly more rounded triangular. Note that *Delaria* is Permian, while *Ditomopyge* is Pennsylvanian.

Anisopyge *(Photo 299)*
Permian period. The last known North American trilobite genus, before the group became extinct. Band in front of glabella not flat but sloped with front of glabella. Glabella widest to the

front and very slightly granulated. Eyes curved and narrow. Pygidium central lobe has many small segments, side lobes distinctly less. Central pygidium lobe extends all the way to the end of a triangular pygidium.

Vidria sp. is known mostly from pygidia, which are rounded but with a long central lobe reaching to edge. Ornament of small tubercles on unworn specimens. It is also a Permian form.

Class Xiphosura — Horseshoe Crabs

Paleolimulus (Photo 300)

Permian period. Shape is almost identical to modern horsehoe crabs. A rare fossil because of the skeleton of chitin and little calcification.

Class Crustacea — Crustaceans

Linuparus (Photos 302, 303, and Color Photo 35)

Upper Cretaceous period, Eagle Ford group. Small crustacean with a long carapace, marked by spiny edges and a central row of spines on the rear portion. Two species are prominent: *L. grimmeri* Stenzel is rather slim with moderate rough texture, and a V-shaped front notch between the front large spines. *L. watkinsi* Stenzel is less slim and a little bulgy along the sides of the carapace. Its surface texture is very rough, and the front notch is distinctly U-shaped. *Astacodes* sp. is a similarly long, thin crustacean, but without a central row of spines on the back part of the carapace, and with a little pointlike rostrum projecting from between the front spines. *A. maxwelli* is found near Roxton, Texas, in uppermost Austin group, Gober Chalk. *A. davisi* Stenzel is found in the Eagle Ford group and has somewhat rougher tubercles on the rear part of the carapace, almost a "pigskin" texture.

Homerus sp. is vaguely similar to the above genera. It produces shrimplike tails with pointy-bottomed segments in the Britton formation of the Eagle Ford group, Upper Cretaceous. Its carapace has a long, side-spined front projection and the rear portion has a central crease. *H. brittonestris* Stenzel and *H. davisi* Stenzel are found in similar strata but *H. davisi* has a rougher front part of the carapace and is larger. The genus *Upogebia* (Photo 305) produces compressed individuals in the Eagle Ford group that have shrimplike tails with round-bottomed segments. It can occur also in Eocene deposits. Fragmentary parts of *Homerus travisensis* Stenzel occur in the Walnut formation of the Lower Cretaceous.

Notopocorystes dichrous Stenzel (Photo 306)

Upper Cretaceous, Eagle Ford group, Britton formation. Broad carapace, a quarter longer than it is wide. Carapace is relatively smooth except for a jagged band along the front edge and somewhat down the sides. The carapace is rougher in front of that line and the front area is bluish as contrasted to a gray rear portion. Hence the name *dichrous*, meaning "two-colored." Only front edge of carapace is spiny. Rear portion of carapace covered with very closely spaced, minute, flat-topped granules.

Cenomanocarcinus vanstraeleni Stenzel (Photos 307, 308)

Upper Cretaceous period, Eagle Ford group, Britton formation. A very broad carapace; slightly broader than long and broadest at the middle. Surface of carapace marked by at least seven rows of prominent tubercles: two radiating off each side, and three running as parallel lines to the rear edge. A rear spine can occur on two rear lobes. *Necrocarcinus* sp. is a similar genus with a carapace broader than long. It has many species ranging from the lower Upper Cretaceous into the upper parts of the Lower Cretaceous. It has a less distinct pattern of tubercled rows on the carapace, and the carapace is broadest slightly in front of center. *N. moseleyi* and *N. renfroae* (Pawpaw formation, Washita division); *N. ovalis* (Eagle Ford group, Upper Cretaceous); *N. scotti* (Denton formation, Washita division). Another very large Upper Cretaceous crab is *Enoploclytia* (Photo 304). Most very huge claws, etc., are ascribed to this genus. *Zanthopsis peytoni* Stenzel (Photo 310) is an Eocene genus closely resembling *Cenomanocarcinus* but capable of four-inch wide carapaces. *Harpactocarcinus* (Photo 309) is another Eocene genus of similar outline but rather smooth carapace of more modest size.

Protocullianassa pleuralum Beikirch and Feldman (Color Photo 34)

Upper Cretaceous, Austin group. Excellently preserved specimens of crablike crustaceans.

Class Ostracoda — Ostracods

A large group of mostly microscopic crustaceans that enclose themselves in two shell halves (valves). The valves are generally longer than tall and rounded on the ends, often kidney-shaped. Space has not permitted this book to deal with this large and diverse group, yet a kidney-shaped ostracod does appear in Text Illustration 8. Shell shape and any exterior ornamentation are the most important identification criteria since the delicate crustacean bodies seldom last as fossils. Their identification is a matter for specialists, but they can be obtained in microfossil washes and viewed through a low-powered binocular microscope.

Class Insecta — Insects

Insects are not often fossilized. Their fragile bodies and often airborne habits require specially fortunate circumstances if they are to be protected and preserved. It has occasionally happened in Texas.

Mesitoblatta — Cockroach (Photo 311, also see Photo 314)

Permian period. One of the oldest known insect fossils from Texas. Often associated with plant fossil layers.

Diospyrae — Termite Nest (Photo 312)

Upper Cretaceous period, Aguja formation, West Texas. Shows cells occupied by fossilized termites. Very rare.

Eodichroma mirifica Cockerell (Photo 313)

Eocene epoch. Often associated with layers containing plentiful plant remains.

Playa Lake Insects (Photos 315, 316)

Pleistocene epoch, Texas Panhandle. Soft-bodied insects, ostrocods, and leaves are trapped in the thin-bedded sediments of the ancient playa (temporary) lakes. Often show wing veins, legs, etc.

Phylum Echinodermata —
Spiny-Skinned Animals

It would be hard to name a more important group of Texas fossil creatures than those in the Phylum Echinodermata, which means "spiny-skinned animals." The phylum contains two very large and dramatic groups of fossils, the crinoids and the echinoids. Cystoids (not found in Texas), blastoids (very rare in Texas), and crinoids make up the echinoderms that attach to the sea floor, while starfish and sea cucumbers are echinoid examples of unattached, free-swimming echinoderms.

Echinoderms have an internal skeleton of calcite plates that are in life covered by a leathery skin. They display a five-part symmetry with an underlying bilateral tendency in more advanced forms.

Echinoderms, whole or in pieces, have left great numbers of fossils in Texas's late Paleozoic and Mesozoic rocks.

Subphylum Pelmatozoa — Attached Echinoderms

Among the echinoderms that are attached by stalks to the sea bottom, the cystoids and blastoids have left almost no fossil record in Texas. Like the crinoids, these two totally extinct groups were attached by a stalk of calcareous segments to the sea bottom. Cystoids had a ball-shaped body chamber (calyx) composed of irregular calcite plates atop a stem. Blastoids are similar, but with a calyx of thirteen regularly arranged plates in a five-part symmetry. Neither the stems nor the arms of cystoids and blastoids preserve well as fossils.

The crinoids alone are preserved as Texas fossils in this subphylum (with a few minor exceptions), but they are very plentiful. Broken remains of crinoids literally fill some of the state's Late Paleozoic rocks (Color Photo 25), while well-preserved specimens are among Texas' most beautiful fossils. Crinoids, although less plentiful than during the Late Paleozoic era, are still present in modern seas.

Class Crinoidea

Crinoids are composed of four main body parts: a rootlike holdfast for sea bottom anchoring; a stem of stacked disks (columnals), which may be many feet long; a body chamber (calyx) composed of regularly arranged calcite plates; and five or more branched or unbranched arms that are fortified by small calcite plates. The crinoid's mouth is at the top of the body chamber, between the arms. The anus is in that same area and can be extended upwards, even above the arms, by an anal tube, which may be fortified by plates and armed with protuding spines. The many interesting variations possible by the crinoid anus have been overlooked in most publications. The Texas species *Pirasocrinus scotti* (Photo 319) is an excellent example of a long anal tube armed with prominent spines. Such spines are distinctive and common Texas fossils. Complete calyxes with arms (crowns) are found in Texas, as the illustrations in this book show, but they are uncommon. The predominant crinoid fossils for easy finding are the stem columnals. Since these are composed of a calcite crystal with a certain amount of internally trapped water, heat from a campfire will cause the columnals to explode, even dangerously. They are often known in rural Texas as "pop rocks."

Crinoid Columnals (Color Photo 25)
Pennsylvanian and Permian periods. These small disks (3 to 20 mm. in diameter) are from the stem of the crinoid animal. They are found free or in short stacks. They are usually round, but may also be oval or starshaped. Each has a central hole, which may be round or five-petaled. There are usually tiny radiating grooves on the flat surfaces. The circular edge may have scars from the attachment of small branches called *cirri*. These may be anchors or sensory organs. Few of these isolated columnals have been identified as to which crinoids produced them. Stacks of columnals do not taper in diameter as do similar-looking fossils, such as straight Orthocerid nautiloids.

Scytalocrinus sansabensis Moore and Plummer (Photo 317)
Lower Pennsylvanian period, Marble Falls formation. Only species of this genus in Texas. Stem round and slender. Cup conical and slightly incurved at top. Arms long and unbranched.

Plaxocrinus perundatus Moore and Plummer (Photo 318)
Pennsylvanian period. A large species, crown approximately

150 mm. tall. Broad and shallowly concave at base. Arms narrow, numerous, and ascending in unruly column. Photos of cup with stubby, sharp, thornlike knobs. Single stacked plates of arms knobbed at intervals. *Pirasocrinus scotti* M. and P. (Photo 319) is very similar but with deeply concave calyx base. Species of this family often exhibit tall anal sacs with long spined anal plates above the arms.

Parathlocrinus watkinsi (Strimple) (Photo 320)
Pennsylvanian period, Millsap Lake formation, Strawn group, Desmoinesian series. Shallow broad cup, no spiky ornamentation. Cup base flat with a large central concavity. Arms short, broad. Named after Bill and Helen Watkins of San Antonio.

Sciadocrinus harrisae Moore and Plummer (Photo 321)
Pennsylvanian period. Like *Plaxocrinus* (Photo 318), but with even shallower basal concavity and a much shorter crown. No knobs amid arms. Radial plates fat and rounded.

Delocrinus graphicus Moore and Plummer (Photo 322)
Pennsylvanian period. A medium-sized crinoid (approx. 70 mm. tall) with a shallow bowl-shaped cup with deep, steep sided basal cavity where stem attaches. *Delocrinus* has an anal plate between the radial plates. Similar genus, *Endelocrinus,* has a much shallower basal depression, while *Paradelocrinus* (Color Photo 28) and *Erisocrinus* have no anal plate in the cup. *Erisocrinus* (Photo 326) also has a flat base. Arms are covered with two rows of plates neatly arranged to appear braided. Arrangement of arms looks like fingers extended of two hands placed palm to palm. This particular species is characterized by finely granular surface, especially on lower parts of arms.

Delocrinus subhemisphericus Moore and Plummer (Photo 323)
Pennsylvanian period. Much like *D. graphicus* (Photo 322), but with taller cup and proportionately shorter arms. Surface without many granules. Radial plates bear spinelike protrusions.

Graffhamicrinus (Photo 328 and Color Photo 27)
Pennsylvanian period. Much like a *Delocrinus,* Photos 322, 323, but with smoother surface texture and no spines on cup.

Erisocrinus elevatus Moore and Plummer (Photo 324)
Pennsylvanian period. Calyx cup with straight sides angling steeply upwards from flat base. No anal plate in cup between the row of radial plates.

Paradelocrinus brachiatus Moore and Plummer (Color Photo 28)
Pennsylvanian period. A rather impressive but simple crinoid, with a shallow bowl-shaped cup. The base of the cup is slightly concave and with the inner plates in the form of a star. The ten arms are unbranched and slightly tapered. The arms have no bumps or spines.

Ulocrinus (Color Photo 26)
Pennsylvanian period. Calyx cup globose. All arms branch evenly one plate above cup. Arms with two rows of plates.

Sellardsicrinus marrsae Moore and Plummer (Photo 325)
Pennsylvanian period. Calyx cup composed of three cycles of plates and is globular in shape. Arms branch three times, giving eight parts to each at top of crown. One of Texas's most branched crinoids.

Ethelocrinus texasensis Moore and Plummer (Photo 326)
Pennsylvanian period. A crinoid known for its cup, which is low and broad and covered heavily with modest-sized tubercles.

Parulocrinus marquisi Moore and Plummer (Photo 327)
Pennsylvanian period. Beautiful crinoid with ten long arms above a bowl-shaped cup. Base of cup flat. Edges of cup plates corrugated. Very slightly ornamented.

Subphylum Eleutherozoa
This subphylum is composed of the free-moving, unattached echinoderms, principally the starfish, brittle stars, and echinoids.

Class Stelleroidea
Subclass Asteroidea
Asteroids, or true starfish, have arms which are broadly connected to their central body mass. Number of arms are usually

five but can be more. Open food groove on lower side of arms, leading to central mouth.

"Mastaster" (Photo 334)

Lower Cretaceous. A pentagonal starfish, in the case of this species, with arms only slightly differentiated from the central disk. Assigned tentatively to this genus by the enlarged marginal plates between the arms and rather few marginal plates altogether.

Austinaster mc-carteri Adkins (Photo 335 and Color Photo 24)

Upper Cretaceous period. Base of the Austin group. Small true starfish. Disk thin and flattened. Arms end in rounded points. Distance of arm points from center of disk just slightly more than twice (2.15x) the distance from center to edge of disk between arms. Disk and arms are composed of irregular small plates with a fine stippling of minute tubercles. *Austinaster* is made a synonym of *Crateraster* in the *Treatise on Invertebrate Paleontology*, by Moore et al. Forgive this book for being a little patriotically slow to haul down such a great Texas name!

A very similar starfish, Photo 333, has been collected in the Del Rio formation, Lower Cretaceous, in McLennan County. It has slightly longer arms relative to the central disk, and the arms are much thinner. It is much like *Comptonia* in arm shape and marginal plate shape.

Subclass Ophiuroidea

The brittle stars; arms very distinct from the central disk. Arms long and sinuous, without food groove on lower arm surface.

Ophiura graysonensis (Photos 329, 330)

Lower Cretaceous period, Del Rio formation. Five long, thin arms coming from a small central disk. When found, these creatures are often in a concentration or "nest." According to Dr. John Fox of Baylor University, a foremost collector of such fossils, the nests are approximately 36 cm. across and 14 cm. deep. Smaller, lighter colored individuals are higher in the nest. Crabs and asteroid starfish, Photos 301, 331, 332, are found in these nests.

Class Echinoidea

The echinoids may be subdivided into sea urchins, which are round when viewed from above and which are somewhat inflated in shape from a side view; sand dollars, which are quite flattened; and heart urchins, which are inflated like the sea urchins but have an oblong shape when viewed from above. Only the sea urchins have their mouths central on their bottom side and their anal opening exactly opposite it at the center of their upper side. The round, symmetrical sea urchins are called regular urchins (Subclass Perischoechinoidea), and the asymmetrical heart urchins are called irregular urchins (Subclass Euechinoidea). In general it is felt that the heart urchins have evolved their oblong shape and forward-positioned mouth as a successful adaptation making movement and feeding more effective. The rear-positioned heart urchin anus is likewise viewed as a successful adaptation for helping keep wastes at a distance. Burrowing in the soft ocean bottom sediment became easier with these changes and provided more food and better protection. As a result, the round, regular, sea urchins are considered a more ancient form than the heart urchins. Texas rocks contain abundant examples of both kinds.

We shall view the mouth (peristome) and anus (peristome) placement in heart urchins as reason to speak of them as having a forward end and rear end for purposes of classification.

The shell of the urchins is called a test. The test is composed of five-sided calcite plates. The plates are perforated in some cases to allow passage of water and bodily secretions. The plates often bear small or large knobs for the attachment of spines varying from hairlike to clublike.

The mouth area of urchins is called the *peristome;* the anal area is called the *periproct.* A central area on the upper side of the urchin, where the plates converge, is called the *apical area.* It is marked by several pores for sperm and egg production and a water-intake opening. In regular urchins, the anus is part of the apical system. In irregular urchins it has moved from the apical area.

One of the most visible characteristics of echinoids is the five-part pattern of perforated plates spreading from the apical area. These are *ambulacra.* The plates between the ambulacra are called *interambulacral areas.* The ambulacra pass water to the hydraulic system of tube-feet, which have a role in movement and in passing food toward the mouth. The mouth of the urchin contains a jaw framework and five calcite teeth. This is called the *Aristotle's lantern* and is seldom preserved in the fossil. (See Color Photo 32.)

Echinoids are present in poorer preservation in the Paleozoic era because most forms were "regular" urchins with tissue-connected plates that soon scattered after death. "Irregular" urchins first appear in the Triassic period. The Mesozoic and Cenozoic eras contained more solidly preserved urchins of both types.

Subclass Perischoechinoidea — Regular Sea Urchins
Echinocrinus (Archaecidaris)(Photo 336)
Pennsylvanian through Lower Permian periods. Large, globular tests usually preserved as only five- or six-sided plates with large central spine knobs or as the spines themselves. The spines have a narrowed, conical base, flat on the end. Spines are side-prickled.

Stereocidaris hudspethensis Cooke (Photo 337)
Lower Cretaceous Washita division. The largest knobby, regular echinoid in Texas. A very impressive, spherical test with bottom and top slightly flattened. Five sinuous ambulacral areas snake down the sides of the test. The interambulacral plates bear singular, large spine base knobs with pitted center, each surrounded by a circlet of smaller bumps. Peristome somewhat larger than periproct. Spines are up to 100 mm. long, thick and blunt.

Phyllacanthus (Leiocidaris) hemigranosus (Shumard) (Photo 338)
This is a very similar echinoid, knobby-spined and smaller, best identified by its Northeast Texas location in the upper half of the Washita division, Lower Cretaceous. Two rather small species occur in the Lower Cretaceous, Glen Rose formation: *P. texanus* and *P. tysoni* Whitney and Kellum. *P. texanus* has straighter ambulacral grooves and smaller main tubercles.

Salenia texana Credner (Photos 339, 340)
Lower Cretaceous, Trinity division, Glen Rose formation.

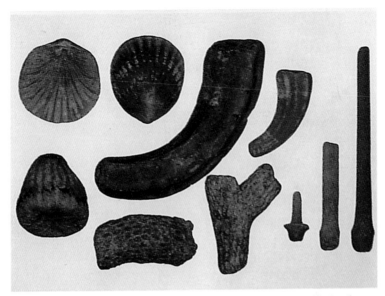

Color Photo 1. Microfossils, Sulfur River gravel, (top l. to r.) two brachiopods, two *Hamites*; (bottom l. to r.) horn coral, two bryozoans, and three urchin spines. Largest specimen 4mm., Upper Cretaceous period, Taylor gr., Delta Co., coll. by Ben Hong.

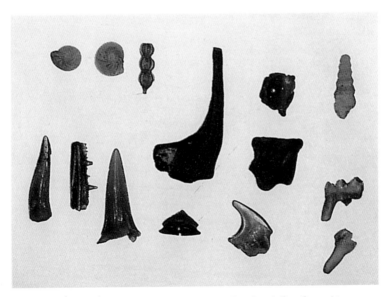

Color Photo 2. Microfossils, Sulfur River gravel, (upper l.) three *foraminifera*; (lower r.) two mammal teeth; (upper r.) snail; others are fish teeth and bone. Largest specimen 4mm., Upper Cretaceous period, Taylor gr., Delta Co., coll. by Ben Hong.

Plate 1

Color Photo 3. Fusilinids in block, 68 mm., Pennsylvanian period, Coleman Co., Texas Memorial Museum, Univ. of Texas at Austin.

Color Photo 4. Oak leaf, *Quercus* sp., 19 mm. long, Early Pleistocene epoch, Rita Blanca fm., Hartley Co., Texas Memorial Museum, Univ. of Texas at Austin.

Plate 2

Color Photo 5. Fern fossil, cf. *Lescuropteris* sp., Pennsylvanian period, Palo Pinto Co., Dr. G. Dennis Campbell and Sharron Schumann.

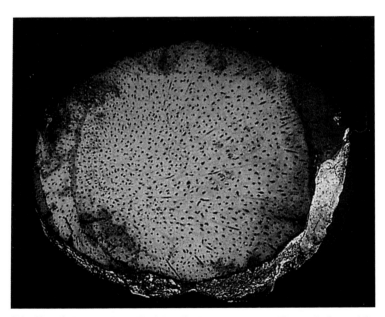

Color Photo 6. Palm wood (salicified), the official Texas state stone; 150 mm., Tertiary period, Houston Co., Dallas Museum of Natural History.

Plate 3

Color Photo 7. Graptolites on slab, 54 mm., *Phyllograptus* (oval); *Tetragraptus* (thin saw-edged blades); Ordovician period, Marathon Limestone, Sul Ross State Univ.

Color Photo 8. Jellyfish imprints, *Kirklandia texana* Caster, approx. 175 mm., Upper Cretaceous period, Woodbine fm., Denton Co., Louis Todd.

Plate 4

Color Photo 9. *Juresania* sp., spiny brachiopods on matrix, 29 mm., Pennsylvanian period, Palo Pinto Co., Frank, Mary, and Stephen Crane Coll., Dallas Museum of Natural History.

Color Photo 10. Snail fossils, *Conus sauridens* Conrad, 37 mm.; *Pseudoliva vetusta* Conrad, 27 mm.; *Athleta petrosus* Conrad, 31 mm.; Tertiary period, Eocene epoch, Stone City fm., Brazos Co., William Lowe.

Plate 5

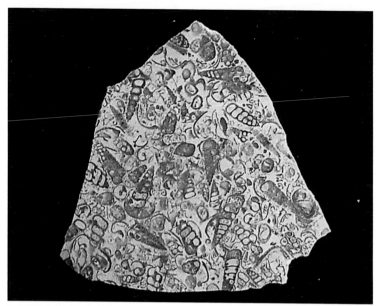

Color Photo 11. 'Turritella" snail limestone, 125 mm., Lower Cretaceous period, Walnut fm., Coryell Co., Dallas Museum of Natural History.

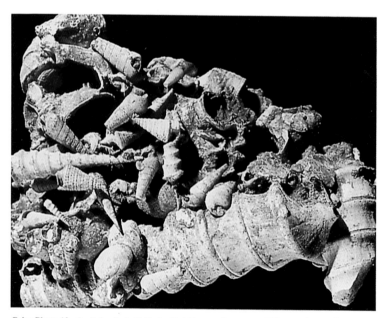

Color Photo 12. Snail fossils (salicified), *Cerithium* et al., approx. 250 mm., Lower Cretaceous period, Edwards fm., Colorado River cliffs, Travis Co., Texas Memorial Museum, Univ. of Texas at Austin.

Plate 6

Color Photo 13. Texas heart shell (clam); *Protocardia texana* Conrad, 72 mm., Lower Cretaceous period, Comanche Peak fm., central Texas, Frank, Stephen and Mary Crane.

Color Photo 14. Reef oyster, *Eoradiolites quadratus* Adkins, 95 mm., Lower Cretaceous period, Edwards fm., Coryell Co., C.D. Homan.

Color Photo 15. Bivalve with unusual growth habit, *Durania* sp., width 197 mm., Upper Cretaceous period, Austin gr., Dallas Co., Dallas Museum of Natural History.

Plate 7

Color Photo 16. Pyritized Lower Cretaceous bivalves, *Neithea* sp., center and left; *Ilymatogyra arietina* (Roemer); Lower Cretaceous period, Washita div., Tarrant Co., Dallas Museum of Natural History.

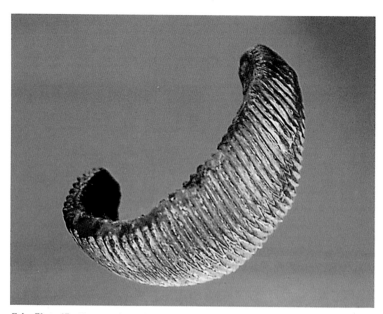

Color Photo 17. "Denture clam," *Rastellum carinatum* (Lamarck), 110 mm., Lower Cretaceous period, Washita div., Coryell Co., C. D. Homan.

Plate 8

Color Photo 18. Fossil pearls, probably from *Inoceramus* oyster; Upper Cretaceous period, Eagle Ford gr., Kamp Ranch member, Dallas Co., Robert Price.

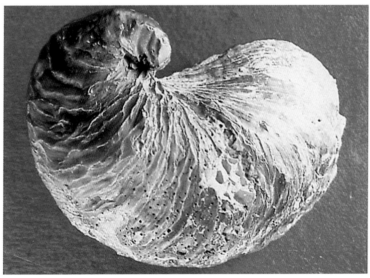

Color Photo 19. "Devil's toenail" oyster, *Exogyra ponderosa* Roemer, Upper Cretaceous period, Taylor gr., Rockwall Co., Dallas Museum of Natural History.

Plate 9

Color Photo 20. Glass Mountains cephalopod (acid etched), Permian period, Word fm., Brewster Co., Don O'Neill.

Color Photo 21. Ammonite, *Sphenodiscus pleurisepta* (Conrad), 135 mm., Upper Cretaceous period, Escondido fm., Jeff Davis Co., Frank, Mary and Stephen Crane.

Plate 10

Color Photo 22. Ammonite showing internal chambers, *Calycoceras (Conlinoceras) tarrantense* (Shumard), 167 mm., sliced on rocksaw; Upper Cretaceous period, Woodbine fm., Tarrant Co., Dallas Museum of Natural History.

Color Photo 23. Ammonite showing complex "suture pattern," *Placenticeras* sp., 205 mm., Upper Cretaceous period, Eagle Ford gr., Dallas Co., Dallas Museum of Natural History.

Plate 11

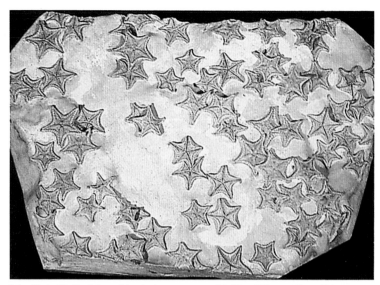

Color Photo 24. Starfish on slab, *Austinaster mc-carteri* Adkins, 535 mm., Upper Cretaceous period, basal Austin gr., Travis Co., Texas Memorial Museum, Univ. of Texas at Austin.

Color Photo 25. Crinoidal limestone, composed largely of crinoid stem fragments; Lower Pennsylvanian period, Lambert Ranch, San Saba Co., Dallas Museum of Natural History.

Plate 12

Color Photo 26. Crinoid stem, cup, and arms, *Ulocrinus* sp.; 116 mm., Pennsylvanian period, Wise Co., Louis Todd.

Color Photo 27. Crinoid "crown," *Graffhamicrinus* sp., 52mm., Pennsylvanian period, Wise Co., Kenneth Craddock.

Color Photo 28. Crinoid "crown," *Paradelocrinus brachiatus* Moore and Plummer, approx. 100 mm., Pennsylvanian period, Strawn gr., Hood Co.,Wm. Watkins.

Color Photo 29. Regular urchin, *Phymosoma texanum* (Roemer), 32mm., Lower Cretaceous period, Comanche Peak fm., Central Texas, Dallas Museum of Natural History.

Plate 13

Color Photo 30. Heart urchin, *Macraster* sp. (Boese), 49 mm., Lower Cretaceous period, Denton fm., Bell Co., John Moody, Sr.

Color Photo 31. Heart urchin, *Holaster simplex* Shumard, 49 man., Lower Cretaceous period, Duck Creek fm., northeast Texas, Dallas Museum of Natural History.

Plate 14

Color Photo 32. *Holectypus* sp. urchin, with Aristotle's Lantern mouthparts in place; Lower Cretaceous period, basal Del Rio fm., Bexar Co., Wm. Watkins.

Color Photo 33. *Echinocorys texanus* (Cragin) urchin, 81 mm. tall, Upper Cretaceous period. Anacacho fm., Medina Co., Stephen Crane.

Plate 15

Color Photo 34. Trilobite, *Paladin morrowensis* (Mather), 40 mm., small band in front of glabella missing, but has one nice cheek spine; Pennsylvanian period, Wise Co., Fred Wessman.

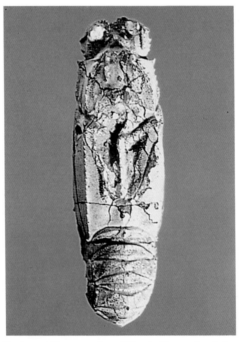

Color Photo 35. Crustacean, *Linuparus grimmeri* Stenzel, 73 mm., dorsal view, Upper Cretaceous, Eagle Ford gr., Dallas Co., Arlene Pike.

Plate 16

Color Photo 36. Crustacean (shrimp-like), *Protocullianassa pleuralum* Beikirch and Feldman, 46 mm., Upper Cretaceous period, Austin gr., Travis Co., Texas Memorial Museum 1238TX1, Univ. of Texas at Austin.

Color Photo 37. Shark vertebra (centrum), approx. 85 mm., Upper Cretaceous period, Eagle Ford gr., Dallas Co., Jim Kinkaid Coll., Dallas Museum of Natural History.

Plate 17

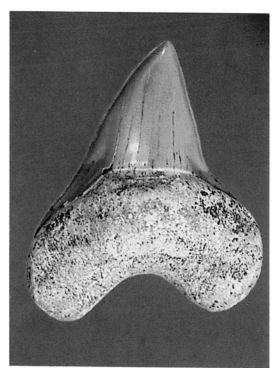

Color Photo 38. Shark tooth, *Cretoxyrhina mantelli* extenta, 36 mm. wide, Upper Cretaceous period, Austin gr., Collin Co., collected by Matt Reeves, Dallas Museum of Natural History.

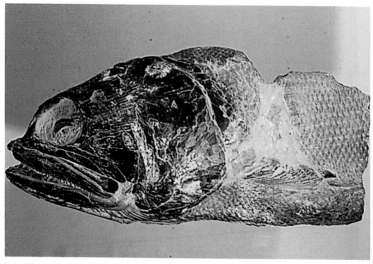

Color Photo 39. Fish fossil, *Pachyrhizodus minimus*, 300 mm., Upper Cretaceous period, Eagle Ford gr., Dallas Co., collected by the Ralph Churchill Family, on display, Dallas Museum of Natural History.

Plate 18

Color Photo 40. Fish fossil, *Tselfatia* sp., 425 mm., Upper Cretaceous period, Austin gr., Dallas Co., Dallas Museum of Natural History.

Color Photo 41. Fish fossil, *Xiphactinus* sp., Upper Cretaceous period, Eagle Ford gr., Collin Co., Texas Memorial Museum, Univ. of Texas at Austin.

Plate 19

Color Photo 42. *Pachyrhizodus caninus* fish, length 8 ft., Eagle Ford gr., Britton fm., Tarrant Co., found by Gary and Eddie Ford, on exhibit, Dallas Museum of Natural History.

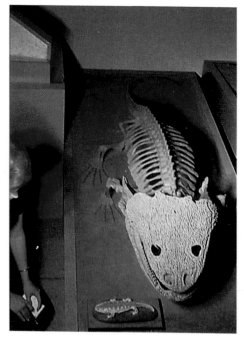

Color Photo 43. Fossil amphibian, *Metoposaurus* sp., Triassic period, Dockum gr., west central Texas, Texas Memorial Museum, Univ. of Texas at Austin.

Plate 20

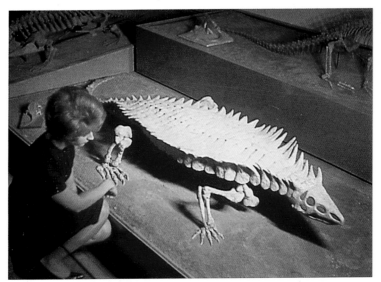

Color Photo 44. Triassic reptile, *Typothorax* sp.; note side spines; Triassic period, Dockum gr., west central Texas, Texas Memorial Museum, Univ. of Texas at Austin.

Color Photo 45. Dinosaur track trail, made by *Acrocanthosaurus*, Lower Cretaceous period, Glen Rose, Tex., Sommervell Co., Dinosaur Valley State Park.

Plate 21

Color Photo 46. Tooth of Pliosaur, *Polytychodon* sp., 148 mm., Upper Cretaceous period, Eagle Ford gr., Lower Britton fm., Dallas Co., collected by C. E. Finsley, Dallas Museum of Natural History.

Color Photo 47. *Tylosaurus* mosasaur, length 32 ft., Upper Cretaceous period, Taylor gr., Rockwall Co., found by the Larry Newman family, on display, Dallas Museum of Natural History.

Plate 22

Color Photo 48. *Protostega* sp. turtle, length approx. 11 feet, Upper Cretaceous period, Taylor gr., Rockwall Co., found by Jimmy Joe Herndon, on exhibit at Dallas Museum of Natural History.

Color Photo 49. *Tenontosaurus* sp. dinosaur, length 26 feet, Lower Cretaceous period, Trinity div., Antlers fm., Wise Co., on exhibit at Dallas Museum of Natural History, permanent loan from Texas Memorial Museum, excavated by D.M.N.H., S.M.U., and T.M.M.

Plate 23

Color Photo 50. Armor plates, *Glyptotherium floridanum* (Simpson), 45mm., Pleistocene epoch, Bee Co., Balcones Vertebrate Paleo. Lab., Univ. of Texas at Austin.

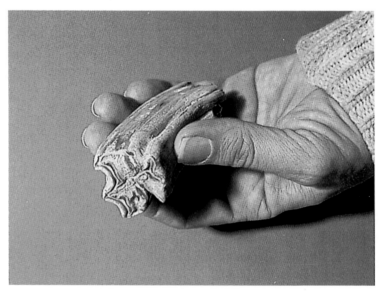

Color Photo 51. *Equus* sp. horse tooth, 32mm., Late Pleistocene epoch, Dallas Co., Dallas Museum of Natural History.

Plate 24

Color Photo 52. Saber-toothed cat sabre, *Smilodon*, canine tooth, 194 mm. long, Late Pleistocene epoch, San Patricio Co., Balcones Vertebrate Paleo. Lab., Univ. of Texas at Austin.

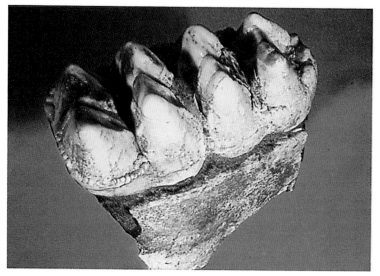

Color Photo 53. Mastodon tooth, *Mammuthus americanus*, molar tooth, 163 mm. long, Late Pleistocene epoch, Dallas Co., Dallas Museum of Natural History.

Plate 25

Color Photo 54. Mammoth tooth, *Elphas sp. cf. columbi,* molar tooth, 95mm. wide, Late Pleistocene epoch, Dallas Co., Dallas Museum of Natural History.

Color Photo 55. Mammoth skeleton, *Elphas sp. cf. columbi,* 13 ft. high, Pleistocene epoch, Dallas Co., collected by and displayed in Dallas Museum of Natural History.

Plate 26

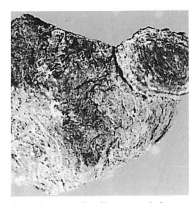

Photo 1. Stromatolite, 72 mm., an algal mound, Precambrian eras, Millican Limestone Hudspeth Co., Texas Memorial Museum, Univ. of Texas at Austin.

Photo 2. *Porocystis globularis* Giebel, 32 mm., an algal fruiting structure, Lower Cretaceous period, Glen Rose fm., Somervell Co., Dallas Museum of Natural History.

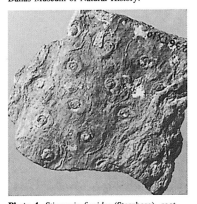

Photo 3. Cone of *Lepidodendropsis corrugata* (Dawson), scale tree cone, 50 mm., Pennsylvanian, Early Morrowan, Brewster Co., Texas Memorial Museum, Univ. of Texas at Austin.

Photo 4. *Stigmaria ficoides* (Sternberg), root fragment of Lepidodendroid scale tree, 78 mm., Pennsylvanian, Palo Pinto Co., Texas Memorial Museum, Univ. of Texas at Austin.

Photo 5. *Stigmaria ficoides* (Sternberg), root of Lepidodendroid scale tree, 158 mm., Pennsylvanian, Strawn gr., Palo Pinto Co., S. Schumann and D. Campbell.

Photo 6. *Sigillaria ichthyolepis* (Presl), leaf scars, bark of scale tree, 68 mm., Penn., Graham gr., Wayland Shale, Montague Co., Texas Memorial Muse., U. T. Austin 1140TX94.

Plate 27

Photo 7. *Calamites suckowi* Brongniart, width 16 mm., Pennsylvanian, Atokan, Burnett Co., Texas Memorial Museum, Univ. of Texas at Austin.

Photo 8. Leaf whorls, calamitid *Asterophyllites equisetiformis* (Schlotheim); long pinna of pecopterid fern *Asterotheca lamuriana* (Heer) Penn., Palo Pinto Co., Tex. Memorial Muse. U. T. 1236TX4.

Photo 9. Leaf whorls of calamitid *Asterophyllites* sp., Pennsylvanian, Cisco gr., Thifty Shale, Montague Co., Texas Memorial Museum, Univ. of Texas at Austin FR16-3.

Photo 10. *Annularia asteris* Bell (now considered a calamitid); area phot'd. 68 mm., Permian, Pueblo fm., Clay Co., Texas Memorial Museum, Univ. of Texas at Austin FP59-2.

Photo 11. *Annularia* sp., 95 mm., Permian, Putnam gr., Montague Co., Texas Memorial Museum, Univ. of Texas at Austin 1139TX-124.

Photo 12. *Sphenophyllum* sp., wide whorled leaves, length 84 mm., Pennsylvanian, Graham gr., Wayland Shale, Montague Co., Texas Memorial Museum, Univ. of Texas at Austin FP14-4.

Plate 28

Photo 13. *Neuropteris ovata* Hoffman, pinna of seed fern, 103 mm. slab, Pennsylvanian, Mineral Wells fm., Erath Co., Texas Memorial Museum, Univ. of Texas at Austin 2273.

Photo 14. *Neuropteris* sp., 50 mm., in concretion, Permian, Harpersville fm., Jack Co., Texas Memorial Museum, Univ. of Texas at Austin.

Photo 15. *Linopteris obliqua* (Bunbury) pinnules of net-veined seed fern, length 12 mm., Penn., Early Desmoinesean index fossil, Milsap fm., Palo Pinto Co., U. T. Austin 1234TX3.

Photo 16. *Alethopteris ambigua* Lesquereux, 88 mm. slab, seed fern, Pennsylvanian, Millsap fm., Palo Pinto Co., Texas Memorial Museum, Univ. of Texas at Austin 1236TX2.

Photo 17. *Megalopteris dawsoni* (Hartt), pinnule of seed fern, 130 mm. slab, Pennsylvanian, Late Morrowan, Marble Falls fm., Lampasas Co., Texas Memorial Museum, Univ. of Texas at Austin 1232TX1.

Photo 18. *Lescuropteris moori* Lesquereux, 148 mm., Permian, Admiral fm., Clay Co., Texas Memorial Museum, Univ. of Texas at Austin.

Plate 29

Photo 19. *Taeniopteris newberryana* Fontaine and White, 113 mm., a seed fern, Permian, Arroyo fm., Taylor Co., Texas Memorial Museum, Univ. of Texas at Austin.

Photo 20. *Callipteris conferta* (Sternberg), 150 mm. slab, indicator of earliest Permian, Wichita gr., late Admiral fm., Clay Co., Tex. Memorial Muse., U. T. Austin.

Photo 21. *Gigantopteris* sp., part of frond of a seed fern, area phot'd 125 mm., Permian, Arroyo fm., Taylor Co., Texas Memorial Museum, Univ. of Texas at Austin.

Photo 22. *Gigantopteris americana* White, a forked seed fern frond, 270 mm. slab, Permian, Clear Fork gr., Arroyo fm., Taylor Co., Tex. Memorial Muse., U. T. Austin.

Photo 23. *Danaeites emersoni* Lesquereux, 170 mm. slab, Permian, Clear Fork gr., Arroyo fm., Taylor Co., Texas Memorial Museum, Univ. of Texas at Austin.

Photo 24. *Delnortea abbottii*, 124 mm., Leonardian series, Permian, Brewster Co., Sul Ross State Univ.

Plate 30

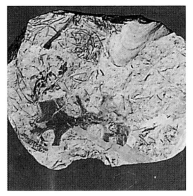

Photo 25. Insect nibbling on fern frond of *Phagophytichnus* sp., 94 mm. slab, Permian, Harpersville fm., Newcastle coal, Jack Co., Tex. Memorial Muse., U. T. Austin.

Photo 26. Common Permian plant, possibly *Rhacophyllum* sp., 197 mm., Permian, Harpersville fm., Jack Co., Texas Memorial Museum, Univ. of Texas at Austin 1185TX67.

Photo 27. *Cordaitean Conifer,* 35mm. (width), Smithwick Pm., Penn. period, Smithwick, Tex., U.T. Austin 1004TX8.

Photo 28. *Walchia (Lebachia) schneideri* (Zeiller), a conifer, 135 mm. slab, Permian, Putnam gr., Montague Co., Texas Memorial Museum, Univ. of Texas at Austin 1139TX44.

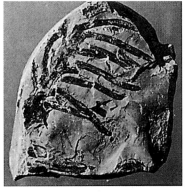

Photo 29. *Walchia (Lebachia) angustifolia* (Florin), 240 mm. slab, a conifer, Permian, Wichita gr., Putnam fm., Montague Co., Texas Memorial Museum, Univ. of Texas at Austin.

Photo 30. *Paleotaxites praecursor* White, 62 mm. slab, a conifer, Permian, Clear Fork gr., Arroyo fm., Jones Co., Texas Memorial Museum, Univ. of Texas at Austin BEG31719.

Plate 31

Photo 31. *Trichopitys* sp., 51 mm. slab, Permian, Putnam gr., Montague Co., Texas Memorial Museum, Univ. of Texas at Austin.

Photo 32. *Frenelopsis* sp., conifer imprint, 48 mm., Lower Cretaceous period, Glen Rose fm., Williamson Co., Texas Memorial Museum, Univ. of Texas at Austin.

Photo 33. Cycad leaves, 105 mm., Lower Cretaceous period, Bisset fm., Brewster Co., Texas Memorial Museum, Univ. of Texas at Austin.

Photo 34. Broadleaf tree leaf, 97 mm. slab, Woodbine fm., Upper Cretaceous period, near Arthur's Bluff, East Texas State Univ.

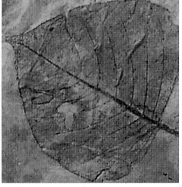

Photo 35. Broadleaf tree leaf, 23 mm. width of leaf, Upper Cretaceous period, Woodbine fm., near Arthur's Bluff, East Texas State Univ.

Photo 36. Broadleaf tree leaf, *Euonymus glanduliferus* Ball, a hypotype, leaf length 163 mm., Tertiary, Paleocene epoch, Bastrop Co., Texas Memorial Museum, Univ. of Texas at Austin 2316TX A526A.

Plate 32

Photo 37. Tufted seed, 9 mm., Pleistocene epoch, Rita Blanca fm., Hartley Co., Texas Memorial Museum, Univ. of Texas at Austin.

Photo 38. *Talpaspongia clavata* King, 73 mm., Permian, Clyde fm., Talpa Limestone, Runnels Co., Texas Memorial Museum, Univ. of Texas at Austin.

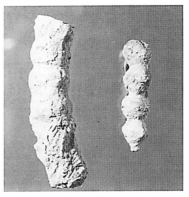

Photo 39. *Heliospongia ramosa* Girty, 148 mm., Pennsylvanian, Graford fm., Wise Co., Texas Memorial Museum, Univ. of Texas at Austin.

Photo 40. *Girtyocoelia* sp., on right, Pennsylvanian, Miles Co.; *Girtycoelia* sp., 28 mm., on left, same locale; Strecker Museum, Baylor Univ.

Photo 41. *Amblysiphonella prosseri* Clarke, 58 mm., plesiotype, Pennsylvanian, Graham gr., McCulloch Co., Texas Memorial Museum 34715, Univ. of Texas at Austin.

Photo 42. *Wewokella* sp., 49 mm., Millsap Lake fm., Pennsylvanian, Palo Pinto Co., Strecker Museum, Baylor Univ.

Plate 33

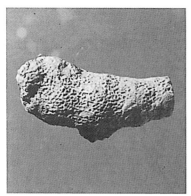

Photo 43. *Maeandrostia kansasensis* Girty, 38 mm., Pennsylvanian, Graford fm., Wise Co., Texas Memorial Museum, Univ. of Texas at Austin.

Photo 44. *Fissispongia jacksboroensis* King, 42 mm., (l.), Penn., Caddo Cr. fm., Jack Co., *F. spinosa* King, (r.), Penn., Millsap fm., Hood Co., U. T. Austin K1467, K1166 (syntypes).

Photo 45. *Conularia* sp., 32.5 mm., Pennsylvanian, Palo Pinto Co., Bill Carpenter.

Photo 46. *Tollina trapezoidalis* Flower, a chain coral, approx. 90 mm., Ordovician period, El Paso Co., Texas Memorial Museum, Univ. of Texas at Austin 1410TX9.

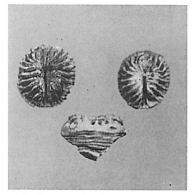

Photo 47. *Cumminsia aplanata* (Cummins), 19 mm., Lower Pennsylvanian, Smithwick Shale, Lampasas series, San Saba Co., Frank, Mary, and Stephen Crane.

Photo 48. *Lophophyllidium spinosum* Jeffords, 28 mm., Pennsylvanian, Finis Shale, Jack Co., Dallas Museum of Natural History.

Plate 34

Photo 49. *Lophophyllidium proliferum,* 29 mm., Pennsylvanian, Graham gr., Stephens Co., collected by George D. Harris, Strecker Museum, Baylor Univ.

Photo 50. *Caninia torquia* (Owen), 120 mm., Pennsylvanian, Jack and Brown cos., Strecker Museum, Baylor Univ.

Photo 51. *Cladophyllia furcifera* Roemer, 48 mm., Lower Cretaceous period, Edwards fm., Barton Creek, Travis Co., Texas Memorial Museum, Univ. of Texas at Austin.

Photo 52. *Adkinsella edwardensis* Wells, 143 mm. slab, Lower Cretaceous period, Edwards fm., Bell Co., Texas Memorial Museum, Univ. of Texas at Austin.

Photo 53. *Favia texana,* 111 mm., Upper Cretaceous period, Austin gr., Travis Co., Texas Memorial Museum, Univ. of Texas at Austin.

Photo 54. *Montastrea roemeriana* (Wells), 69 mm., Lower Cretaceous period, Edwards fm., Hill Co., Dallas Museum of Natural History.

Plate 35

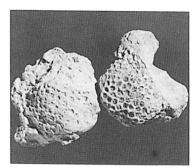
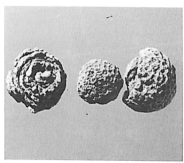

Photo 55. *Septastrea* sp., 25 mm., Lower Cretaceous period, Edwards fm., Hill Co., Frank, Mary, and Stephen Crane.

Photo 56. *Siderastrea tuckerae* Wells, 38 mm., Lower Cret. period, Denton fm., West Texas equivalent, Pecos Co., Tex. Memorial Muse., U. T. Austin 21337.

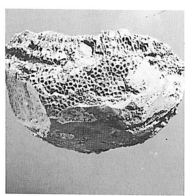

Photo 57. *Astrocoenia guadalupae* Roemer, 123 mm. slab, Lower Cretaceous period, Edwards fm., Devil's River, Texas Memorial Museum, Univ. of Texas at Austin.

Photo 58. *Blothrocyathus harrisi* Wells, 180 mm., Lower Cretaceous period, Glen Rose fm., Hays Co., Texas Memorial Museum, Univ. of Texas at Austin UT 11472.

Photo 59. *Turbinolia* sp., corals 14 mm. ea., Paleocene, Midway gr., near Commerce, Tex., East Texas State Univ.

Photo 60. *Paracyathus* sp., corals, 15 mm., Paleocene, Midway gr., Hunt Co., East Texas State Univ.

Plate 36

Photo 61. *Parasimilia* sp., 20 mm., type specimen, Lower Cretaceous period, Comanche Peak fm., Bosque Co., Texas Memorial Museum, Univ. of Texas at Austin.

Photo 62. *Flabellum lerchi* Vaughan, 17 mm., Eocene, near Smithville, Tex., Strecker Museum, Baylor Univ.

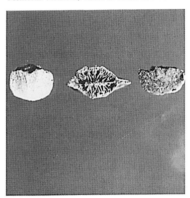

Photo 63. *Endopachys maclurii* (Lea), w. 18 mm., Eocene, near Smithville, Tex., Strecker Museum, Baylor Univ.

Photo 64. *Balanophyllia ponderosa,* 30 mm., Paleocene, Midway gr., C. D. Homan.

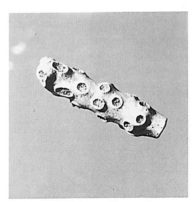

Photo 65. *Archohelia* sp., 37 mm., Eocene epoch, Hurricane Lentil fm., Houston Co., Texas Memorial Museum, Univ. of Texas at Austin.

Photo 66. *Chaetetes milleporaceous* Edwards and Haime, 135 mm., Pennsylvanian, Palo Pinto Co., Dallas Museum of Natural History.

Plate 37

Photo 67. *Polypora* sp., 18 mm., Pennsylvanian, Cisco series, Graham gr., Trickham Shale, Coleman Co., Frank, Mary, and Stephen Crane.

Photo 68. Lacy bryozoan *aff. Fenestella*, 44 mm., Lower Pennsylvanian, Kickapoo Falls Limestone, Lampasas series, Hood Co., Frank, Mary, and Stephen Crane.

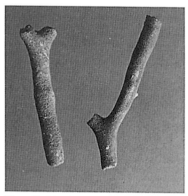

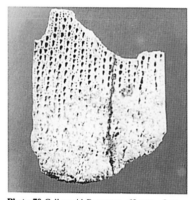

Photo 69. *Rhombopora lepidodendroidea* (Meek), 37 mm., Pennsylvanian, Harpersville fm., Stephens Co., Dallas Museum of Natural History.

Photo 70. Calloporid Bryozoan, 62 mm., Lower Cretaceous period, Edwards fm., Travis Co., Texas Memorial Museum, Univ. of Texas at Austin.

Photo 71. *Linguella* sp., 7 mm., faint traces of fingernail-like inarticulate brachiopods, Upper Cambrian, Cap Mt. fm., Strecker Museum, Baylor Univ.

Photo 72. *Lingula subspatulata* Hall and Meek, 12 mm., Upper Cretaceous period, Woodbine fm., Tarrant Co., Dallas Museum of Natural History.

Plate 38

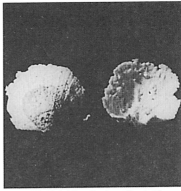

Photo 73. *Billingsella coloradoensis* (Shumard), 67 mm. slab, Upper Cambrian, Morgan Ck. Lime fm., Wilberns fm., Burnett Co., Tex. Memorial Muse., U. T. Austin.

Photo 74. *Finkelnburgia obesa* Cloud, 15 mm., Ordovician period, Ellenburger-Tanyard fms., index fossil, Mason Co., Texas Memorial Museum, Univ. of Texas at Austin 159-T-66.

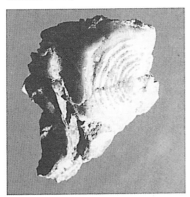

Photo 75. *Leptaena analoga* (Phillips), brachiopod, 18 mm., Mississippian, Chappel fm., Lampasas Co., Texas Memorial Museum, Univ. of Texas at Austin.

Photo 76. *Derbyia crassa* (Meek and Hayden), Pennsylvanian, Canyon gr., near Rochelle, Tex., C. D. Homan.

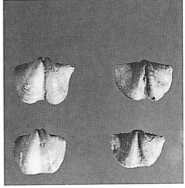

Photo 77. *Chonetes granulifer* Owen, 18 mm., Pennsylvanian, Strawn gr., Palo Pinto Co., Strecker Museum, Baylor Univ.

Photo 78. *Chonetina flemingi* (Norwood and Pratten), 9 mm., Pennsylvanian, Grayford fm., Palo Pinto Co., Strecker Museum, Baylor Univ.

Plate 39

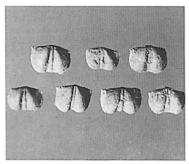

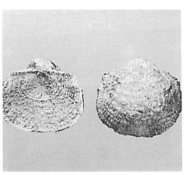

Photo 79. *Mesolobus inflexus* (Girty), 14 mm., Middle Pennsylvanian, Millsap fm., Parker Co., Texas Memorial Museum, Univ. of Texas at Austin.

Photo 80. *Juresania symmetrica* (McChesney), 31 mm., Pennsylvanian, Canyon gr., near Rochelle, Tex., C. D. Homan.

Photo 81. *Marginifera muricatina* (Dunbar and Condra), 18 mm., Pennsylvanian, Millsap Lake gr., Erath Co., Strecker Museum, Baylor Univ.

Photo 82. *Marginifera lasallensis* (Worthen), 22 mm., Pennsylvanian, Finis Shale, Jack Co., Strecker Museum, Baylor Univ.

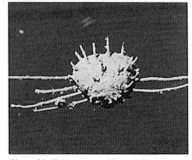

Photo 83. *Liosotella* sp., 40 mm., Permian, Word fm., Brewster Co. (acid-etched Glass Mts. material), Sul Ross State Univ.

Photo 84. *Echinaris* sp., 55 mm., Permian, Word fm., Brewster Co. (acid-etched Glass Mts. material), Sul Ross State Univ.

Plate 40

Photo 85. *Echinaris* sp. brachiopods dominate limestone slab, 245 mm., Permian, Word fm., Brewster Co., (acid etched Glass Mts. rock), Dr. David Rohr and S. Rudine, Sul Ross Univ.

Photo 86. *Collemataria (Lyttonia) nobilis americanus* (Girty), odd brachiopod, 54 mm., Permian, Word fm., Glass Mts., Brewster Co., U. T. Austin, type specs., 10650, 10572.

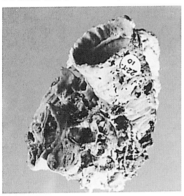

Photo 87. *Prorichtofenia (Richtofenia) permiana* (Shumard), 42 mm., odd brachiopod, Permian, Word fm., Brewster Co., Glass Mts., Tex. Memorial Muse., U. T. Austin UT7038.

Photo 88. *Reticulatia portlockianus* (Norwood and Pratten), 39 mm., Pennsylvanian, Millsap Lake fm., Palo Pinto Co., Strecker Museum, Baylor Univ.

Photo 89. *Reticulatia bassi* (McKee), 54 mm., Permian, Moran fm., near Moran, Tex., Frank, Mary, and Stephen Crane.

Photo 90. *Echinoconchus knighti* Dunbar and Condra, 63 mm., Pennsylvanian, Millsap Lake fm., Palo Pinto Co., Texas Memorial Museum, Univ. of Texas at Austin.

Plate 41

Photo 91. *Linoproductus prattenianus* (Norwood and Pratten), 43 mm., Pennsylvanian, Millsap Lake gr., Palo Pinto Co., Strecker Museum, Baylor Univ.

Photo 92. *Composita ovata* (Mather), 20 mm., Pennsylvanian, Cisco gr., near Eastland, Tex., Strecker Museum, Baylor Univ.

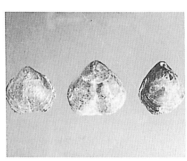

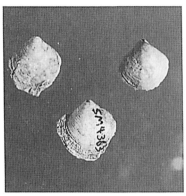

Photo 93. *Composita subtilita* (Sheppard), 28 mm., Pennsylvanian, Graham gr., near Cisco, Tex., C. D. Homan.

Photo 94. *Cleiothyridina* sp., 15 mm., Pennsylvanian, Strawn gr., Palo Pinto Co., Strecker Museum, Baylor Univ.

Photo 95. *Neospirifer cameratus* (Morton), 21 mm., Pennsylvanian, Millsap Lake gr., Parker Co., Strecker Museum, Baylor Univ.

Photo 96. *Neospirifer alatus* (Dunbar and Condra), 82 mm., Pennsylvanian, Millsap fm., Palo Pinto Co., Texas Memorial Museum, Univ. of Texas at Austin.

Plate 42

Photo 97. *Punctospirifer kentuckiensis* (Shumard), 21 mm., Pennsylvanian, Strawn gr., Palo Pinto Co., Dallas Museum of Natural History.

Photo 98. *Phricodothyris perplexa* (McChesney), 18 mm., Pennsylvanian, Mineral Wells gr., Strecker Museum, Baylor Univ.

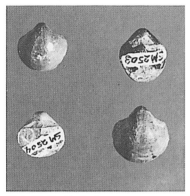

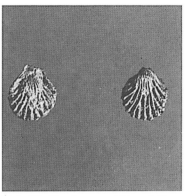

Photo 99. *Crurithyris planoconvexa* (Shumard), 14 mm., Pennsylvanian, Strecker Museum, Baylor Univ.

Photo 100. *Hustedia mormoni* (Marcou), 7 mm., Pennsylvanian, Mineral Wells gr., Palo Pinto Co., Strecker Museum, Baylor Univ.

Photo 101. *Kingena wacoensis* (Roemer), 24 mm., Lower Cretaceous period, Denton fm., Denton Co., Dallas Museum of Natural History.

Photo 102. *Euphemites nodocarinatus* (Hall), 33 mm., Pennsylvanian, Millsap Lake fm., Palo Pinto Co., Strecker Museum, Baylor Univ.

Plate 43

Photo 103. *Pharkidonotus* sp., 29 mm., Pennsylvanian, Millsap Lake fm., Palo Pinto Co., Texas Memorial Museum, Univ. of Texas at Austin.

Photo 104. *Bellerophon crassus* (Meek and Worthen), 33 mm., Pennsylvanian, along Colorado River, Mills Co., Dallas Museum of Natural History.

Photo 105. *Straparollus (Euomphalus),* 14 mm., Pennsylvanian, Jack Co., Dallas Museum of Natural History.

Photo 106. *Trepospira discoidalis* Newell, 18 mm., Pennsylvanian, Jack Co., collected by M. Seifert, Dallas Museum of Natural History.

Photo 107. *Glabrocinculum grayvillense* (Norwood and Pratten), 17 mm., Pennsylvanian, Jack Co., collected by M. Seifert, Dallas Museum of Natural History.

Photo 108. *Worthenia tabulata* (Conrad), 20 mm., Pennsylvanian, Canyon gr., Palo Pinto Co., Dallas Museum of Natural History.

Plate 44

Photo 109. *Goniasma lasallensis* (Worthen), 31 mm., Pennsylvanian, Millsap Lake fm., Parker Co., Strecker Museum, Baylor Univ.

Photo 110. *Meekospira choctawensis* Girty, 14 mm., Pennsylvanian, Millsap Lake fm., Palo Pinto Co., Texas Memorial Museum, Univ. of Texas at Austin.

Photo 111. *Strobeus* sp., 30 mm., Pennsylvanian, Finis Shale, Jack Co., Frank, Mary, and Stephen Crane.

Photo 112. *Olivellites plummeri* Fenton and Fenton, holotype, snail burrow, 14 mm. width, Penn., Graham gr., Wayland Sh. fm., Tx. Memorial Muse., U. T. Austin BEG 35681.

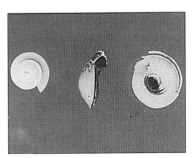

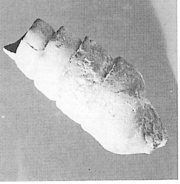

Photo 113. *Architectonica scrobiculata* (Conrad), 13 mm., Eocene epoch, Cook Mt. fm., Brazos Co., collected by Wm. Lowe.

Photo 114. *Cerithium bosquense* Shumard, 87 mm., Lower Cretaceous period, Comanche Peak fm., Hood Co., Texas Memorial Museum, Univ. of Texas at Austin.

Plate 45

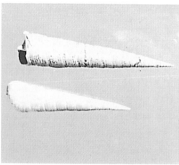

Photo 115. *Mesalia (Turritella) seriatim-granulata* (Roemer), 42 mm., Lower Cretaceous period, Comanche Peak fm., Bosque Co., Frank, Mary, and Stephen Crane.

Photo 116. *Mesalia claibornensis* Harris, 53 mm., Eocene epoch, Stone City fm., Brazos Co., Wm. Lowe.

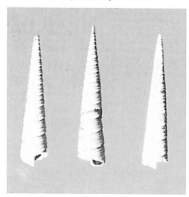

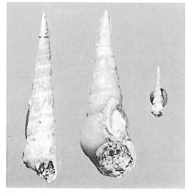

Photo 117. *Turritella* sp., 23 mm., Eocene epoch., Stone City fm., Brazos Co., Wm. Lowe.

Photo 118. *Turritella hilli,* 52 mm., left; *Turritella aldrichi,* 54 mm., center and right; Paleocene epoch, Midway gr., near Mexia, Tex., C. D. Homan.

Photo 119. *Anchura mudgeana* Whitney, 45 mm., Lower Cretaceous period, Goodland fm., Tarrant Co., Dallas Museum of Natural History.

Photo 120. *Anchura monilifera* Gabb, 64 mm., Lower Cretaceous period, Glen Rose fm., Bosque Co., Frank, Mary, and Stephen Crane.

Plate 46

Photo 121. *Gyrodes (Sohlella) spillmani* Gabb,
64 mm., Upper Cretaceous period, Navarro gr.,
Paris, Texas, Don O'Neill.

Photo 122. *Polinices* sp., 59 mm., Upper
Cretaceous period, Taylor gr., Sulphur River,
Don O'Neill.

Photo 123. *Amaurellina alabamensis*, 23
mm., left; *Epitonium cookei*, 27 mm., right;
Paleocene epoch, Midway gr., near Kosse,
Tex., C. D. Homan.

Photo 124. *Sinum declive* (Conrad), 17 mm.,
Eocene epoch, Cook Mt. fm., Brazos Co.,
Wm. Lowe.

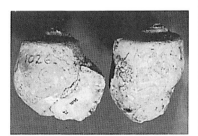

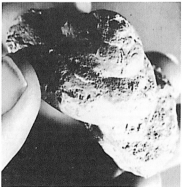

Photo 125. *Amauropsis pecosensis* Adkins, a
paratype, 113 mm., Lower Cretaceous period,
Upper Fredericksburg fm., Pecos Co., Texas
Memorial Museum, Univ. of Texas at Austin
34056, 34057.

Photo 126. *Leptomaria austinensis* (Shumard),
62 mm.(a syntype), Lower Cretaceous period,
Ft. Worth fm., McLennan Co., Texas Memorial
Museum, Univ. of Texas at Austin 17602, a
sytype.

Plate 47

Photo 127. *Tylostoma tumidum* Shumard, 48 mm., Lower Cretaceous period, Goodland fm., Tarrant Co., Frank, Mary, and Stephen Crane.

Photo 128. *Levifusus mortoniopsis* (Gabb), 20 mm., Eocene epoch, Claiborne gr., Stone City fm., Brazos Co., Frank, Mary, and Stephen Crane.

Photo 129. *Lyria wilcoxiana,* left, 20 mm.; *Levifusus pagoda,* right, 23 mm.; Paleocene epoch, Midway gr., Falls Co., C. D. Homan.

Photo 130. *Architectonica* sp., 20 mm., (l.); *Tritonium* sp., 40 mm., (cent.); *Cypraea* sp., 26 mm., (r.); Paleocene epoch, Midway gr., Kaufman Co., Frank, Mary and Stephen Crane.

Photo 131. *Calytraphorus popenoe* Gardner, left, 24 mm.; *Cypraea* sp., center, 8 mm.; *Coronia mediavia,* right, 20 mm.; Paleocene epoch., Midway Group, Falls Co., C. D. Homan.

Photo 132. *Mangelia schotti* Gardner, 11 mm., Paleocene epoch, Midway gr., Kinkaid fm., Kaufman Co., Frank, Mary, and Stephen Crane.

Plate 48

Photo 133. *Distorsio septemdentata* Gabb, 26 mm., Eocene epoch, Cook Mt. fm., Brazos Co., Wm. Lowe.

Photo 134. *Falsifusus ludovicianus* (Johnson), 25 mm., Eocene epoch, Stone City fm., Brazos Co., Wm. Lowe.

Photo 135. *Volutocorbis texana* Gardner, left, 27 mm.; *Volutocorbis rugatus* (Conrad), center and right, 29 mm.; Paleocene epoch, Midway gr., Falls Co., C. D. Homan.

Photo 136. *Athleta petrosus* (Conrad), 54 mm., Eocene epoch, Cook Mt. fm., Brazos Co., Wm. Lowe.

Photo 137. *Lapparia crassa* Stenzel and Turner, 43 mm., Eocene epoch, Cook Mt. fm., Brazos Co., Wm. Lowe.

Photo 138. *Lapparia mooreana* (Gabb), 50 mm., Eocene epoch, Claiborne gr., Burleson Co., Walter Davis II.

Plate 49

Photo 139. *Pseudoliva vestusta* Conrad, 31 mm., Eocene epoch, Cook Mt. fm., Brazos Co., Wm. Lowe.

Photo 140. *Pseudoliva scalina* Gardner, left, 29 mm.; *Mesalia alabamensis* Gardner, right, 49 mm.; Paleocene epoch, Midway gr., Falls Co., C. D. Homan.

Photo 141. *Pseudoliva ostrarupis*, 8 mm., (l.); *Polinices* sp., 24 mm., (cent.); *Pleurotomella whitfieldi*, 34 mm., (r.); Paleocene epoch, Midway gr., Falls Co., C. D. Homan.

Photo 142. *Cochlespira engonata* Conrad, 20 mm., Eocene epoch, Stone City fm., Brazos Co., Wm. Lowe.

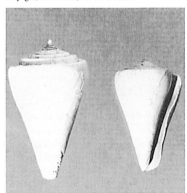

Photo 143. *Conus sauridens* Conrad, 37 mm., Eocene epoch, Stone City fm., Brazos Co., Wm. Lowe.

Photo 144. *Orthosurcula longispersa* (Gardner), left, 48 mm.; *Orthosurcula francescae* Gardner, center, 30 mm.; *Orthosurcula adeona* (Whitfield), right, 21 mm.; Paleocene epoch, Midway gr., Falls Co., C. D. Homan.

Plate 50

Photo 145. *Protosurcula gabbii* (Conrad), 46 mm., Eocene epoch, Stone City fm., Brazos Co., Wm. Lowe.

Photo 146. *Conocardium* sp., a rostroconch, a primitive ancestor of bivalves, 28 mm., Pennsylvanian, Palo Pinto Co., East Texas State Univ. ET 5011, L 467-1.

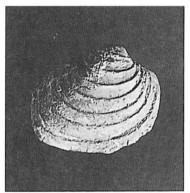

Photo 147. *Nucula (Nuculopsis) girtyi* (Schenck), 17 mm., Pennsylvanian, Graford fm., Palo Pinto Co., Dallas Museum of Natural History.

Photo 148. *Astartella concentrica* (Conrad), 24 mm., Pennsylvanian, Gunsight fm., Stephens Co., Dallas Museum of Natural History.

Photo 149. *Yoldia glabra* Beede and Rogers, 32.5 mm., Pennsylvanian, Canyon series, Finis Shale, Jack Co., Frank, Mary, and Stephen Crane.

Photo 150. *Allorisma terminale* Hall, 97 mm., Permian, Admiral fm., Coleman Co., Texas Memorial Museum, Univ. of Texas at Austin.

Plate 51

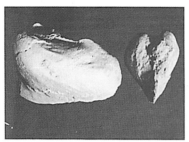

Photo 151. *Arca simondsi* Whitney, 83 mm., Lower Cretaceous period, Glen Rose fm., Bandera Co., Frank, Mary, and Stephen Crane.

Photo 152. *Cucullaea kaufmanensis,* 31 mm., Paleocene epoch, Midway gr., Kaufman Co., C. D. Homan.

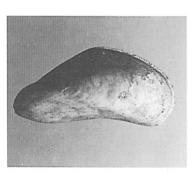

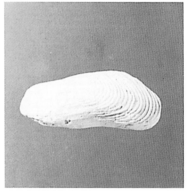

Photo 153. *Brachidontes filisculptus* (Cragin), 59 mm., Upper Cretaceous period, Woodbine fm., Denton Co., Kenneth Craddock.

Photo 154. *Modiolus* sp, 32 mm., Lower Cretaceous period, Glen Rose fm., Kerr Co., Dallas Museum of Natural History.

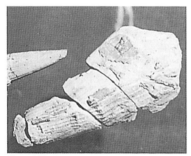

Photo 155. *Pinna comancheana* Cragin, 144 mm., Lower Cretaceous period, Goodland fm., Tarrant Co., Dallas Museum of Natural History.

Photo 156. *Myalina copei* Whitfield, 88 mm., Permian period, Stephens Co., Dallas Museum of Natural History.

Plate 52

Photo 157. *Myalina subquadrata* Shumard, 98 mm., Pennsylvanian period, Canyon gr., Jack Co., Dallas Museum of Natural History.

Photo 158. *Inoceramus labiatus* Schlotheim, 98 mm., Upper Cretaceous period, Eagle Ford gr., Dallas Co., Dallas Museum of Natural History.

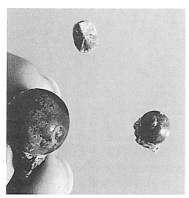

Photo 159. Fossil pearls, 13 mm., possibly from *Inoceramus* oysters, Upper Cretaceous period, Eagle Ford gr., Kamp Ranch member, Dallas Co., Robert Price.

Photo 160. *Inoceramus comancheanus* Cragin, 140 mm., Lower Cretaceous period, Duck Creek fm., Grayson Co., Frank, Mary, and Stephen Crane.

Photo 161. *Neithea texana* Roemer, 41 mm., Lower Cretaceous period, Ft. Worth fm., McLennon Co., C. D. Homan.

Photo 162. *Neithea georgetownensis* Kniker, 42 mm., a syntype, Lower Cretaceous period, Georgetown fm., Travis Co., Texas Memorial Museum, Univ. of Texas at Austin.

Plate 53

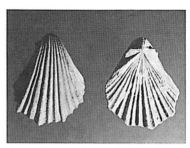

Photo 163. *Neithea subalpina* Boese, 38 mm., Lower Cretaceous period, Walnut fm., Coryell Co., C. D. Homan.

Photo 164. *Neithea irregularis* (Boese), 30 mm., Lower Cretaceous period, Comanche Peak fm., Bosque Co., Frank, Mary, and Stephen Crane.

Photo 165. *Neithea wrighti* (Shumard), 32 mm., a hypotype, Lower Cretaceous period, Georgetown fm., Travis Co., Texas Memorial Museum, Univ. of Texas at Austin 36171.

Photo 166. *Neithea roemeri* (Hill), 44 mm., a hypotype, Lower Cretaceous period, Buda fm., Travis Co., Texas Memorial Museum, Univ. of Texas at Austin.

Photo 167. *Neithea duplicicosta* (Roemer), 32 mm., a syntype, Lower Cretaceous period, Edwards fm., Travis Co., Texas Memorial Museum, Univ. of Texas at Austin 30061.

Photo 168. *Neithea casteeli* Kniker, 33 mm., a syntype, Upper Cretaceous period, Austin gr., Travis Co., Texas Memorial Museum, Univ. of Texas at Austin 30054-B.

Plate 54

Photo 169. *Pectin (Aequipectin) perplanus* Morton, 43 mm., Lower Cret. period, lower part of middle Duck Creek fm., Gainesville, Tex., Frank, Mary and Stephen Crane.

Photo 170. *Aviculopecten gryphus* Newell, 47 mm. slab, Permian, Word fm., Brewster Co., Texas Memorial Museum, Univ. of Texas at Austin.

Photo 171. *Plicatula subgurgitis* Boese, 9 mm., Lower Cretaceous period, Weno fm., Denton Co., Dallas Museum of Natural History.

Photo 172. *Plicatula dentonensis* Cragin, 8 mm., Lower Cretaceous period, Upper Marl, Duck Creek fm., Tarrant Co., Frank, Mary, and Stephen Crane.

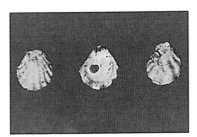

Photo 173. *Plicatula filimentosa* Conrad, 11 mm., Eocene epoch, Cook Mt. fm., Brazos Co., Wm. Lowe.

Photo 174. *Spondylus hilli* Cragin, 53 mm., Lower Cretaceous period, Ft. Worth fm., Williamson Co., Texas Memorial Museum 19724, Univ. of Texas at Austin.

Plate 55

Photo 175. *Lima wacoensis* Roemer, 29 mm., Lower Cretaceous period, Goodland fm., Tarrant Co., Frank, Mary, and Stephen Crane.

Photo 176. *Lima pecosensis* Stanton, 28 mm., Lower Cretaceous period, Edwards fm., Hill Co., Frank, Mary, and Stephen Crane.

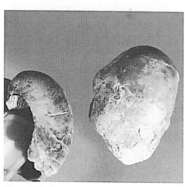

Photo 177. *Pycnodonte newberryi* (Stanton), 30 mm., Upper Cretaceous period, Anacacho fm., Uvalde Co., Frank, Mary, and Stephen Crane.

Photo 178. *Pycnodonte mutabilis* (Morton), a hypotype, 97 mm., Upper Cretaceous period, Escondido fm., Medina Co., Texas Memorial Museum, Univ. of Texas at Austin 34067.

Photo 179. *Texigryphea mucronata* (Gabb), 77 mm., Lower Cretaceous period, Grayson fm., Denton Co., Dallas Museum of Natural History.

Photo 180. *Texigryphea marcoui* (Hill and Vaughan) (now considered same as *T. mucronata*), 38 mm., Lower Cretaceous period, Comanche Peak fm., Bosque Co., Frank, Mary, and Stephen Crane.

Plate 56

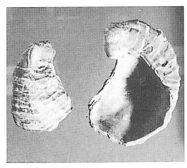

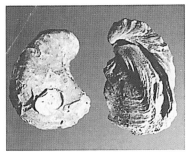

Photo 181. *Texigryphea graysonana* Stanton (now considered same as *G. roemeri*), 68 mm., Lower Cretaceous period, Upper Grayson fm., Denton Co., Frank and Mary Crane.

Photo 182. *Texigryphea navia* (Hall), 48 mm.; small round patch on the left specimen is an "oyster spate" attachment point of a younger oyster; Lower Cretaceous period, Kiamichi fm., Johnson Co., Frank and Mary Crane.

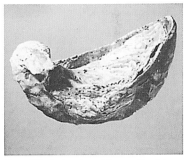

Photo 183. *Texigryphea washitaensis* (Hill), 58 mm., Lower Cretaceous period, Washita div., Denton Co., Dallas Museum of Natural History.

Photo 184. *Texigryphea gibberosa* (Cragin), 77 mm., Lower Cretaceous period, Duck Creek fm., McLennon Co., C. D. Homan.

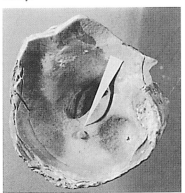

Photo 185. Interior of *Exogyra ponderosa* Roemer, 85 mm., with 4 mm. pearl, Upper Cretaceous period, Taylor gr., basal Pecan Gap fm., Hunt Co., collected by Donna Baker Spinato for East Texas State Univ. ET 5298.

Photo 186. *Exogyra laeviuscula* Roemer, 138 mm., Upper Cretaceous period, Austin gr., Bell Co., C. D. Homan.

Plate 57

Photo 187. *Exogyra costata* Say, a hypotype, 114 mm., Upper Cretaceous period, Navarro gr., Bowie Co., Texas Memorial Museum, Univ. of Texas at Austin 34068.

Photo 188. *Exogyra erraticostata* Stephenson, 123 mm., Upper Cretaceous period, Taylor and Austin grs., Bell Co., C. D. Homan.

Photo 189. *Amphidonte walkeri* (White), 133 mm., left valve, Lower Cretaceous period, Ft. Worth fm., Denton Co., Louis Todd.

Photo 190. *Ceratostreon texanum* (Roemer), 84 mm., Lower Cretaceous period, Walnut fm., Coryell Co., C. D. Homan.

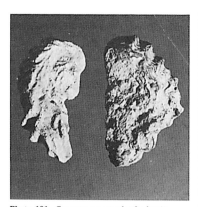

Photo 191. *Ceratostreon weatherfordensis* (Cragin), 30 mm., Lower Cretaceous period, Comanche Peak fm., Frank, Mary, and Stephen Crane.

Photo 192. *Ilymatogyra arietina* (Roemer), 41 mm., Lower Cretaceous period, Washita div., Del Rio fm., Denton Co., Frank, Mary, and Stephen Crane.

Plate 58

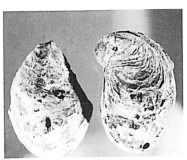

Photo 193. *Gyrostrea cartledgei* (Boese), 62 mm., cotype, both valves, Lower Cret. period, Del Rio fm., Brewster Co., Tex. Memorial Museum, U. T. Austin.

Photo 194. *Crassostrea soleniscus* (Meek), 83 mm., Upper Cretaceous period, Woodbine fm., Fannin Co., Texas Memorial Museum, Univ. of Texas at Austin.

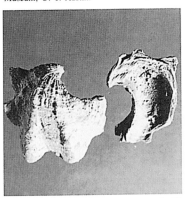

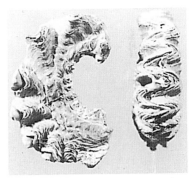

Photo 195. *Lopha quadriplicata* (Shumard), 39 mm., Lower Cret. period, contact of Denton and Weno fms., Denton Co., M. Seifert collector, Dallas Muse. of Nat. Hist.

Photo 196. *Agerostrea falcata* (Morton), 45 mm., Upper Cretaceous period, Navarro gr., Sulphur River area, Robert Price.

Photo 197. *Ostrea crenulimarginata,* 39 mm., Paleocene epoch, Midway gr., near Mexia, Tex., C. D. Homan.

Photo 198. *Lopha subovata* (Shumard), 143 mm., Lower Cretaceous period, Denton fm., Denton Co., Don O'Neill.

Plate 59

Photo 199. *Lopha travesana* (Stephenson), 115 mm., small individual cemented to larger, Upper Cretaceous period, Austin gr., Williamson Co., C. D. Homan.

Photo 200. *Chondrodonta* sp., 125 mm., Lower Cretaceous period, Fredericksburg div., Edwards fm., central Texas, Dallas Museum of Natural History.

Photo 201. *Trigonia clavigera* Cragin, 85 mm., Lower Cretaceous period, Walnut fm., central Texas, Dallas Museum of Natural History.

Photo 202. *Pterotrigonia guadalupe* (Boese), 54 mm., Lower Cretaceous period, Walnut fm., near Clifton, Texas, C. D. Homan.

Photo 203. *Venericardia wenoensis* Adkins, 18 mm., Lower Cretaceous period, Washita div., Lower Weno fm., Denton Co., Frank, Mary, and Stephen Crane.

Photo 204. *Venericardia planicosta densata* (Conrad), 43 mm., Eocene epoch, Cook Mt. fm., Brazos Co., Wm. Lowe.

Plate 60

Photo 205. *Venericardia smithii* Aldrich, 29 mm., internal mold, Paleocene epoch, Kincaid fm., Kaufman Co., Dallas Museum of Natural History.

Photo 206. *Venericardia mediaplata,* 44 mm., Paleocene epoch, Midway gr., near Buffalo Mop, Tex., C. D. Homan.

Photo 207. *Magicardium* sp., 39 mm., Paleocene epoch, Midway gr., east Texas, C. D. Homan.

Photo 208. *Callocardia kempae* Gardner, 36 mm., Paleocene epoch, Kincaid fm., Kemp, Tex., Kaufman Co., Dallas Museum of Natural History.

Photo 209. *Callocardia haetofi* Gardner, 31 mm., Paleocene epoch, Midway gr., east Texas, C. D. Homan.

Photo 210. *Callocardia pteleina* Gardner, 24 mm., Paleocene epoch, Midway gr., Kinkaid fm., Kaufman Co., Frank, Mary, and Stephen Crane.

Plate 61

Photo 211. *Crassatella antestricta* Gabb, 28 mm., Eocene epoch, Cook Mt. fm., Brazos Co., Wm. Lowe.

Photo 212. *Crassatellites gabbi* (Safford), 34 mm., Paleocene epoch, Kincaid fm., Kaufman Co., C. D. Homan.

Photo 213. *Protocardia texana* (Conrad), 79 mm., Lower Cretaceous period, Comanche Peak fm., central Texas, Frank, Mary, and Stephen Crane.

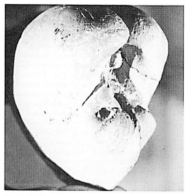

Photo 214. *Arctica roemeri* (Cragin), 100 mm., Lower Cretaceous period, Glen Rose fm. Hood Co., Texas Memorial Museum, Univ. of Texas at Austin.

Photo 215. *Artica medialis* (Conrad), 48 mm., Lower Cretaceous period, Glen Rose fm., Bandera Co., Frank, Mary, and Stephen Crane.

Photo 216. *Dentonia leveretti* (Cragin), 37 mm., syntype, Upper Cretaceous period, Woodbine fm., Denton Co., Texas Memorial Museum, Univ. of Texas at Austin.

Plate 62

Photo 217. *Cyprimeria washitaensis* Adkins, holotype, 57 mm., with original shell, Lower Cret. period, Weno fm., Grayson Co., Texas Memorial Muse., U. T. at Austin.

Photo 218. *Cyprimeria texana* (Roemer), 78 mm., Lower Cretaceous period, Comanche Peak fm., Lampasas Co., Frank, Mary, and Stephen Crane.

Photo 219. *Tapes decepta* (Hill), 36 mm., Lower Cretaceous period, Glen Rose fm., Bandera Co., Frank, Mary, and Stephen Crane.

Photo 220. *Corbula* sp., 43 mm., Paleocene epoch, Midway gr., Kinkaid fm., Kaufman Co., Martin Seifert Coll., Dallas Museum of Natural History.

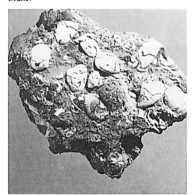

Photo 221. *Corbula basiniformis* Adkins, slab 150 mm., paratypes, Lower Cretaceous period, Weno fm., Grayson Co., Texas Memorial Museum, Univ. of Texas at Austin 21452.

Photo 222. *Homomya* sp., 54 mm., Lower Cretaceous period, Goodland fm., Tarrant Co., Dallas Museum of Natural History.

Plate 63

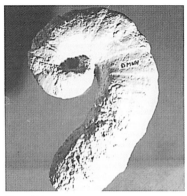

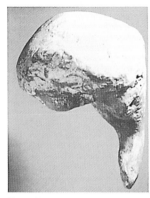

Photo 223. *Caprina occidentalis* Conrad, 155 mm., both valves, Lower Cretaceous period, Edwards fm., central Texas, Dallas Museum of Natural History.

Photo 224. *Sellaea* sp., 130 mm., Lower Cretaceous period, Edwards fm., Coryell Co., C. D. Homan.

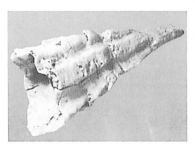

Photo 225. *Eoradiolites davidsoni* (Hill), 103 mm., Lower Cretaceous period, Edwards fm., Coryell Co., C. D. Homan.

Photo 226. *Durania* sp., width 197 mm., Upper Cretaceous period, Austin gr., Dallas Co., Dallas Museum of Natural History.

Photo 227. *Sauvagesia acutocarinata* Adkins, 150 mm., holotype, Upper Cretaceous period, Travis Co., Texas Memorial Museum, Univ. of Texas at Austin WSA 12222.

Photo 228. *Pholadomya sanctisabae* Roemer, 24 mm., Lower Cretaceous period, Comanche Peak fm., Bosque Co., Frank, Mary, and Stephen Crane.

Plate 64

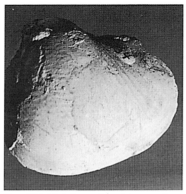

Photo 229. *Pholadomya shattucki* Boese, 62 mm., Lower Cretaceous period, Duck Creek fm., Grayson Co., Frank, Mary, and Stephen Crane.

Photo 230. *Pholadomya lincecumi* Shumard, 70 mm., Upper Cretaceous period, Taylor gr., Delta Co., C. D. Homan.

Photo 231. *Pholadomya papyracea,* 73 mm., Upper Cretaceous period, Taylor gr., Delta Co., C. D. Homan.

Photo 232. *Laternula simondsi* Whitney, 69 mm., Lower Cretaceous period, Glen Rose fm., Bandera Co., Frank, Mary, and Stephen Crane.

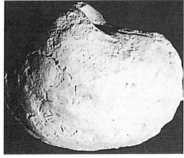

Photo 233. *Laternula texana* (Cragin), 130 mm., a syntype, Lower Cretaceous period, Buda fm., Denton Co., Texas Memorial Museum, Univ. of Texas at Austin 245-T-27.

Photo 234. *Liopistha jurafacies* (Cragin), 88 mm., Lower Cretaceous period, Glen Rose fm., Bandera Co., Frank, Mary, and Stephen Crane.

Plate 65

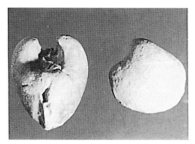

Photo 235. *Liopistha banderaensis* Whitney, 65 mm., Lower Cretaceous period, Trinity div., Glen Rose fm., Bandera Co., Frank, Mary, and Stephen Crane.

Photo 236. *Liopistha walkeri* Whitney, 89 mm., Lower Cretaceous period, Glen Rose fm., Bandera Co., Frank, Mary, and Stephen Crane.

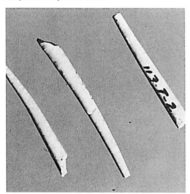

Photo 237. *Dentalium* sp., scaphopods, 30 mm., Eocene epoch, Landrum fm., Houston Co., Texas Memorial Museum, Univ. of Texas at Austin.

Photo 238. *Michelinoceras* ssp., 70 mm., Pennsylvanian, Palo Pinto Co., Kenneth Smith.

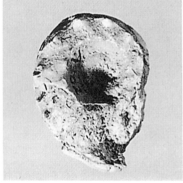

Photo 239. *Protocycloceras* sp., 40 mm., Pennsylvanian, Cisco gr., Palo Pinto Co., Dallas Museum of Natural History.

Photo 240. *Cooperoceras texanum* (Miller), 38 mm., Permian, Moran fm., Coleman Co., Alice Frost and Gilbert Norris.

Plate 66

Photo 241. *Paraceltites elegans* Girty, 38 mm., plesiotype, Permian, Delaware fm., Culberson Co., Texas Memorial Museum, Univ. of Texas at Austin 34556.

Photo 242. *Neoglyphioceras entogonum* (Gabb), 38 mm., plesiotype, Mississippian Period, Barnett fm., Lampasas Co., Texas Memorial Museum, Univ. of Texas at Austin P7545.

Photo 243. *Gonioloboceras goniolobum* (Meek), 50 mm., Pennsylvanian, Trickham Shale fm., Graham gr., Brown Co., Frank, Mary, and Stephen Crane.

Photo 244. *Schistoceras smithi* Boese, 92 mm., plesiotypes, Pennsylvanian, Graford fm., Wise Co., Texas Memorial Museum, Univ. of Texas at Austin P6180 and 34478.

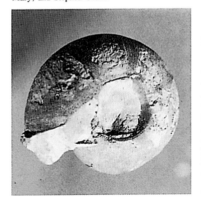

Photo 245. *Eoasianites* sp., 35 mm., Pennsylvanian, Graham gr., north central Texas, Texas Memorial Museum, Univ. of Texas at Austin P1269.

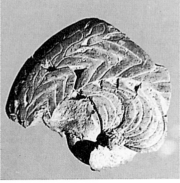

Photo 246. *Neodimorphoceras texanum* (Smith), 42 mm., Pennsylvanian period, Graham gr., Young Co., Texas Memorial Museum, Univ. of Texas at Austin.

Plate 67

Photo 247. *Waagenoceras guadalupensis* Girty, 52 mm., type specimens, Permian, Delaware fm., Culberson Co., Tex. Memorial Muse., U. T. at Austin 34453, 34465.

Photo 248. *Perrinites hilli* (Smith), 97 mm., the holotype, Permian, Stonewall Co., Texas Memorial Museum, Univ. of Texas at Austin.

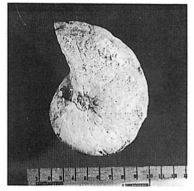

Photo 249. *Paracymatoceras texanum* (Roemer), 49 mm., Lower Cretaceous period, Ft. Worth fm., Tarrant Co., Frank, Mary, and Stephen Crane.

Photo 250. *Paracymatoceras hilli* (Shattuck), 83 mm., Lower Cretaceous period, central Texas, Frank, Mary, and Stephen Crane.

Photo 251. *Cimomia vaughani*, 85 mm., Paleocene epoch, Midway gr., Raines Co., East Texas State Univ. ET 5176.

Photo 252. *Hercoglossa* sp., 164 mm., in a concretion, Paleocene epoch, Kinkaid fm., Midway gr., Kaufman Co., Joseph Kane.

Plate 68

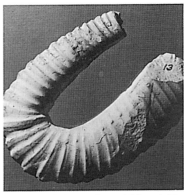

Photo 253. *Aturia brazoensis* Stenzel, 187 mm., (largest), holotype, Eocene epoch, Stone City and Weches fms., Burleson Co., Tex. Memorial Muse., U. T. Austin 20908, 20912.

Photo 254. *Idiohamites fremonti* (Marcou), 75 mm., Lower Cretaceous period, Washita div., Northeast Texas, John Moody, Sr.

Photo 255. *Idiohamites fremonti* (Marcou), 120 mm., Lower Cretaceous period, Washita div., Wise Co., Jerry Askey.

Photo 256. *Didymoceras* sp., 71 mm., Upper Cretaceous period, Navarro gr., Kemp Clay, Williamson Co., Don O'Neill.

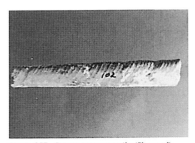

Photo 257. *Sciponoceras gracile* (Shumard), 133 mm., formerly *Baculites gracilis,* Upper Cretaceous period, Eagle Ford gr., Dallas Co., Dallas Museum of Natural History.

Photo 258. *Baculites taylorensis* Adkins, 28 mm. diam., showing flank nodes; Upper Cretaceous period, Taylor fm., Pecan Gap Chalk, Travis Co., East Texas State Univ.

Plate 69

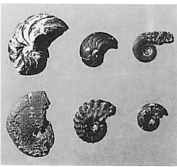

Photo 259. *Plesioturrilites brazoensis* (Roemer), 133 mm., Lower Cretaceous period, Georgetown fm., Williamson Co., John Moody, Sr.

Photo 260. *Adkinsia,* 24 mm., top (l., c.); *Scaphites,* top (r.); *Engonoceras,* lower (l.); *Mantelliceras,* lower (c.); *Adkinsia,* lower (r.); all in pyrite, L. Cret., Del Rio fm., McLennan Co., J. W. Fox Coll., Baylor Univ.

Photo 261. *Trachyscaphites springer variety ariki,* 63 mm., Upper Cretaceous period, Taylor gr., Fannin Co., John Moody, Sr.

Photo 262. *Exiteloceras annulatum* (Shumard), 53 mm., Upper Cretaceous period, Eagle Ford gr., Britton fm., Texas Memorial Museum, Univ. of Texas at Austin 19820.

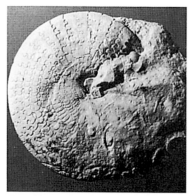

Photo 263. *Engonoceras pierdenale* (Buch), 110 mm., Lower Cretaceous period, Comanche Peak fm., Johnson Co., Don O'Neill.

Photo 264. *Metengonoceras* sp., 89 mm. (some authors consider this the same as *Engonoceras*), Lower Cretaceous period, Walnut fm., Grayson Co., John Moody, Sr.

Plate 70

Photo 265. *Placenticeras* sp., 227 mm., Upper Cretaceous period, Eagle Ford gr., Dallas Co., Frank and Mary Crane.

Photo 266. *Oxytropidoceras* sp., 173 mm., Lower Cretaceous period, Goodland fm., Cooke Co., Dallas Museum of Natural History.

Photo 267. *Manuiceras* sp., 110 mm., Tarrant Co., Dallas Museum of Natural History.

Photo 268. *Adkinsites* sp., 280 mm., Lower Cretaceous period, Kiamichi fm., near Blum, Tex., Frank, Mary, and Stephen Crane.

Photo 269. *Eopachydiscus marcianus* (Shumard), 379 mm., Lower Cretaceous period, Duck Creek fm., Lake Texoma, Frank, Mary, and Stephen Crane.

Photo 270. *Eopachydiscus laevicanaliculatum* (Lasswitz), 240 mm., Lower Cretaceous period, Duck Creek fm., Tarrant Co., Frank, Mary, and Stephen Crane.

Plate 71

Photo 271. *Mortoniceras equidistans* Cragin 270 mm., Lower Cretaceous period, Lower Washita div., Grayson Co., Frank, Mary, and Stephen Crane.

Photo 272. *Drakeoceras wintoni,* 58 mm., Lower Cretaceous period, Duck Creek fm., Grayson Co., Frank, Mary, and Stephen Crane.

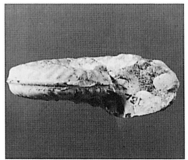

Photo 273. *Drakeoceras drakei,* 124 mm., Lower Cretaceous period, Weno fm., McLennan Co., John Moody, Sr.

Photo 274. *Mortoniceras* sp., 124 mm., Lower Cretaceous period, Duck creek fm., Grayson Co., Frank, Mary, and Stephen Crane.

Photo 275. *Schloenbachia leonensis* Conrad, var. *serratescens,* 143 mm., the holotype, Lower Cretaceous period, Duck Creek fm., Grayson Co., Texas Memorial Museum, Univ. of Texas at Austin 19515.

Photo 276. *Budaiceras whitneyi* Archer, 58 mm., left; *B. boesi* Archer, center; *B. simondsi* Archer, right; all are Lower Cretaceous period, Buda fm., Travis Co., Texas Memorial Museum, Univ. of Texas at Austin.

Plate 72

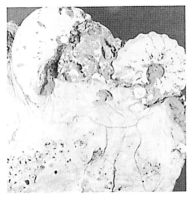

Photo 277. *Metoicoceras whitei* Hyatt, slab 360 mm., Upper Cretaceous period, Eagle Ford gr., Britton fm., Dallas Co., Dallas Museum of Natural History.

Photo 278. *Calycoceras (Conlinoceras) tarrantense* (Adkins), 117 mm., formerly *Acanthoceras* Adkins, Upper Cret. period, Woodbine fm., Tarrant Co., John Moody, Sr.

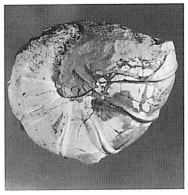

Photo 279. *Calycoceras (Conlinoceras) tarrantense* (Adkins), 60 mm., sliced open to show internal chambers; Upper Cretaceous period, Woodbine fm., Tarrant Co., Kenneth Smith.

Photo 280. *Desmoceras* sp., 49 mm., Upper Cretaceous period, Eagle Ford gr., Britton fm., Dallas Co., Jimmy Green.

Photo 281. *Prionocyclus* sp., 43 mm., Upper Cretaceous period, Eagle Ford gr., Kamp Ranch member, Dallas Co., Dallas Museum of Natural History.

Photo 282. *Belemnitella* sp., 116 mm., Upper Cretaceous period, Eagle Ford gr., Dallas Co., Vicki Krumke (larger) and Jan Saunders Scherrer (smaller).

Plate 73

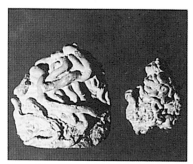

Photo 283. *Serpula* sp., 31 mm., worm tubes, Lower Cretaceous period, Washita div., Lake Arlington, Tarrant Co., C. B. Willis, collector, Dallas Museum of Natural History.

Photo 284. *Serpula texana* Giebel, 38 mm. slab, worm tubes, a large species, Lower Cretaceous period, Washita div., Lower Weno fm., Denton Co., Frank, Mary, and Stephen Crane.

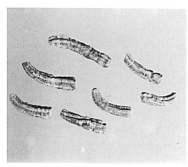

Photo 285. *Hamulus* sp., 26 mm., worm tubes, Upper Cretaceous period, Taylor gr., Ozan fm., near Ladonia, Tex., East Texas State Univ. ET 5277.

Photo 286. *Thalassinoides* sp., burrows, 297 mm., slab, Upper Cret. period, Taylor gr., upper Pecan Gap fm., inclusions of Marlbrook fm. from above, Hunt Co., East Tex. State U.

Photo 287. *Elvinia roemeri* (Shumard), cephalon only, 21 mm., Upper Cambrian, Wilberns fm., central Texas, Texas Memorial Museum, Univ. of Texas at Austin 27T837A.

Photo 288. Asaphid Trilobite, possibly *Isoteloides* sp., length 48 mm., Montoya fm., Ordovician period, Culberson Co., Texas Memorial Museum, Univ. of Texas at Austin P 10474.

Plate 74

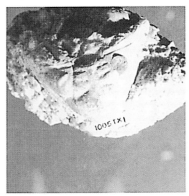

Photo 289. *Lygdozoon arkansanum* (Van Ingen), 34 mm. wide, Silurian period, Starke Lms., Burnett Co., Texas Memorial Museum, Univ. of Texas at Austin 1005TX1.

Photo 290. *Ditomopyge scitula* (Meek and Worthen), 20 mm. long, Pennsylvanian period, Marble Falls Lms., near Bend, Tex., Don O'Neill.

Photo 291. *Ditomopyge scitula* (Meek and Worthen), 15 x 19 mm., enrolled view of cephalon, Pennsylvanian, Wolf Mt. Shale, Lake Bridgeport, Wise Co., Don O'Neill.

Photo 292. *Ditomopyge scitula* (Meek and Worthen), 15 x 19 mm., enrolled view of pygidium, Pennsylvanian, Wolf Mt. Shale, Lake Bridgeport, Wise Co., Don O'Neill.

Photo 293. *Ditomopyge scitula* (Meek and Worthen), 15 mm., typically worn pygidia, Pennsylvanian, Canyon gr., Graford fm., Palo Pinto Co., Dr. R. J. Moiola.

Photo 294. *Ditomopyge scitula* (Meek and Worthen), imprint showing cheek spines, 28 mm., Pennsylvanian, Marble Falls fm., Sloan Community, San Saba Co., Texas Memorial Museum, Univ. of Texas at Austin.

Plate 75

Photo 295. *Ameura major* (Shumard), 14 mm. wide, enrolled view of cephalon, Pennsylvanian, Graham gr., near Mineral Wells, Don O'Neill.

Photo 296. *Ameura major* (Shumard), 14 mm. wide, enrolled view of pygidium, Pennsylvanian, Graham gr., near Mineral Wells, Don O'Neill.

Photo 297. *Paladin morrowensis* (Mather), 32 mm., Pennsylvanian, Wise Co., Kenneth Smith.

Photo 298. *Delaria antigua* (Girty), 11 mm. width of largest specimen, Permian, Camp Creek Shale, Don and Hollis O'Neill.

Photo 299. *Anisopyge* sp., 9 mm. long, pygidium only on Glass Mts. slab, Permian period, Word fm., Brewster Co., Sul Ross State Univ.

Photo 300. *Paleolimulus* sp., a Horseshoe Crab, 27 mm. wide, Permian period, Runnels Co., Texas Memorial Museum, Univ. of Texas at Austin 1420TX2.

Plate 76

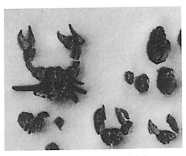

Photo 301. Crabs from *Ophiura* brittle star nests, 28 mm., Lower Cretaceous period, Del Rio fm., McLennan Co., J. W. Fox Coll., Baylor Univ.

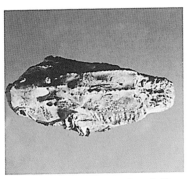

Photo 302. *Linuparus grimmeri* Stenzel, 70 mm., Upper Cretaceous period, Eagle Ford gr., Dallas Co., Ken Craddock.

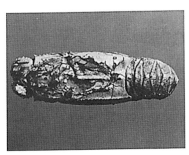

Photo 303. *Linuparus grimmeri* Stenzel, 73 mm., dorsal view, Upper Cretaceous period, Eagle Ford gr., Dallas Co., Arlene Pike.

Photo 304. *Enoploclytia* sp. 45 mm. width, crab claw, Upper Cretaceous period, Eagle Ford gr., Britton fm., Dallas Co., Dallas Museum of Natural History.

Photo 305. *Upogebia rhacheochir* Stenzel, 22 mm., Upper Cretaceous period, Eagle Ford gr., Dallas Co., Arlene Pike.

Photo 306. *Notopocorystes dichrous* Stenzel, 36 mm., Upper Cretaceous period, Eagle Ford gr., Dallas Co., Louis Todd.

Plate 77

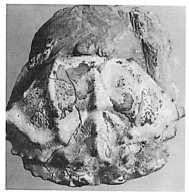

Photo 307. *Cenomanocarcinus vanstraeleni* Stenzel, 40 mm., carapace only, Upper Cretaceous period, Eagle Ford gr., Dallas Co., Louis Todd.

Photo 308. *Cenomanocarcinus vanstraeleni* Stenzel, 75 mm., claws, Upper Cretaceous period, Eagle Ford gr., Dallas Co., Kenneth Craddock.

Photo 309. *Harpactocarcinus americanus* Rathbun, 54 mm., type specimen, Eocene epoch, Crockett fm., Brazos Co., Texas Memorial Muse., U. T. Austin 21152.

Photo 310. *Zanthopsis peytoni* Stenzel, a large crab carapace, 103 mm., Eocene epoch, Weches fm., Leon Co., Texas Memorial Museum, Univ. of Texas at Austin 21157.

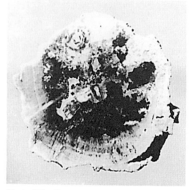

Photo 311. *Mesitoblatta* sp., cockroach wing, 27 mm., Permian, Little Wichita River, Texas Memorial Museum, Univ. of Texas at Austin.

Photo 312. *Diospyrae* termite nest, 55 mm. wide, Upper Cretaceous period, Aguja fm., Brewster Co., Sul Ross State Univ.

Plate 78

Photo 313. *Eodichroma mirifica* Cockerell, dragonfly wing, 22 mm., Eocene, Brazos Co., Texas Memorial Museum, Univ. of Texas at Austin, O. M. Ball Coll. 1371.

Photo 314. Cockroach Wing, 25 mm. Pennsylvanian period, Millsap Lake fm., Parker Co. Kenneth Craddock.

Photo 315. Aquatic insect, 16 mm., note preservation of legs; Pleistocene epoch, Rita Blanca fm., Hartley Co., Texas Memorial Museum, Univ. of Texas at Austin.

Photo 316. Insect with wings, 18 mm. long, Pleistocene epoch, Rita Blanca fm., Hartley Co., Balcones Vertebrate Paleo. Lab., Univ. of Texas at Austin.

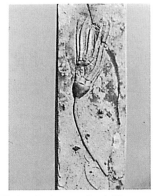

Photo 317. *Scytalocrinus sansabensis* Moore and Plummer, 82 mm., Lower Pennsylvanian, Marble Falls fm., San Saba Co., Frank, Mary, and Stephen Crane.

Photo 318. *Plaxocrinus perundatus* Moore and Plummer, 63 mm., Pennsylvanian, Wise Co., Kenneth Craddock.

Plate 79

Photo 319. *Pirasocrinus scotti* Moore and Plummer, 87 mm., paratype, Pennsylvanian, Millsap Lake fm., Parker Co., Texas Memorial Museum, Univ. of Texas at Austin P8190.

Photo 320. *Parathlocrinus watkinsi* (Strimple), 70 mm., Pennsylvanian, Millsap Lake fm., Strawn gr., collected by Bill and Helen Watkins. Crane Collection, Dallas Museum of Natural History.

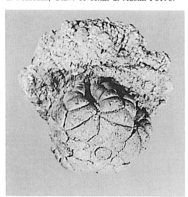

Photo 321. *Sciadocrinus harrisae* Moore and Plummer, 37 mm., Pennsylvanian, Parker Co., Louis Todd.

Photo 322. *Delocrinus graphicus* Moore and Plummer, 50 mm., Pennsylvanian, Graford fm., Lake Bridgeport, Wise Co., Don and Hollis O'Neill.

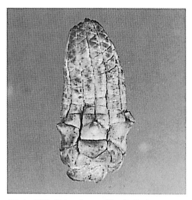

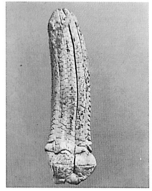

Photo 323. *Delocrinus subhemisphericus* Moore and Plummer, 31 mm., Pennsylvanian, Wise Co., Louis Todd.

Photo 324. *Erisocrinus elevatus* Moore and Plummer, 71 mm., Pennsylvanian, Wise Co., Louis Todd.

Plate 80

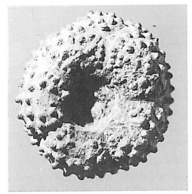

Photo 325. *Sellardsicrinus marrsae* Moore and Plummer, 66 mm. tall, holotype, Pennsylvanian, Strawn fm., Parker Co., Texas Memorial Muse., U. T. Austin P12372.

Photo 326. *Ethelocrinus texasensis* Moore and Plummer, 37 mm., holotype, base of cup, Pennsylvanian, Marble Falls fm., San Saba Co., Texas Memorial Muse., U. T. Austin 34620.

Photo 327. *Parulocrinus marquisi* Moore and Plummer, 125 mm. tall, holotype, Pennsylvanian, Canyon gr., near Mason, Tex., Texas Memorial Museum, Univ. of Texas at Austin P8188.

Photo 328. *Graffhamicrinus* sp., 52 mm., Pennsylvanian, Wise Co., Kenneth Craddock.

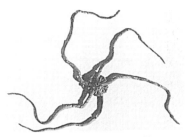

Photo 329. *Ophiura graysonensis,* 108 mm., Lower Cretaceous period, Del Rio fm., McLennan Co., J. W. Fox Coll., Baylor Univ.

Photo 330. *Ophiura* "nest" slab, 100 mm., Lower Cretaceous period, Del Rio fm., McLennan Co., J. W. Fox Coll., Baylor Univ.

Plate 81

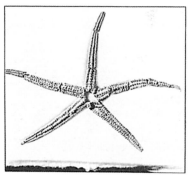

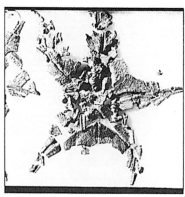

Photo 331. Thin-armed giant asteroid starfish, 107 mm., found in *Ophiura* "nests," Lower Cretaceous period, Del Rio fm., McLennan Co., J. W. Fox Coll., Baylor Univ.

Photo 332. Giant asteroid starfish, 180 mm., found in *Ophiura* "nests," Lower Cretaceous period, Del Rio fm., McLennan Co., J. W. Fox Coll., Baylor Univ.

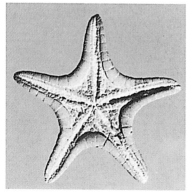

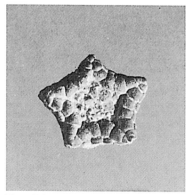

Photo 333. Unidentified asteroid starfish, 43 mm., bottom view, Lower Cretaceous period, Del Rio fm., McLennan Co., J. W. Fox Coll., Baylor Univ.

Photo 334. *"Mastaster,"* approx. 21 mm., Lower Cretaceous period, Denton fm., Denton Co., Kenneth Craddock.

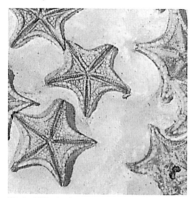

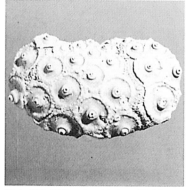

Photo 335. *Austinaster mc-carteri* Adkins, close-up of 535 mm. slab, basal Austin gr., Travis Co., Texas Memorial Museum, Univ. of Texas at Austin. See full slab in color section.

Photo 336. *Echinocrinus (Archaeocidaris)* sp., 46 mm., Pennsylvanian, Colony Creek Shale, Brown Co., Mike Murphy.

Plate 82

Photo 337. *Stereocidaris hudspethensis*
Cooke, 108 mm., Lower Cretaceous period,
Washita div., Hudspeth Co., Frank, Stephen,
and Mary Crane.

Photo 338. *Phyllacanthus (Leiocidaris)*
hemigranosus (Shumard), 95 mm. x 75 mm.,
Lower Cretaceous period, Ft. Worth fm.,
Grayson Co., Henry Doshier.

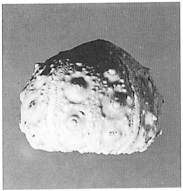

Photo 339. *Salenia texana* Credner, 29 mm.,
side view, Lower Cretaceous period, Glen
Rose fm., Travis Co., Frank Crane.

Photo 340. *Salenia texana* Credner, 29 mm.,
oral view, Lower Cretaceous period, Glen
Rose fm., Travis Co., Frank Crane.

Photo 341. *Salenia mexicana* Schluter, 11-17
mm., Lower Cretaceous period, Comanche
Peak fm., near Clifton, Tex., Frank, Mary,
and Stephen Crane.

Photo 342. *Salenia volana* Whitney, 16 mm.,
Lower Cretaceous period, Grayson fm., Grayson Co., John Moody, Sr.

Plate 83

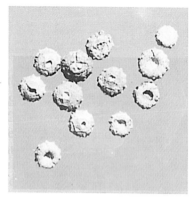

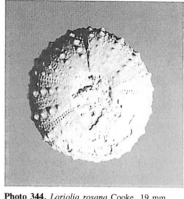

Photo 343. *Goniophorus scotti* Lambert, 6 mm., Lower Cretaceous period, Upper Marl, Duck Creek fm., Tarrant Co., Frank, Mary, and Stephen Crane.

Photo 344. *Loriolia rosana* Cooke, 19 mm., apical view, Lower Cretaceous period, Glen Rose fm., Kendall Co., Frank, Mary, and Stephen Crane.

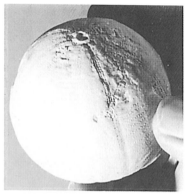

Photo 345. *Loriolia rosana* Cooke, 18 mm., oral view, Lower Cretaceous period, Glen Rose fm., Kendall Co., Frank, Mary, and Stephen Crane.

Photo 346. *Dumblea symmetrica* Cragin, 59 mm., Lower Cretaceous period, Boracho fm., Reeves Co., Frank Crane.

Photo 347. *Tetragramma taffi* (Cragin), 70 mm., Lower Cretaceous period, Comanche Peak fm., central Texas, Frank, Mary, and Stephen Crane.

Photo 348. *Tetragramma streeruwitzi* (Cragin), 39 mm., apical view, Lower Cretaceous period, Grayson fm., Grayson Co., John Moody, Sr.

Plate 84

Photo 349. *Tetragramma streeruwitzi* (Cragin), 39 mm., oral view, Lower Cretaceous period, Grayson fm., Grayson Co., John Moody, Sr.

Photo 350. *Phymosoma texanum* (Roemer), (r.), 47 mm., Comanche Peak fm.; *P. mexicanum*, Boese, (l.), Ft. Worth fm.; apical view, Lower Cret., Frank Crane.

Photo 351. *Phymosoma texanum* (Roemer), (r.), 47 mm., Comanche Peak fm.; *P. mexicanum*, Boese, (l.), Ft. Worth fm.; side view, Lower Cret., Frank Crane.

Photo 352. *Phymosoma texanum* (Roemer), right, 47 mm., Comanche Peak fm.; *Phymosoma mexicanum* Boese, left, 30 mm., Ft. Worth fm.; side views, both Lower Cretaceous period, Frank Crane.

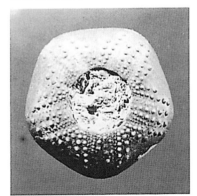

Photo 353. *Codiopsis texana* Whitney, 32 mm., holotype, Lower Cretaceous period, Buda fm., Travis Co., Texas Memorial Museum, Univ. of Texas at Austin. Oral view.

Photo 354. *Codiopsis texana* Whitney, 32 mm., holotype, Lower Cretaceous period, Buda fm., Travis Co., Texas Memorial Museum, Univ. of Texas at Austin. Anal view.

Plate 85

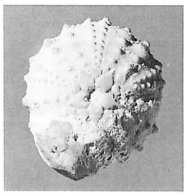

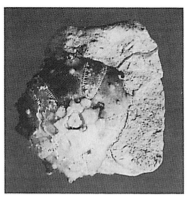

Photo 355. *Goniopygus zitteli* Clark, 26 mm., Lower Cretaceous period, Edwards fm., Travis Co., Don O'Neill.

Photo 356. *Goniopygus stockonensis* Smiser, 23 mm., Lower Cretaceous period, Boracho fm., Pecos Co., Kenneth Smith.

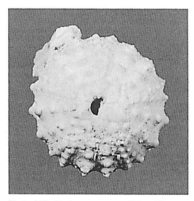

Photo 357. *Goniopygus texanus* Ikins, 19 mm., Lower Cretaceous period, Edwards fm., Coryell Co., Kenneth Smith.

Photo 358. *Coenholectypus engerrandi* Lambert, 41 mm., Lower Cretaceous period, Trinity div., Glen Rose fm., Comal Co., Frank, Mary, and Stephen Crane.

Photo 359. *Coenholectypus limitis* (Boese), based on double-pointed periproct that is rather small for this species; 42 mm., Lower Cretaceous period, Washita div., Main St. fm., Tarrant Co., Kenneth Smith.

Photo 360. *Coenholectypus castilloi* (Cotteau), 52 mm., Lower Cretaceous period, Main St. fm., Denton Co., Frank, Mary, and Stephen Crane.

Plate 86

Photo 361. *Coenholectypus planatus* (Roemer), 23 mm., shows five apical pores, Lower Cretaceous period, Walnut fm., Taylor Co., Frank, Mary and Stephen Crane.

Photo 362. *Coenholectypus transpecosensis* (Cragin), 69 mm. width, Lower Cretaceous period, Washita div., Buda fm., near Dryden, Tex., Frank, Mary, and Stephen Crane Coll.

Photo 363. *Anorthopygus texanus* Cooke, 33 mm., Lower Cretaceous period, Boracho fm., San Martine member, Culberson Co., Kenneth Smith.

Photo 364. *Conulus stephensoni* Cooke, 38 mm., Upper Cretaceous period, Austin gr., Bexar Co., Frank, Mary, and Stephen Crane.

Photo 365. *Globator parryi* (Hall), 32 mm., Lower Cretaceous period, Boracho fm., San Martine member, Culberson Co., Kenneth Smith.

Photo 366. *Phyllobrissus cubensis* (Weisbord), 31 mm., Upper Cretaceous period, Navarro gr., Escondido fm., Medina Co., Frank, Mary, and Stephen Crane.

Plate 87

Photo 367. *Nucleopygus (Echinobrissus) angustatus* (Clark), 15 mm., apical view, Lower Cretaceous period, Washita div., Buda fm., Travis Co., Frank, Mary, and Stephen Crane.

Photo 368. *Nucleopygus (Echinobrissus) angustatus* (Clark), 15 mm., oral view, Cretaceous period, Washita div., Buda fm., Travis Co., Frank, Mary and Stephen Crane.

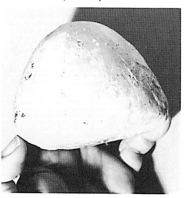

Photo 369. *Holaster simplex* Shumard, 43 mm., Lower Cretaceous period, Washita div., Duck Creek fm., Tarrant Co., Frank, Mary, and Stephen Crane.

Photo 370. *Echinocorys texanus* (Cragin), 81 mm., Upper Cretaceous period, Anachacho fm., Medina Co., Frank, Mary, and Stephen Crane.

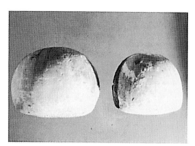

Photo 371. *Pseudananchys completa* (Cragin), 38 mm., right; *Pseudananchys supernus* (Cragin), 44 mm., left; both Lower Cretaceous period, Grayson fm., Grayson Co., Henry Doshier.

Photo 372. *Heteraster mexicanus* (Cotteau), 29 mm. wide, apical view, Lower Cretaceous period, Walnut fm., Cooke Co., John Moody, Sr.

Plate 88

Photo 373. *Heteraster mexicanus* (Cotteau), 33 mm. long, side view, Lower Cretaceous period, Walnut fm., Cooke Co., John Moody, Sr.

Photo 374. *Heteraster obliquatus* (Clark), 41 mm. wide, Lower Cretaceous period, Glen Rose fm., Bandera Co., Frank, Mary, and Stephen Crane.

Photo 375. *Heteraster adkinsi* Lambert, 33 mm. wide, Lower Cretaceous period, Fredericksburg div., Tarrant Co., John Moody, Sr.

Photo 376. *Heteraster bohmi* (de Loriol), 28 mm. long, side view, Lower Cretaceous period, Ft. Worth fm., Grayson Co., John Moody, Sr.

Photo 377. *Heteraster texanus* (Roemer), 32 mm. wide, Lower Cretaceous period, Walnut and Comanche Peak fms., near Evant, Tex., Frank, Mary, and Stephen Crane.

Photo 378. *Lambertiaster ficheuri* Dalloni and Lambert, 35 mm. wide, apical view, Lower Cretaceous period, Duck Creek fm., Grayson Co., John Moody, Sr.

Plate 89

Photo 379. *Lambertiaster ficheuri* Dalloni and Lambert, 38 mm., long, side view, Lower Cretaceous period, Duck Creek fm., Grayson Co., John Moody, Sr.

Photo 380. *Macraster texanus* Roemer, 78 mm. wide, apical view, Lower Cretaceous period, Ft. Worth fm., Grayson Co., Henry Doshier.

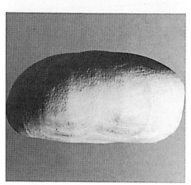

Photo 381. *Macraster texanus* Roemer, 85 mm., long, side view, Lower Cretaceous period, Ft. Worth fm., Grayson Co., Henry Doshier.

Photo 382. *Macraster elegans* (Shumard), 63 mm. wide, apical view, Lower Cretaceous period, Ft. Worth fm., Johnson Co., John Moody, Sr.

Photo 383. *Macraster elegans* (Shumard), 69 mm. long, side view, Lower Cretaceous period, Ft. Worth fm., Johnson Co., John Moody, Sr.

Photo 384. *Macraster pseudoelegans* Adkins, 68 mm. wide, apical view, Lower Cretaceous period, Ft. Worth fm., Bell Co., John Moody, Sr.

Plate 90

Photo 385. *Macraster pseudoelegans* Adkins, 76 mm. long, side view, Lower Cretaceous period, Ft. Worth fm., Bell Co., John Moody, Sr.

Photo 386. *Macraster nodopyge* Lambert, 51 mm. wide, Lower Cretaceous period, Duck Creek fm., Grayson Co., John Moody, Sr.

Photo 387. *Macraster roberti var. ovatus* Smiser, 23 mm., apical view, Lower Cretaceous period, Duck Creek fm., Grayson Co., John Moody, Sr.

Photo 388. *Macraster roberti var. ovatus* Smiser, 24 mm., side view, Lower Cretaceous period, Duck Creek fm., Grayson Co., John Moody, Sr.

Photo 389. *Macraster solitariensis* Smiser, 46 mm. (l) x 48 mm. (w), 29 mm. (h), Lower Cretaceous period, Duck Creek fm., Grayson Co., John Moody, Sr.

Photo 390. *Macraster obesus* Adkins, 95 mm. wide, apical view, Lower Cretaceous period, Weno fm., Coryell Co., John Moody, Sr.

Plate 91

Photo 391. *Macraster obesus* Adkins, 101 mm. long, side view, Lower Cretaceous period, Weno fm., Coryell Co., John Moody, Sr.

Photo 392. *Macraster subobesus* (Adkins), 86 mm. wide, apical view, Lower Cretaceous period, Weno fm., Coryell Co., John Moody, Sr.

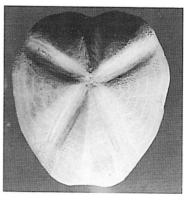

Photo 393. *Macraster subobesus* (Adkins), 93 mm. long, side view, Lower Cretaceous period, Weno fm., Coryell Co., John Moody, Sr.

Photo 394. *Macraster denisonensis* Smiser, 65 mm. wide, apical view, Lower Cretaceous period, Duck Creek fm., Grayson Co., John Moody, Sr.

Photo 395. *Macraster denisonensis* Smiser, side view, Lower Cretaceous period, Duck creek fm., Grayson Co., John Moody, Sr.

Photo 396. *Macraster washitae* Lambert, 47 mm. wide, Lower Cretaceous period, Duck Creek fm., Grayson Co., John Moody, Sr.

Plate 92

Photo 397. *Macraster kentensis* Adkins, 45 mm. wide, Lower Cretaceous period, Duck Creek fm., Grayson Co., John Moody, Sr.

Photo 398. *Hemiaster texanus* Roemer, 45 mm. wide, three views, Upper Cretaceous period, Anacacho fm., Uvalde Co., Frank, Mary, and Stephen Crane.

Photo 399. *Hemiaster calvini* Clark, 24 mm. wide, Lower Cretaceous period, Grayson fm., Denton Co., Dallas Museum of Natural History.

Photo 400. *Hemiaster jacksoni* Maury, 14 mm. wide, Upper Cretaceous period, Eagle Ford gr., Val Verde Co., Frank, Mary, and Stephen Crane.

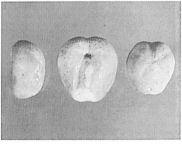

Photo 401. *Hemiaster bexari* Clark, 24 mm., Upper Cretaceous period, Taylor gr., Corsicana Marl, Bexar Co., Frank, Mary, and Stephen Crane.

Photo 402. *Palhemiaster comanchei* (Clark), 32 mm. wide, Lower Cretaceous period, Glen Rose fm, Bandera Co., Frank, Mary, and Stephen Crane.

Plate 93

Photo 403. *Washitaster riovistae* Adkins, 24 mm., topotypes, Lower Cretaceous period, Paw Paw fm., near Rio Vista, Tex., Frank, Mary, and Stephen Crane.

Photo 404. *Washitaster inflatus* (Cragin), 37 mm. wide, apical view, Lower Cretaceous period, Grayson fm., Grayson Co., John Moody, Sr.

Photo 405. *Washitaster inflatus* (Cragin), 43 mm., side view, Lower Cretaceous period, Grayson fm., Grayson Co., John Moody, Sr.

Photo 406. *Washitaster wenoensis* Adkins, 32 mm., apical view, Lower Cretaceous period, Weno fm., Grayson Co., John Moody, Sr.

Photo 407. *Washitaster wenoensis* Adkins, 35 mm., side view, Lower Cretaceous period, Weno fm., Grayson Co., John Moody, Sr.

Photo 408. *Plesiaster americanus* (Stephenson), 45 mm., Upper Cretaceous period, Austin gr., Bexar Co., Frank, Mary, and Stephen Crane.

Plate 94

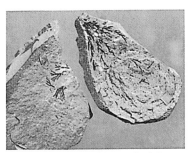

Photo 409. Graptolites, 54 mm., Cambrian period, Wilberns fm., Mason Co., Texas Memorial Museum, Univ. of Texas at Austin.

Photo 410. *Loganograptus* sp. (graptolite), 45 mm., Ordovician period, Ft. Pena fm., Brewster Co., Sul Ross State Univ.

Photo 411. *Phyllograptus* sp. (graptolite), 88 mm., Ordovician period, Brewster Co., Sul Ross State Univ.

Photo 412. *Orthacanthus* teeth, 10-18 mm., Lower Permian, Wichita gr., Archer Co., Louis Todd.

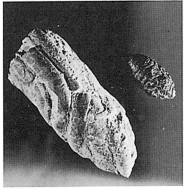

Photo 413. *Orthacanthus* coprolites, 37-79 mm. long, Lower Permian, Wichita gr., Archer Co., Louis Todd.

Photo 414. Spiral coprolites, 95 mm. and 35 mm., larger is Upper Cretaceous period, smaller is Paleocene, both east Texas, East Texas State Univ.

Plate 95

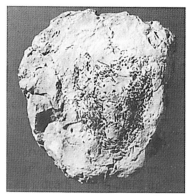

Photo 415. *Petalodus* tooth, 36 mm. wide, Pennsylvanian, north Texas, Dallas Museum of Natural History.

Photo 416. Lungfish burrows with tiny bones of the fish itself, 85 mm., Permian, north central Texas, Dr. Walter Dalquest, Midwestern State Univ.

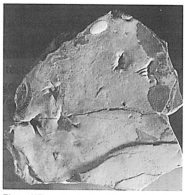

Photo 417. Reptile tracks, 103 mm. slab, Permian, north central Texas, T. T. Broun Coll., East Texas State Univ.

Photo 418. Lower Cretaceous shark teeth, 20 mm., similar to *Cretolamna* sp., Del Rio fm., McLennan Co., John Fox Coll., Baylor University.

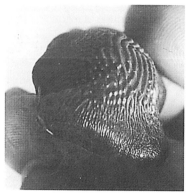

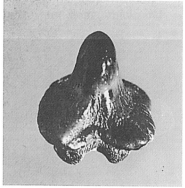

Photo 419. *Ptychodus decurrens*, 28 mm., Upper Cretaceous period, Eagle Ford gr., Dallas Co., Robert Price.

Photo 420. *Ptychodus whipplei* Marcou, tooth, 27 mm. height, Upper Cretaceous period, Eagle Ford gr., Ellis Co., Dallas Museum of Natural History.

Plate 96

Photo 421. *Ptychodus mortoni,* teeth in block 61 mm. wide, Austin gr., Dallas Co., Dallas Museum of Natural History.

Photo 422. *Uranoplosus pychnodont* teeth, slab 43 mm. wide, Lower Cretaceous period, Ft. Worth fm., Tarrant Co., Don O'Neill.

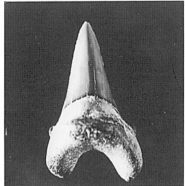

Photo 423. *Scapanorhynchus* sp., 40 mm., Upper Cretaceous period, Grayson Co., Jimmy Green.

Photo 424. *Cretoxyrhina mantelli oxyrhinoides* Savage, 36 mm., Upper Cretaceous period, Eagle Ford gr., Dallas Co., Jimmy Green.

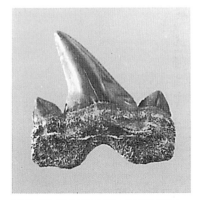

Photo 425. *Cretolamna appendiculata* (Agassiz) (called *Otodus* sp. by some authors), 25 mm., Upper Cretaceous period, Eagle Ford gr., Ellis Co., Jimmy Green.

Photo 426. *Leptostyrax crassidens,* shark teeth, largest 38 mm., Upper Cretaceous period, Eagle Ford gr., Dallas Co., John Hodge.

Plate 97

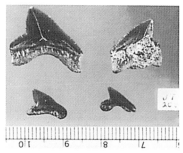

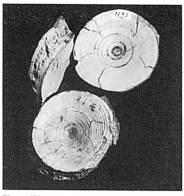

Photo 427. *Squalicorax* sp. tiger shark teeth, 16 mm., Upper Cretaceous period, Eagle Ford gr., Eagle Ford-Austin contact, Ellis Co., coll. by Mr. John Tutor.

Photo 428. Shark vertebral centrums, 78 mm., Upper Cretaceous period, Eagle Ford gr., Britton fm., Tarrant Co., Jim Kinkaid, Dallas Museum of Natural History 1193.

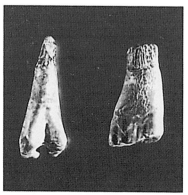

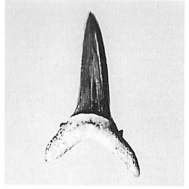

Photo 429. *Ischyrhiza* sp., worn roots of spines of sawfish bill, Upper Cretaceous period, Taylor gr., Sulphur River area, northeast Texas, Jimmy Green.

Photo 430. *Odontaspis,* 30 mm., Eocene, Stone City fm., Burleson Co., William Lowe.

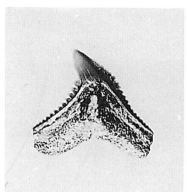

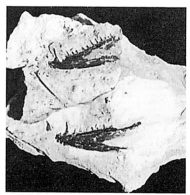

Photo 431. *Galeocerdo* sp., 19 mm., Eocene epoch, Stone City fm., Burleson Co., William Lowe.

Photo 432. *Enchodus* sp., fish jaws, 75 mm, length, Upper Cretaceous period, Eagle Ford gr., Lower Britton fm., chalky layer, Dallas Co., James Bryant, in Dallas Museum of Natural History.

Plate 98

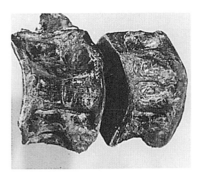

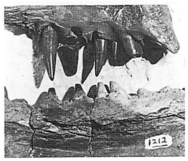

Photo 433. *Xiphactinus audax,* vertebral centrums, 50 mm. high., Upper Cretaceous period, Eagle Ford gr., Collin Co., Dallas Museum of Natural History.

Photo 434. *Xiphactinus audax* teeth (above) and *Pachyrhizodus caninus* teeth (below), Upper Cretaceous period, Eagle Ford gr., Dallas Co., Robert Price and Lloyd Hill.

Photo 435. *Pachyrhyzodus minimus,* 300 mm., Upper Cretaceous period, Eagle Ford gr., Dallas Co., Ralph Churchill family.

Photo 436. *Apsopelix angelicus* (Dixon), 275 mm., Upper Cretaceous period, Austin gr., Ellis Co., Texas Industries, Inc.

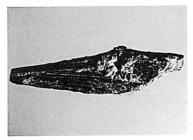

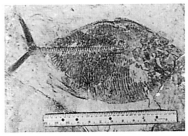

Photo 437. *Belonostomus* sp. head, 173 mm., Upper Cretaceous period, Eagle Ford gr., Dallas Co., Don O'Neill.

Photo 438. *Tselfatia* sp., 425 mm. long, Upper Cretaceous period, Austin gr., Dallas Co., Dallas Museum of Natural History.

Plate 99

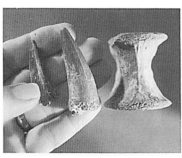

Photo 439. Playa lake fish, 28 mm., Pleistocene epoch, Rita Blanca fm., Hartley Co., Texas Memorial Museum, Univ. of Texas at Austin.

Photo 440. *Rutiodon* sp. phytosaur teeth and vertebra, vert. 58 mm. long, Triassic period, Dockum fm., Crosby Co., coll. by Emory Swenson, donated to Dallas Museum of Natural History.

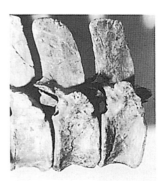

Photo 441. *Tenontosaurus* sp., 160 mm. high, dinosaur vertebrae, Lower Cretaceous period, Trinity div., Antlers fm., Wise Co., on display, Dallas Museum of Natural History.

Photo 442. *Tenontosaurus* sp., dinosaur skin impressions, largest slab 40 mm., Lower Cretaceous period, Trinity div., Antlers fm., Wise Co., on display, Dallas Museum of Natural History.

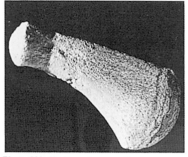

Photo 443. Plesiosaur vertebrae, 87 mm. largest, Upper Cretaceous period, Taylor gr., Fannin Co., John Moody, Sr.

Photo 444. Plesiosaur humerus (front upper leg bone), 192 mm., Upper Cretaceous period, Eagle Ford gr., Britton fm., Tarrant Co., Ron Almarez.

Plate 100

Photo 445. Mosasaur teeth, 33 mm., Upper Cretaceous period, Taylor gr., Sulphur River area, northeast Texas, Martin Seifert Coll., Dallas Museum of Natural History.

Photo 446. *Mosasaurus* sp., ventral view of mosasaur vertebra, fused chevron attachments; 82 mm., Upper Cret., Navarro gr., S. Sulphur River, E. Tex. State U. L-609-1.

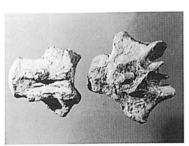

Photo 447. *Clidastes* sp., two vertebrae, 75 mm. ea., Upper Cretaceous period, Roxton Limestone, near Gober, Tex., East Texas State Univ. ET 4278.

Photo 448. *Halisaurus* sp., mosasaur vertebra (convex end), 73 mm., Upper Cretaceous period, Taylor gr., Fannin Co., East Texas State Univ. ET 4371.

Photo 449. *Halisaurus* sp., mosasaur vertebra (concave end), 73 mm., Upper Cretaceous period, Taylor gr., Fannin Co., East Texas State Univ. ET 4371.

Photo 450. *Tylosaurus proriger* (Cope), vertebra, 125 mm. length, Upper Cretaceous period, Taylor gr., Rockwall Co., collected by Mr. Malone, in Dallas Museum of Natural History.

Plate 101

Photo 451. *Globidens alabamaensis* Gilmore, 69 mm., teeth, Upper Cretaceous period, Taylor gr., Ozan fm. redbeds, Fannin Co., East Texas State Univ. ET 4303.

Photo 452. Mosasaur bone with shark tooth scratches, 101 mm., Upper Cretaceous period, Taylor gr., Sulphur River area, East Texas State Univ. ET 4319.

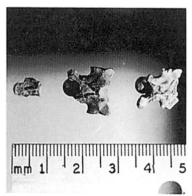

Photo 453. *Coniasaurus* sp., vertebrae, 12 mm., a small aquatic reptile, Upper Cretaceous period, Eagle Ford gr., Britton fm., Denton Co., Lloyd Hill.

Photo 454. *Coniasaurus* sp., teeth, Upper Cretaceous period, Eagle Ford gr., Britton fm., Denton Co., Lloyd Hill.

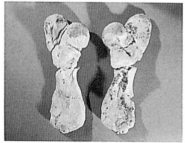

Photo 455. Crocodile scute, 67 mm., Upper Cretaceous period, Navarro gr. in eroded material (float), Hunt Co., collected by Lewis Smith for East Texas State Univ.

Photo 456. Fossil sea turtle, upper front leg bones (left and right humerus), 283 mm., Upper Cretaceous period, Woodbine fm., Tarrant Co., donated to Dallas Museum of Natural History by Mr. Jimmy Payne.

Plate 102

Photo 457. *Geochelone* sp., approx. 900 mm., Pleistocene epoch, northeast Texas, Shuler Museum of Paleo., Southern Methodist Univ.

Photo 458. *Glossotherium harlani* (Owen), phalanx (sloth claw), 170 mm., Late Pleistocene epoch, Hill-Schuler fauna, Dallas Co., Kenneth Smith.

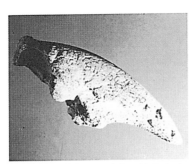

Photo 459. *Mylodon* sp., phalanx (sloth claw), 167 mm., Pleistocene epoch, Stonewall Co., Balcones Vertebrate Paleo. Lab., Univ. of Texas at Austin.

Photo 460. *Mylodon* sp., sloth tooth, 27 mm. wide, Pleistocene epoch, Stonewall Co., Balcones Vertebrate Paleo. Lab., Univ. of Texas at Austin.

Photo 461. *Glyptotherium floridanum* (Simpson), 180 mm. slab width, scutes (armor plates), Pleistocene epoch, Bee Co., Balcones Vertebrate Paleo. Lab., Univ. of Texas at Austin.

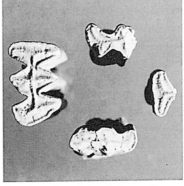

Photo 462. *Glyptotherium floridanum* (Simpson), teeth, 20 mm., Pleistocene epoch, Bee Co., Balcones Vertebrate Paleo. Lab., Univ. of Texas at Austin.

Plate 103

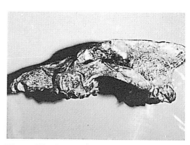

Photo 463. *Canis dirus* cranium, 313 mm. (length), a dire wolf; top view, Late Pleistocene epoch, San Patricio Co., Balcones Vert. Paleo Lab., U. T. Austin.

Photo 464. *Canis dirus* cranium, 313 mm. (l.), side view, a dire wolf, Late Pleistocene epoch, San Patricio Co., Balcones Vertebrate Paleo. Lab., Univ. of Texas at Austin.

Photo 465. *Canis dirus* carnassial tooth, 30 mm. crown width, Late Pleistocene epoch, Innerspace Caverns, bonebed III, Williamson Co., Balcones Vertebrate Paleo. Lab. Univ. of Texas at Austin.

Photo 466. *Smilodon californicus,* a saber-toothed cat, worn canine tooth, in hand; *Smilodon fatalis,* right mandibular ramus, 204 mm. (l.); both are from Texas saber-toothed cats of the Late Pleistocene epoch, San Patricio Co., Balcones Vertebrate Paleo. Lab., Univ. of Texas at Austin.

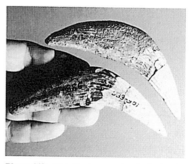

Photo 467. *Homotherium,* a saber-toothed cat, cranium, Late Pleistocene epoch, Freisenhahn Cave, Balcones Vertebrate Paleo. Lab., Univ. of Texas at Austin.

Photo 468. *Homotherium,* a saber-toothed cat, canines, 124 mm. and 122 mm. lengths, Late Pleistocene epoch, Freisenhahn Cave, Balcones Vertebrate Paleo. Lab., Univ. of Texas at Austin.

Plate 104

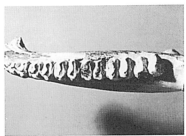

Photo 469. *Equus* sp., lower tooth row, 155 mm., Late Pleistocene epoch, Innerspace Caverns (Laubach Cave II), Williamson Co., Balcones Vertebrate Paleo. Lab., Univ. of Texas at Austin.

Photo 470. *Tapirus excelus,* lower tooth row, 144 mm., Late Pleistocene epoch, Ingleside, Texas fauna, Balcones Vertebrate Paleo. Lab., Univ. of Texas at Austin.

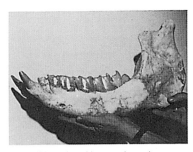

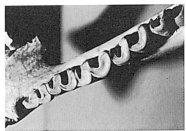

Photo 471. Extinct rhinoceros lower jaw, Pliocene epoch, West Texas, Joe Kennedy.

Photo 472. Extinct rhinoceros, lower tooth row, Pliocene epoch, West Texas, Joe Kennedy.

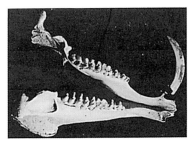

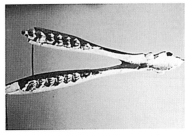

Photo 473. *Platygonus compressus,* lower jaw, 213 mm., Late Pleistocene epoch, Innerspace Caverns (Laubach Cave), Williamson Co., Balcones Vertebrate Paleo. Lab., Univ. of Texas at Austin.

Photo 474. *Tanupolama mirifica,* lower jaw, 113 mm. (tooth row), Late Pleistocene epoch, San Patricio Co., Balcones Vertebrate Paleo. Lab., Univ. of Texas at Austin.

Plate 105

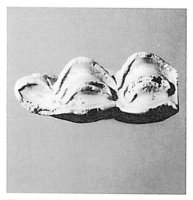

Photo 475. *Camelops* sp., lower third molar tooth, 53 x 19 mm., Late Pleistocene epoch, San Patricio Co., Balcones Vertebrate Paleo. Lab., Univ. of Texas at Austin.

Photo 476. *Camelops* sp., canine teeth, 52 mm., Late Pleistocene, San Patricio Co., Balcones Vertebrate Paleo. Lab., Univ. of Texas at Austin.

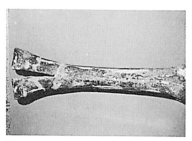

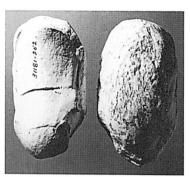

Photo 477. *Camelops* sp., metapodial, "cannon" bone (ankle), 373 mm., note "splayed" end; Late Pleistocene epoch, Stonewall Co., Balcones Vertebrate Paleo. Lab., Univ. of Texas at Austin.

Photo 478. Camel patellae (knee caps), 123 mm., Pleistocene epoch, Blanco fm., Crosby Co., Balcones Vertebrate Paleo. Lab., Univ. of Texas at Austin.

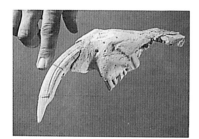

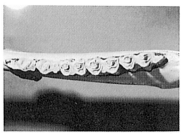

Photo 479. *Castoroides* sp. (fossil beaver), lower jaw with giant incisor tooth (much of tooth imbeds in jaw), entire tooth is 11 inches long, Late Pleistocene epoch, Fannin Co., Dallas Museum of Natural History, found by Frank Glover.

Photo 480. *Bison* sp. cf. *antiquus*, tooth row, 27 mm. wide, Late Pleistocene epoch, San Patricio Co., Balcones Vertebrate Paleo. Lab., Univ. of Texas at Austin.

Plate 106

Photo 481. *Equus* horse molar tooth and *Bison* molar tooth, each approx. 30 mm. wide, show different enamel patterns, Late Pleistocene Epoch, Dallas Co., Jerry Hightower Coll. at Dallas Museum of Natural History.

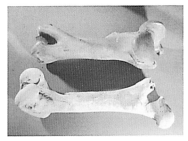

Photo 482. *Bison* leg bones (humerus, above; femur, below), longest is approx. 16 in., Late Pleistocene Epoch, Dallas Co., Dallas Museum of Natural History.

Photo 483. *Bison* "ankle bones," metacarpals, approx. 9 in., top bone shows age deformity (paleopathology), Late Pleistocene Epoch, Dallas Co., Dallas Museum of Natural History.

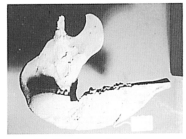

Photo 484. *Glyptotherium floridanum* mandible (lower jaw), Pleistocene Epoch, South Texas, University of Texas at Austin.

Photo 485. Wide-horned bison skull, probably *Bison latifrons* although somewhat mid-sized and curved like *Bison antiquus*, University of Texas at Austin.

Photo 486. Skull of modern species of bison with stone scraper, *Bison bison*, horn spread 30 in., Dallas Co., found by the Dallas County Archeological Society.

Plate 107

Cordova Shellstone (aka Golden Shellstone and "Austin" Stone), Lower Cretaceous period, Walnut fm., central Texas. The quarry strikes the shell layer at a certain level; the less fossiliferous rock above the shellstone is called Cordova Creme.

This photo shows the fossils of Cordova Shellstone as used on the lobby walls of the Dallas Museum of Natural History. This beautiful stone contains the molds of *Trigonia* clams and *Turritella* snail fossils in abundance. It is commercially available.

Plate 108

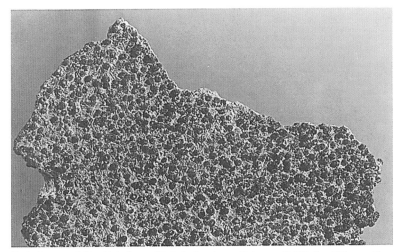

Goniophorus scotti slab with background bed of spines, Lower Cretaceous, Del Rio fm., McLennan Co. This palm-sized slab of hundreds of tiny sea urchins lying in death on a bed of their own spines is indeed an unusual Texas fossil. It is from the large Frank, Mary, and Stephen Crane collection at the Dallas Museum of Natural History.

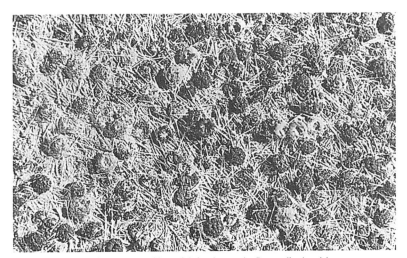

Close-up of the *Goniophorus scotti* urchins and their spines on the Crane collection slab.

Plate 109

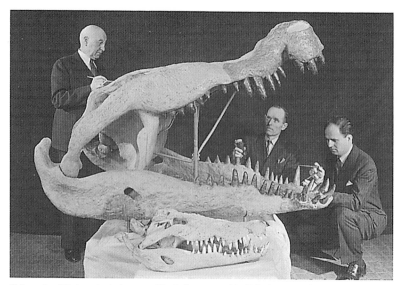

Deinosuchus (Phobosuchus) giant crocodile skull, as restored in 1940, from area of present Big Bend National Park, collected by Barnum Brown and R. T. Bird, American Museum of Natural History. A Cretaceous contemporary of *Tyrannosaurus rex*. (l. to r.) Dr. Brown, R. T. Bird, and Dr. Schlaikjer. (Photo 318651, courtesy of Library Services, A.M.N.H.)

Parapuzosia americana Scott and Moore, width 38 in., Upper Cretaceous, Austin fm., near Eagle Pass, Texas. Many collectors consider "large" ammonites to come from the Lower Cretaceous around Lake Texoma or Lake Whitney, but the largest in Texas are from the Upper Cretaceous Austin Chalk. The Dallas Museum of Natural History has two 48-inch specimens. The one shown is at Texas Christian University in Fort Worth.

Plate 110

Baculites claviformis Stephenson, a giant straight ammonite, length as reconstructed over 5 feet, Upper Cretaceous period, Navarro gr., Nacatoch fm., Kaufman Co. The specimen shown in this old Smithsonian photo is reconstructed from several perhaps unrelated fragments. The gentleman shown is Dr. T. W. Stanton. The Dallas Museum of Natural History has a specimen from Kaufman Co., collected by Phillip Virgil, that can be reconstructed at 7 ft. in length. (Courtesy of the U.S. National Museum, Smithsonian Institution, #31618.)

The Waco Mammoth Site, Late Pleistocene epoch, McLennan Co. Discovered in 1978, this site has yielded to date the skeletal remains of 22 mammoths and one camel. It may have been a mass kill resulting from a flash flood and engulfing mud flow. Both adult and juvenile mammoths are found here, and digging still continues. (Courtesy of the Strecker Museum Complex, Baylor University, Waco, Texas.)

Plate 111

One of the four large plastron (belly) plates of the giant *Protostega* sea turtle from Rockwall Co., Taylor gr., approximately 75 million years old. This turtle, now on exhibit in the Dallas Museum of Natural History, has an 8-foot-long carapace (shell). It is the second largest sea turtle in the world (see also Color Photo 48).

Vertebra of mosasaur, a 70-million-year-old swimming reptile of the Upper Cretaceous period, showing part of adjacent vertebra fused to it in life by arthritis. This is an example of *paleopathology* (the study of ancient illness) and *uniformitarianism* (how present experience can be a key to understanding the past).

Plate 112

Small to medium, somewhat globose regular echinoid. Slightly elevated at top. Interambulacral areas much wider than the narrow ambulacral areas. Two main rows of ambulacral tubercles very close. Periproct slightly off center in apical system, but in all *Salenia*s it will adjoin an ambulacral area. Apical disk with rounded, wavy edges. The fairly sparse, large interambulacral tubercles, evenly spaced over the test surface, give the impression of an antenna-covered communications satellite. Tubercles are crenulate and imperforate.

Salenia mexicana Schluter (Photo 341)
Lower Cretaceous, Fredericksburg division, Walnut and Kiamichi formation. Smaller than *S. texana*, Photos 339, 340. Two main rows of ambulacral tubercles wider apart than *S. texana*. Ambulacral pore pairs slanted. Ambulacral tubercles eighteen or so. Peristome larger proportionately than *S. texana*. Apical system more ornate. *S. leanderensis* Ikins has very large peristome but only twenty-four ambulacral tubercles in two rows. It is found in the Walnut formation. *S. phillipsae* Whitney, Glen Rose formation, has a pentagonal apical system and only five ambulacral tubercles per row, and is a squat little test. It is found in the Glen Rose formation. *S. hondoensis* Cooke is a similar species of the Upper Cretaceous, Anacacho formation.

Salenia volana Whitney (Photo 342)
Lower Cretaceous, upper parts of Washita division, Denton and Main Street formations. Differs from *S. texana* and *S. mexicana* in being more depressed at the top. Differs from *S. mexicana* and others by having sixteen ambulacral tubercles per row.

Goniophorus scotti (Photo 343)
Lower Cretaceous, Washita division, Duck Creek, Grayson, and Del Rio formations. Very small test. Each interambulacral plate has one large primary tubercle decorated with a ring of small tubercles. Ambulacral areas have two rows of small tubercles and alternating small pits. In this species the apical disk at top of test is pentagonal, periproct slightly offset but adjoining an interambulacral area always. Tubercles crenulate and imperforate. *G. whitneyi* Ikins is found in the Lower Cretaceous, Del Rio formation, and is larger (perhaps approaching 12-15 mm. wide).

Loriolia texana (Clark) (Compare to Photos 344, 345)

Lower Cretaceous, Fredericksburg and Trinity divisions. This is a medium to small regular echinoid with top and bottom flattened and parallel, edges rounded. Test much wider than high. The periproct, atop the test, has a sharp notch on one side. Ambulacral areas narrow with two rows of eleven to twelve tubercles per row. Interambulacral areas wide with two rows of larger tubercles. *L. rosana* Cooke (Photos 344, 345) is an especially Glen Rose formation species with top rounded and ambulacral areas larger. All main tubercles are of similar size. *L. clarki* Cooke is similar but with a subconical higher test profile and all tubercles much the same. It is from the Washita division, much younger.

The "loriola" side slit in the periproct area is only the largest of five points. Peristome far less than half of base. Loriolia tubercles are crenulate and perforate. *Polydiadema arguta* (Clark) is smaller than *Loriolia* with no side slit in the apical system and a more granular surface. It is in the Washita division, Grayson to Del Rio formations.

Dumblea symmetrica Cragin (Photo 346)

Lower Cretaceous, Duck Creek through Paw Paw formations, also Georgetown and Boracho formations. Test a medium- to large-sized fat-sided cone. Ambulacra nearly half as wide as the interambulacra. Peristome strongly notched. Apical system very small with a large madreporite. Tubercles of nearly same size in eight to nine rows in interambulacral areas and three to four rows per ambulacral plate. Surface finely and uniformly textured with tubercles. *Pedinopsis* sp. are similar in having many fine rows of even-sized tubercles. The largest finest tubercled species is *P. pondi* Clark in the Austin group, Upper Cretaceous. Another large species with fewer and slightly coarser tubercles is *P. texana* Cooke in the upper Washita division of the Lower Cretaceous.

Two smaller species are found in the Walnut formation, Lower Cretaceous. One of those *P. yarboroughi* Ikins is more inflated and less flattened above and below.

Tetragramma taffi (Cragin) (Photo 347; also compare to Photos 348, 349)

Lower Cretaceous, Fredericksburg division, especially Comanche Peak formation. A large, flattened, very regularly tubercled regular urchin. Looks like *Phymosoma* but has six or eight rows of tubercles on interambulacral areas at sides of test, instead of four. Mouth medium-sized and ten-pointed; peristome medium-sized and five-pointed. Ambulacral areas have two rows of tubercles, reducing to one row near mouth. Tubercles are perforate in all *Tetragramma* species. *T. streeruwitzi* (Cragin) (Photos 348, 349) is a smaller species, but still of medium size, prominent in the Washita division, Upper Fort Worth and Weno formations. Its tubercles are all about the same size, and the mouth is smaller. Its top is less flattened than *T. taffi*. *T. texanum* (Roemer) is a smaller species still, with perforate tubercles and in two rows per ambulacral area and four rows per interambulacral area. It is found in the Trinity division, Lower Cretaceous, Glen Rose and Fredericksburg formations.

Phymosoma texanum (Roemer) (Photos 350, 351, 352 and Color Photo 29)

Lower Cretaceous, Fredericksburg through Lower Washita divisions. A regular echinoid with a round test quite flattened but decidedly convex above. Test medium to medium-large. Peristome wide, periproct large. Tubercles large and in paired rows. All *Phymosoma* tubercles are imperforate. At the test's widest point, there are four rows of large tubercles between the ambulacral areas. *P. mexicanum* Boese (Photos 350, 351, 352) is smaller and quite flattened on both top and bottom, with finer tubercles. It is found in the lower parts of the Washita division down into the Comanche Peak and Edwards formations of the Fredericksburg division, Lower Cretaceous. Test is more subpentagonal in outline than other species of the genus. *P. volanum* (Cragin) is smaller yet, with slightly elevated upper surface. Its peristome is rounder than *P. mexicanum,* periproct large and with a strong, sharp notch in one corner (apical scar). Most common in upper parts of the Washita division, Lower Cretaceous. Its tubercles are uniform size and fairly large compared to other species.

Codiopsis texana Whitney (Photos 353, 354)

Lower Cretaceous period, Upper Washita division. Genus is

characterized by a strongly pentagonal shape and a small periproct. Peristome is slightly pentagonal. Ambulacral areas are on the pentagonal corners. Tubercles are low on sides and on bottom surface. C. sellardsi Ikins is from the Fredericksburg division, Lower Cretaceous, and has weaker tubercles and an oblong peristome. *C. stephensoni* Cooke is an Upper Cretaceous species from the Navarro group, Escondido formation. It has a larger peristome than the other species.

Goniopygus zitteli Clark (Photo 355)

Lower Cretaceous, Fredericksburg division. Test small to medium-sized. Round when viewed from above. Rounded-conical in side profile. Base flattened. Apical system star-shaped with five, long genital plates extending beyond the other apical plates. Ambulacral areas and interambulacral areas each have two rows of tubercles. The interambulacral tubercles are larger, so a rotation of two small and two large rows proceeds around test. This changes on the base where tubercles are nearly equal size. Ambulacral areas straight. Peristome only slightly less than half of base diameter. *G. stocktonensis* Smiser (Photo 356) is similar but smaller and more conical. Genital and other plates of equal length. Found in Ft. Worth through Denton fm. equivalents in Trans-Pecos Texas possibly earlier. G. budaensis Whitney is smaller, with less than 10 large tubercles per row and in the Washita Division, usually Buda fm. Its apical system is different from the star or petal-like plates of most Goniopygus, being composed of small plates with radiating ridges and the periproct diamond shaped with a raised lip. Peristome very large. The Glen Rose formation has a small, flattened species, *G. guadalupae* Whitney, and the Edwards formation has *G. texanus* Ikins (Photo 357), which resembles *G. zitteli* but has a star-shaped apical system with only four small tubercles on the five plates surrounding the periproct.

The Holectypoids

The old catch-all genus *Holectypus* has been changed to *Coenholectypus* in cases where specimens have all five of the small plates in the apical area perforated. Much uncertainty surrounds those species where such details are unknown. We have often followed Akers and Akers, 1987, in such decisions, as it is the best present source on Texas urchins. Many more *Holectypus* will end up *Coenholectypus* eventually.

Coenholectypus planatus Roemer (Photo 361; see also Color Photo 32)

Lower Cretaceous, Washita and Fredericksburg divisions. Test is often round when viewed from above, giving this genus a relationship to the regular echinoids. But test also often has a rounded pentagonal look from above. From side test is a low, even tapered cone. Peristome is in center of test bottom, but periproct is also on under surface, unlike regular urchins. Periproct large, pointed on inner end and rounded on outer if such detail remains. Surface has only tiny perforate tubercles and appears fairly smooth. Ambulacral areas have straight, diverging lines, widest at the test's edge. This species has rather narrow ambulacra. Its apical system shows five perforated plates, clearly making it a *Coenholectypus*. *Holectypus planus* Giebel is very similar but less tall and very concave on bottom with numerous bottom tubercles. Periproct very large. *C. limitis* Boese (Photo 359) has wide ambulacra (average 5-7 mm.) and a smaller periproct, which is slightly pointed on both ends. *Holectypus charltoni* Cragin is a very large species from the Mid-Washita division, Lower Cretaceous of East or Central Texas, and the Boracho formation of Trans-Pecos Texas. It has a small oval periproct near test's underside edge. Peristome also small. A very similar form from similar strata is *Coenholectypus castilloi* (Cotteau) (Photo 360), which has larger tubercles on its lower surface and a definite five-perforated apical system. *Coenholectypus transpecosensis* Cragin (Photo 362) is a very large species from the Washita division, Lower Cretaceous of West Texas with slightly pentagonal, conical test and small periproct rounded on inner end, pointed on the outer end. Peristome almost twice the size of the periproct or more. Two additional *Holectypus* occur in the Fredericksburg division, Lower Cretaceous. Both have periprocts that cut into the edge of the test. *H. adkinsi* Smiser is fat, conical, and more pentagonal than *H. engerrandi* Lambert (Photo 358). *H. engerrandi* has a very large periproct, pointed slightly on at least the inner end. *Coenholectypus nanus* (Cooke) is thumbnail-size or less with the periproct in the test edge. It is a Pawpaw formation form. In the Upper Cretaceous, Taylor group, Anacacho formation in south-central Texas: look for a very rounded, medium-sized *Coenholectypus* look-alike, *Lanieria uvaldana* Cooke. Two other *Coenholectypus*-like echinoids are *Anorthopygus* (Photo 363), from the Lower Cretaceous, and *Conulus* (Photo 364), from the Upper Cretaceous, southern Austin group.

Globator (Photo 365)
Lower Cretaceous, except for *G. vaughani* Cooke, which is Upper Cretaceous, Taylor group, Anacacho formation. Fat, roundish tests, slightly flattened below, peristome central and periproct on the test side, high or low. *G. parryi* (Hall) (Photo 365) is the most plentiful species, found in Lower Cretaceous, Washita division, especially Fort Worth formation and into the Fredericksburg division. Its test is off-round to slightly pentagonal, and somewhat flattened on top. *G. clarki* (Boese) is off-round and has a small off-center peristome beneath. It is small. *G. inaudita* (Boese) is a Washita division species with a round test viewed from above and a high large periproct. *G. bulloides* (Cragin) is also roundish, but with a smaller, usually pointed-top periproct, mid-test in height. *G. whitneyae* Ikins is round, high domed, and has a large low periproct. It is a Georgetown formation species from Central Texas.

Phyllobrissus cubensis (Weisbord) (Photo 366)
Upper Cretaceous, Taylor group, Anacacho formation and Navarro group, Escondido formation (good specimens in D.M.N.H.). Oval, somewhat flattened test, a little wider to the rear. Periproct is in a slit groove on the upper side of the test. *Nucleolites texanus* (Clark) is very similar small species, but with periproct in a wider groove and test front slightly flattened. *Nucleolites wilderae* Ikins is medium-sized and more flat-topped than *N. texanus*. Both *Nucleolites* sp. are in the Austin formation, Upper Cretaceous. *Nucleopygus angustatus* (Clark) (Photos 367, 368) is another small echinoid with the periproct in a narrow groove on the top side of the test. It is from older strata, Buda formation, Washita division, Lower Cretaceous. It is fat in shape with a very concave lower surface, sinking the peristome in a good depression. These three genera were all at one time called *Echinobrissus*.

Periarchus lyelli (Conrad) — a "sand dollar"

Eocene epoch, Claiborne group. Sand-dollar-shaped but with thin test edge, becoming somewhat thinner as it approaches the abruptly raised apical system. Underside flat. Small mouth central beneath with periproct midway to underside edge of test. Circular in shape, averaging 60-70 mm. width. *Protoscutella mississippiensis* (Twitchell) is similar but with periproct at underside edge in small notch. *Mortonella* sp., also in similar age of rock, has a heavy, thick-edged test by comparison.

Holaster simplex Shumard (Photo 369 and Color Photo 31)

Lower Cretaceous, lower half of Washita division. Test very high-domed with flat base. Mouth moved toward forward edge beneath. Periproct on test side at rear above the base. There is a "low phase," with widest part of test at base, and a "high phase," broader above the base. *H. nanus* Cragin is a somewhat shorter species, with nearly equal ambulacral areas when viewed from above. Test is also slightly constricted in the rear. Found in the Grayson formation or its equivalents, especially in West Texas. Tubercles perforate. No fasiole.

Cardiaster leonensis Stephenson (Compare to Photo 369)

Upper Cretaceous, Taylor and Navarro groups. Very similar to *Holaster* in shape, but in very much younger strata. It has a weak marginal fasiole, which also serves to separate it from *Holaster*.

Echinocorys texanus (Cragin) (Photo 370 and Color Photo 33)

Upper Cretaceous, Austin and Taylor groups. Test medium-large to very large. Probably the largest Texas echinoid. Base oval and flattened, shape domed to conical, tall. Mouth and periproct at opposite basal edges. Ambulacral areas not in depressions, diverging straight and regularly from peak of test. Ambulacral pore pairs nearly round, not elongate. Tubercles crenulate and perforate. An even rarer high-domed or conical genus, also from the Austin formation, is *Conulus stephensoni* Cooke (Photo 364). On the underside, it has a central oval peristome turned slightly to one side. It has more and larger tubercles than *Echinocorys*.

Pseudananchys completa (Cragin) (Photo 371)

Lower Cretaceous, Upper Washita division, especially the Main Street formation. A domed test with ambulacral areas merely marked on surface by elongate pore rows. That distinguishes it from *Echinocorys* (Photo 370), which has round pores and usually a more conical dome. Base nearly flat to slightly concave. Tubercles crenulate and perforate. Peristome on base and periproct only slightly above base on the rear. That divides it from *Holaster* (Photo 369), which has periproct higher above base and a forward but basal peristome. *Holaster* also shows a frontal indentation caused by a mildly deep front ambulacral groove. This species has little overhang on domed sides of test. *P. supernus* (Cragin) (Photo 371) is very large with test sides overhanging base. *P. stephensoni* Cooke is an Upper Cretaceous, Austin group species often mistaken for *Echinocorys,* except for the elongate pores and very flat base.

Order Spatangoida — True Heart Urchins
The *Heterasters*

An important *Heteraster* character is unequal-length ambulacral areas, with the unpaired ambulacral groove very deep. Apical system small.

Heteraster mexicanus (Cotteau) (Photos 372, 373)

Lower Cretaceous, Fredericksburg division, especially Comanche Peak and Kiamichi formations, with very similar species earlier. Viewed from side, test slopes toward mouth end. Mouth much forward of bottom center in depressed area. The forward ambulacral groove is deep and extends over the end of the test around to the mouth underneath. The other ambulacra meet somewhat rear of center, the rear pair much shorter and less curved near the tips. Ambulacra consist of rows of slit-shaped pores of alternating lengths. On the base, from the mouth to the rear margin, is a broad V-shaped area of abundant tubercles. Periproct high on broadly truncated rear of test. No fasioles. In older sources this genus is called *Enallaster.*

Heteraster obliquatus (Clark) (Photo 374)

Lower Cretaceous, Trinity division, especially in the Glen Rose formation. Like a squashed *H. mexicanus* (Photos 372,

373), with a very low, broad test. Apical system is off-center to the rear of the test, and ambulacral areas are narrower. Periproct is oval and in an oval, vertical depression. Generally narrower in the rear, view from above, than *H. mexicanus.*

Heteraster texanus (Roemer) (Photo 377)
Lower Cretaceous, Fredericksburg and Trinity divisions. This is the best place to put the historic catch-all species *Enallaster texanus* (Roemer). A medium-sized *Heteraster* with a prominent rear truncation and also somewhat narrowed to the front end of the test. Peristome very narrowed oval. Test somewhat raised between rear ambulacra. Very short rear ambulacral pair. May be a bit narrower than other species, but no doubt this is a hard identification to make certain; this should be the general run-of-the-mill *Heteraster*. *H. adkinsi* Lambert (Photo 375) has been identified as being fatter than *H. texanus* and with narrow ambulacra and a small high periproct. It may be more frequent in West Texas. *H. bohmi* (de Loriol) (Photo 376) is another fat look-alike for *H. texanus,* with the high point of the test near center.

The Macrasters
Macrasters are good indicators of zones in the Lower Cretaceous strata, and identifying them must take into account where they are found geographically and stratigraphically as well as simple characteristics. Slight variants are common. A helpful *Macraster* character is nearly equal-length ambulacral areas, in nearly equal depth grooves.

Macraster texanus Roemer (Photos 380, 381)
Lower Cretaceous period, Washita division, Fort Worth through Upper Duck Creek formations. Medium-sized urchin. Test oval, but slightly longer than wide. Ambulacral grooves long and straight in wide, shallow depressions. This species represents the "flat-topped" members of the genus. Top should have at least some level area.

Macraster elegans (Shumard) (Photos 382, 383)
Lower Cretaceous, Washita division, Fort Worth through Weno formations. Test medium in size and well tubercled. Viewed from above, test is only very slightly narrowed and trun-

cated at rear. Test mostly looks roundish and just a little longer than wide. Ambulacral grooves short, wide, slightly curved, moderately deep, with interambulacral areas elevated. Periproct above middle of rear of test and vertically elongate.

Macraster pseudoelegans Adkins (Photos 384, 385)

Lower Cretaceous period, Washita division, Fort Worth through Denton formations. Test medium in size and smoother than *M. elegans* (Photos 382, 383). Test definitely narrowed in rear and slightly elongate. Ambulacral grooves long, narrow, straight and deep. Highest point of test on a mid-ridge just behind apical system. Periproct not above middle of rear of test, moderately vertically elongate.

Macraster nodopyga Lambert (Photo 386)

Lower Cretaceous, Middle Washita division, Weno and Paw Paw formations. A small species with a low side profile, short, narrow, and straight ambulacral grooves, and two concentrations of nodules or tubercles on the rear face, around the periproct. Periproct at or below middle rear of test.

Macraster aquilerae (Boese) (Color Photo 30; compare to Photos 387, 388)

Lower Cretaceous, Washita division, Fort Worth through Weno formations. Medium-sized test, width and length nearly equal. An oval viewed from above. Straight ambulacra in modest grooves. A fresh specimen can be well tubercled. Rear of test slightly flat, with a little overhang. *M. wenoensis* (Adkins) may be the same species but is described as being smaller and more elongate, with slightly curved and very shallow ambulacral grooves. Both have ambulacra longer than *M. nodopyga* (Photo 386). *M. roberti var. ovatus* Smiser (Photos 387, 388), Duck Creek formation, is another very round species when viewed from above, the most so among very small species. It has a vertically flattened rear with a high periproct. Its ambulacra are shallow. *M. solitariensis* Smiser (Photo 389), from the Trinity division, Glen Rose formation, has more angular equal proportions viewed from above and deeper ambulacra. It also has a granule between the pore pair slits of the front (unpaired) ambulacral area. Although first identified in far West Texas, collectors in Northeast Texas have identified it there by all the criteria except geography.

Macraster obesus Adkins (Photos 390, 391)

Lower Cretaceous, Washita division, Fort Worth through Weno formations. Test very large and very rotund. Viewed from side, there is far less overhang on front end, than there is on *M. subobesus* (Photo 393). Both ends overhang about equally. Rear end rather broadly rounded, viewed from above. Ambulacral grooves are long and even, radiating from near the test's top center. They may show a slight curvature.

Macraster subobesus (Adkins) (Photos 392, 393)

Lower Cretaceous, Washita division, Duck Creek through Fort Worth formations. Large and rotund like *M. obesus* (Photo 390) but slightly narrowed toward rear, as viewed from above. Side view shows a definitely greater overhang on the front end of the test, a so-called "nose." Ambulacra are long and straight in moderate grooves. *M. kentensis* Adkins (Photo 397) is a smaller, less rotund variety, quite constricted in the rear, found usually in Trans-Pecos Texas but identified by serious collectors in Northeast Texas as well. It was once a subspecies of *M. subobesus.*

Macraster denisonensis Smiser (Photos 394, 395)

Lower Cretaceous, Washita division, Duck Creek formation. A medium-sized, rather tall species. Elongated rear of test is truncated, with a slight concavity. Test has an angular shoulder forward of center viewed from above. Pore slits in the unpaired ambularal area are chevron-shaped, separated by a granule. Periproct slightly upright oval. A very confusingly similar species is *M. washitae* Lambert (Photo 396), from similar strata. It is more rounded on the sides and has in purest forms a circular periproct, which should be "low" on a rear truncation.

The Hemiasters

An important "hemiaster" character is fairly short, paired, moderately unequal, ambulacral areas, with the unpaired ambulacral area in a modest groove. Apical system large but madreporite moderately perforated.

Hemiaster texanus Roemer (Photo 398)

Upper Cretaceous, Austin and Taylor groups, especially Anacacho formation. Test broadly wedge-shaped when viewed from side, higher to rear. Front ambulacral groove much wider and longer; all are definitely deep. Base is flat. Rear end truncated with slight angle. Mouth and periproct elongate. This is one of the few urchins found in the Austin group. Ambulacral areas deep, wide (petaloid), with the rear pair about half the size of the front pair. A fasiole of small bumps enclose the four smaller ambulacral areas as a group. Slightly larger bumps cover other areas. *H. americanus* Giebel is in similar rock layers but has a high, evenly rounded side profile and a circular mouth and periproct.

Hemiaster calvini Clark (Photo 399)

Lower Cretaceous, upper parts of the Washita division, Weno, Buda, especially Grayson and Del Rio formations. Test moderately tall, angular viewed from above. Base flat. Posterior margin with slanted truncation and a high oval periproct. Ambulacral areas in very deep, sometimes steep sided grooves. Ambulacral areas surrounded by band of small, round, double pores, a fasiole (most of which are faint at best). *H. cranium* Cooke, from the Weno formation, is similar in having depressed ambulacral grooves, but the grooves are short and the test is less angular and fatter. The peristome is set about one-third of the way back from the front of the test.

Hemiaster jacksoni Maury (Photo 400)

Upper Cretaceous, Eagle Ford group and its equivalents in especially West Texas. A moderately small species, generally occurring in large numbers where found. Ambulacral areas surrounded by double band of small, round pores. With deeply set ambulacral grooves, it gives the impression of a small *H. calvini* (Photo 399) but occurs in much younger rock layers and has a less angular outline viewed from above.

Hemiaster bexari Clark (Photo 401)

Upper Cretaceous, especially the Navarro group. Much like *H. cranium,* with a subrounded test and depressed, short ambulacral grooves, but in drastically younger strata. Periproct round and high on a truncated rear end. *H. benhurensis* Stephenson is in similar rock layers, but with a vertically long periproct and a much rounder text viewed from above.

Hemiaster whitei Clark (Compare to Photos 378, 379, Lambertiaster)

Lower Cretaceous, Fredericksburg and Trinity divisions, Goodland and Glen Rose formations, most often in North or Central Texas. This medium-sized echinoid is one of several species that have been called *Epiaster whitei* (Clark) in the past. Test is heart-shaped but with a vertically truncated rear. Front ambulacral groove moderately deep, depressing front test margin. Periproct high on rear truncation. Some fasiole. In West Texas, the Fredericksburg division, Kiamichi formation, produces *Toxaster inflatus* (Smiser), once called *Pliotoxaster inflatus* Smiser. It is similar to *Hemiaster whitei* but never has a fasiole and slightly less deep front ambulacral groove and an especially long, thin apical system.

The Lower Cretaceous, Washita division, Duck Creek formation, as well as the Fredericksburg division, Goodland formation, has another very similar species, *Lambertiaster ficheuri* Dalloni and Lambert (Photos 378, 379). Like the *Hemiaster*, it has a peripetalous fasiole, but it has a nonlabiate, slightly subpentagonal peristome. All three of these species have been misidentified as *Epiaster,* an old genus, now with no Texas species.

Palhemiaster comanchei (Clark) (Photo 402)

Lower Cretaceous, Lower Fredericksburg and Trinity division, most abundant in the Glen Rose formation. Medium-sized test. Ambulacral areas in moderately deep grooves. Rear pair of ambulacra shorter than others. Highest point on test slightly to the front of center. Test a rather rounded dome in side view. Periproct high on sloping rear surface, clearly visible from above. Good specimen should show a fasiole of small tubercles around the ambulacral area. Called *Hemiaster comanchei* Clark by older authors.

The *Washitasters*

An important *Washitaster* character is a large apical system with four pock-marked perforations very visible. With a deep forward ambulacral groove for the unpaired ambulacral area, this genus looks like the most "squashed" *Heterasters.*

Washitaster riovistae (Adkins) (Photo 403)

Lower Cretaceous, Washita division, especially the Main Street, Weno, and Paw Paw formations. Test outline oval viewed from above. Test height moderately depressed. Apical system and highest point near rear of test. Front ambulacral groove very long and in wide groove. Rear pair of ambulacra very short. On fine specimen, a multiple series of fine tubercled fasiole bands extend along sides of test, leading roughly toward the periproct. Front ambulacral pores separated by a tubercle. A similar Weno formation species is *W. wenoensis* Adkins (Photo 406); it has a deep but shorter and less exaggerated front groove. A very similar species, *W. bravoensis* (Boese), occurs in the Washita division, Georgetown formation, and is somehat wider and less elongate. *W. longisulcus* (Adkins and Winton) is very similar but even more squashed-looking, with apical system even farther to the rear of the test. It occurs especially in the top few feet of the Fort Worth formation. *W. inflatus* (Cragin) (Photos 404, 405) is a very tall, fat form from the Lower Cretaceous, Washita division, Grayson formation. It still shows the typical rear-positioned apical system and long, front ambulacral groove. Because of its similar shape to several *Heterasters,* the four large pock-marked perforations in the apical system are helpful. *Proraster dalli* (Clark) has a long, wide *Washitaster*-like front ambulacral groove and a low profile. It has an almost hexagonal-shape viewed from above, with both ends somewhat notched; it is however, an Upper Cret., Navarro and Taylor gr., Corsicana Marl and Anacacho fms. It was formerly called *Hemiaster dalli* Clark.

Linthia variabilis Slocum

Upper Cretaceous. Navarro Group. Test small to medium size and moderately tall. Ambulacral grooves deep and with steep contours. Rear pair of ambulacra small and separated by a ridge. Rear of test truncated, periproct high and oblong. Front of test sharply notched by wide front ambulacral groove.

Plesiaster americanus (Stephenson) (Photo 408)

Upper Cretaceous, Austin and Navarro groups. A medium-sized test with a swollen base, especially at the rear of the test, causing a slope from rear to front. A circular ring-shaped fasiole is situated under the high upright oval periproct. A peripetalous fasiole is seen on good specimens. *Micraster uddeni* Cooke is a similar form found in the Austin group. Its rear pair of ambulacra are slightly shorter compared to *P. americanus*, and the periproct is only halfway up the rear truncation.

Phylum Hemichordata
Class Graptolithina — Graptolites

Loganograptus (Photo 410)

Ordovician period. Multi-branching carbonized marks, radiating crudely from central junctions. In the Ordovician shales of West Texas. Some saw-toothed edges may appear on very well-preserved specimens.

Phyllograptus (Photo 411 and Color Photo 7)

Ordovician period. Branches very broad and long oval-shaped.

Tetragraptus (Color Photo 7)

Ordovician period. Saw-toothed blades spreading from a central point, but less widely than *Loganograptus*.

Cambrian Graptolites (Photo 409)

Cambrian period, Llano Uplift area, Central Texas. Branching dark lines on the Cambrian marbles and shales. On close examination, some sawtoothed edges can be seen.

Phylum Chordata — The Chordates

If one were to take a human evolutionary perspective, chordates would be considered the most advanced animals. They are characterized by a cartilagenous or bony structure, called a *notochord*, generally along the dorsal side, for stiffening a spine to support the body.

The vertebrates — fish, amphibians, reptiles, birds, and mammals — provide some of the largest and most dramatic fossil material in Texas and elsewhere. As a result, they generate a great deal of interest in paleontology. Yet they are only one part of the fossil record, not really significantly more important to science than any other group of fossils.

Class Chondrichthyes (Sharks, Cartilagenous Fishes)

Orthacanthus or Xenacanthus (Photo 412, Text Illustration 12)

Permian period. A common freshwater or brackish water shark known primarily by its two equal-bladed teeth and numerous coprolites (fossilized dung). Especially common in the Lower Permian. Also called Pleuracanthus or Xenacanthus.

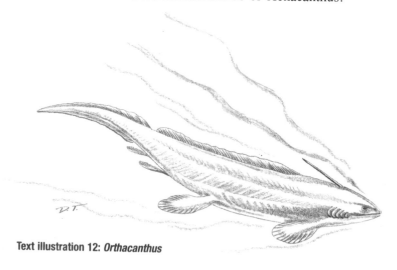

Text illustration 12: *Orthacanthus*

Permian Fish Coprolites (Fossilized Excrement) (Photo 413)

Permian period. Rather common fossils in areas in which *Orthacanthus* shark teeth are also common, and associated with them. Coprolites of later fish are shown in Photo 414.

Petalodus (Photo 415)

Permian period. A shark best known by teeth with a short, pointed crown and a long tapering root. Root length is approximately four times longer than the crown.

"Lungfish" Burrows (Photo 416)

Permian period. Cylindrical plugs of mudstone containing hundreds of tiny fish fragments of a lungfish that perished in its burrow.

Permian Reptile Tracks (Photo 417)

Permian period. Tracks appear to show claw marks in what must once have been a soft muddy sediment more than 250 million years ago.

Ptychodus (Photos 419, 420, 421)

Upper Cretaceous, Woodbine through Eagle Ford groups. Shell-crushing shark, known mostly from teeth. Teeth are low-crowned, knobby rather than sharp, usually with some slight central elevation. Grinding surface is marked with ridges resembling a fingerprint. Several species; the flattest and broadest is *P. decurrens*, Photo 419. It can have a slightly raised center area but is best told by its finely marked marginal area of delicate, often radiating ridges. *P. anonymus* is similar but has a margin of concentric ridges with less refinement than *decurrens*. *P. whipplei*, Photo 420, is characterized by a very high central cusp. *P. mammilaris* also has a high cusp, but the central area is more coarsely ridged and slightly off-center on the tooth. *P. rugosus* has a less slender central knob than *whipplei*. The knob on *rugosus* is squarish in shape and intermediate in height for this genus. The odd member of the genus is *P. mortoni* (Photo 421), with strongly radiating central ridges. Beware! *Ptychodus* teeth (with cross-ridges and raised central areas) are often mistaken by amateurs for trilobites! Trilobites became extinct more than 100 million years earlier and are never found in Mesozoic rocks.

Uranoplosus ("Pychnodont") (Photo 422)

Lower Cretaceous. Small, shiny, long-oval teeth, obviously for a grinding feeding habit. Often in rows forming a pavement.

Ischyrhiza mira Leidy (Photo 429)

Upper Cretaceous. Taylor group to redeposited Paleocene. Large blade with a conical root. Root notched at base. A "sawfish" tooth. *I. schneideri* Slaughter and Steiner have a stumpier blade compared to the root, and the blade is inclined at

a slight angle to the root. Pulp cavity in base is also smaller than
I. mira.

Odontaspis (Photo 430)
Upper Cretaceous through Eocene. Small, smooth or very
finely striated, with small lateral cusps. Moderately small forked
root with nutrient groove that stops short of crown base. *O.
subulata* Agazziz is Upper Cretaceous. *O. macrota* is Eocene.

Scapanorhynchus rhapiodon Agassiz (Photo 423)
Upper Cretaceous. Slender S-curved blade with well-spaced,
obvious striations on the lingual side almost to tip. Root deeply
forked with a strong vertical groove. *S. rapax* is generally larger
than *rhapiodon,* with a broader blade, and striations only halfway up blade on lingual side only. *S. texanus* has striations on
both blade faces.

Cretoxyrhina mantelli oxyrhinoides Savage (Photo 424; also compare to Color Photo 38)
Upper Cretaceous. Central cusp moderately broad at base, but
the overall look is still elongate. Root large and somewhat
forked. May or may not have side cusps, but if it does the cusps
are smaller than *Cretolamna,* Photo 425. Inner (lingual) side of
tooth very flat. *Cretoxyrhina mantelli extenta* Leidy, in the
Austin group, Color Photo 38, has a very broad, triangular blade,
very slightly inclined. Blade curves gently outward at base to
nearly reach the edges of the root. Root is large with a deep,
rounded basal notch. Tooth usually lacks side cusps. Lingual face
is very flat. Older authors call *Cretoxyrhina* by the genus *Isurus.*

Cretolamna appendiculata (Agassiz) (Photo 425)
Upper Cretaceous. Blade broadly triangular; usually has side
cusps. Never a nutritive groove. Base has a much shallower
notch than similar genera. Bottom of base often has flat areas and
often a small secondary·notch. Lingual face of tooth flat as in
Cretoxyrhina, Photo 424. In Tertiary strata, teeth with broad
blades, prominent side cusps, and shallow basal notch are assigned to the genus *Lamna,* as in *L. mediavia,* which has out-
wardly inclined side cusps in the Midway group, Paleocene
epoch.

Leptostyrax crassidens (Photo 426)

Upper Cretaceous. Blade somewhat narrower than *Cretolamna,* Photo 425, and usually has side cusps. Blade may show faint striations. Broad U-shaped root with root tips that point nearly straight downward on each side of a deep notch. *L. macrorhiza* Pictet and Campiche have a large root, moderately slender blade, and striations on both faces. *L. semiplicatus* (Agassiz) is similar but with well-developed striations on both faces.

Squalicorax (Photo 427)

Cretaceous. From Washita division, Lower Cretaceous, to Navarro group, Upper Cretaceous. This genus has a broad, usually serrate-edged blade terminating in a broad point, usually slanted at least slightly to one side. Generally the various species increase in size and are less slanted in progressively younger rocks. The Washita division Lower Cretaceous has a *Squalicorax* with a very narrow, small blade, acutely slanted and with indistinct serrations. *Squalicorax curvatus* Williston in the Woodbine and Lower Eagle Ford groups has a blade slanted nearly ninety degrees. *S. falcatus* Agassiz in the Upper Eagle Ford and Lower Austin groups has a blade slanted just less than ninety degrees. *S. obliquus* Reuss in the uppermost Eagle Ford and Lower Austin has a blade that is small compared to its root, and only a forty-five degree slant. *S. kaupi* in the Taylor group has a broad blade, nearly upright. *S. pristodontis* from the Upper Taylor group through the Navarro group and reworked in the Paleocene, is the largest Texas species of this genus and has a very upright point on a very broad blade. *Pseudocorax laevis* Leriche is found in the Austin and Taylor groups. It has a narrow, smooth, or only slightly serrate blade but a prominent nutritive groove. *Galeocerdo* (Photo 431), from the Eocene epoch, is also small, triangular, and somewhat more serrated on both edges.

Class Osteichthyes (Bony Fish)

Xiphactinus audax (Photos 433, 434, Color Photo 41)

Upper Cretaceous period, Eagle Ford through Austin groups. A very large fish, ten-foot-length fairly common. In a family, *Ichthyodectidae,* that is characterized by vertebral centrums with strut-like ridges on their sides. This genus has very irregularly sized teeth. *Ichthyodectes* sp. has moderately irregular teeth. *Gillicus* sp. has rather regular teeth, but characteristically ichthyodectid struted vertebrae:

Pachyrhizodus caninus (Photos 434, 435)
Upper Cretaceous period. A moderately large fish, up to eight feet in length. Vertebral centrums with fine, irregular striations on their sides, but no large struts. Teeth short, conical with large roots. *P. minimus,* Photos 435 and Color Photo 39, is a small species often found preserved three-dimensionally in the Eagle Ford group.

Enchodus (Photo 432)
Upper Cretaceous period. Small to medium-sized fish. Most identifiable remains are long curved teeth with a very slight S-shape. Some teeth show a number of fine grooves running up concave side of tooth. One edge of tooth sharp-angled.

Belonostomus (Photo 437)
Upper Cretaceous, Eagle Ford group. Medium-sized fish with long snout.

Tselfatia (Photo 438, Color Photo 40)
Upper Cretaceous, Austin group. Small to medium-sized fish with flat, wide body profile.

Shark Centrums (Vertebrae) (Photo 428, Color Photo 37)
Upper Cretaceous through Eocene. Flat disks, usually less than one-fifth thick as wide. Concave on both faces, usually with concentric growth rings showing. Vertebrae of other kinds of fish (bony fish) are much thicker but also double concave on the faces.

Playa Lake Fish (Photo 439)
Pleistocene epoch, Rita Blanca formation. Well-preserved small fish occur in the thin-bedded sediments of the temporary (playa) lakes of the Texas high plains in the Panhandle.

Class Amphibia

Eryops (Text illustration 13; also compare to Metoposaurus, Text illustration 14 and Color Photo 43)

Lower Permian period. A carnivorous amphibian of which many skeletons have been found in north central Texas. Length was five to six feet. Broad flattened cranium provides many fragments as fossils. Not to be confused with the similar Triassic period amphibian *Metoposaurus,* Text Illustration 14 and Color Photo 43, also called *Buettnaria.* The Triassic genus has closerset, oval eye sockets and a somewhat sharper snout on a flatter cranium.

Seymouria baylorensis (Text Illustration 15)

Lower Permian period. A very important and much-debated Texas fossil. Shares many amphibian characteristics, such as cranial shape, with many reptilian characters, such as five-toed feet. It is sometimes considered a reptile, but present thinking places it as a very evolved amphibian. Named after the town of Seymour, Texas.

Diplocaulus (Text Illustration 16)

Permian period. A salamander with a broad triangular head and small limbs. Length about two feet.

Class Reptilia

Edaphosaurus and Dimetrodon (Text Illustrations 17, 18)

Permian period. *Edaphosaurus* is a fin-backed reptile with small side projections on the fin ray bones, unlike *Dimetrodon.* Has small peg-like teeth that were certainly less violently carnivorous than the long, sharp teeth of *Dimetrodon.* It is important in understanding reptilian evolution to note that *Edaphosaurus* and *Dimetrodon* have the sprawling stance of early reptiles and are pre-dinosaur entirely and not to be confused with dinosaurs.

Desmatosuchus (Text Illustration 19)

Late Triassic period. An armor-covered, long, low reptile about six to eight feet long. Side armor plates have moderate spines, but each shoulder has a large, horn-like spine up to twelve inches long. *Typothorax,* Photo 440 and Color Photo 44, is similar but without the shoulder spine. Its side spines are mostly longer than on *Desmatosuchus.*

Rutiodon (Text Illustration 20)

Late Triassic period. One of a group of "phytosaurs." Resemble crocodiles, because they lived a similar lifestyle in watery places. The nasal openings are are far back on the skull, near the eyes. Both nose and eyes are near the top of the skull for use while swimming. The snout is very long, with front teeth enlarged to aid in catching prey. The tail vertebrae are tall-spined to act as a paddle in swimming. *Phytosaur* means "plant eating reptile," but all are sharp-toothed meat eaters.

Text illustration 13: *Eryops*

Text illustration 14: *Metoposaurus*

Text illustration 15: *Seymouria baylorensis*

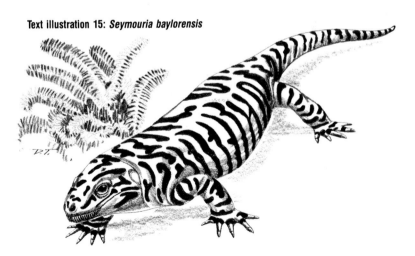

Text illustration 16: *Diplocaulus*

Text illustration 17: *Edaphosaurus*

Text illustration 18: *Dimetrodon*

Text illustration 19: *Desmatosuchus*

Text illustration 20: *Rutiodon*

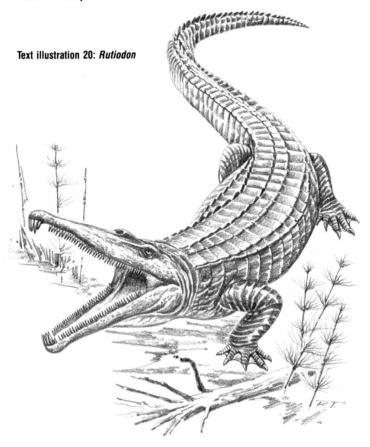

Superfamily Chelonioidea (Sea Turtles)
Protostega (Photo 456)
Upper Cretaceous. Rather large sea turtles. Jaws with large crushing surfaces. Vertebrae with flat, roughened articulating surfaces. Limb bones short and massive. *Archelon* is an even larger relative, the carapace reaching ten feet in diameter. It differs from *Protostega* by having a large, curved toothless beak like that of an eagle. *Toxochelys* is a much smaller turtle of the Texas Upper Cretaceous.

Superfamily Pliosauroidea (Short-Necked Pliosaurs)
Geochelone (Photo 457)
It is common in Texas to call creatures whose vertebrae have flat or slightly concave faces and bottom nutrient foramina

"plesiosaurs." The group is divided into two parts, the long-necked and the short-necked. From individual vertebrae this is hard to distinguish, but some authors suggest that those with shorter vertebrae as compared to width are the short-necked species. This is at best a crude estimation.

Polyptychodon (Color Photo 46 — Tooth; also compare Photos 443, 444)

Upper Cretaceous, Eagle Ford group. Before its discovery in the Texas Upper Cretaceous, this genus and its entire family were thought to have become extinct in the Jurassic. Its teeth are distinctive, having a large hollow root longer than the dark enameled crown. The crown is round in cross-section, with definite striations nearly to the tip. The vertebrae are shorter than wide and may possess a doub'·- ib facet on the side if not worn. Articulating faces of the v e'rae are mildly concave and often mildly lipped around the .culating surface. The faces of the vertebrae may have a roughened or raised area in the center. Two small nutrient pits on the ventral surface of the vertebra. Tail vertebrae may show areas of attachment for V-shaped chevron bones between articulating surfaces of two vertebrae. In this species the forelimbs are only slightly smaller than the hindlimbs, unlike most pliosaurs.

Trinacromerum (Text Illustration 21; compare Photos 443, 444)

Upper Cretaceous, Eagle Ford group. The most complete pliosaur skeletons found in Texas are of this genus. The vertebrae have slightly concave faces, generally with some center pit or slight depression. Neural spines are rectangular and blade-like on the middle vertebrae. Tail vertebrae show well-developed pedestals on their rear edges for chevron bone attachments. All vertebrae show at least two nutrient pits on the lower surface. The teeth are long, sharp, and recurved, with slightly less distinct striations and smoother tips than *Polyptychodon*. The crowns are less round in cross-section and can have a sharp front and back edge. Two other genera of the same family occur in Texas: *Polycotylus,* with central mammillae on the faces of at least the thoracic vertebrae and *Brachauchenius,* with never any nutrient foramina on the bottom of each vertebra.

Superfamily Plesiosauroidea (Long-Necked Plesiosaurs)
Elasmosaurus (Text Illustration 22)

Upper Cretaceous, Eagle Ford group. Swimming reptiles often forty feet long, with four nearly equal-sized paddlelike appendages. Vertebral centrums usually longer than tall, especially in the neck. Centrum usually compressed top to bottom. Ribs single-headed in all "elasmosaurs." Teeth relatively small. At least two other genera occur in Texas in the Upper Cretaceous: *Thalassomedon*, which is to be considered in all giant long-necked plesiosaur discoveries; and *Alzadasaurus*, in the case of smaller individuals.

Text illustration 21: *Trinacromerum*

Text illustration 22: *Elasmosaurus*

Family Mosasauridae (Mosasaurs)

Isolated vertebrae are the most-often-found fossils of the mosasaurs. Such vertebrae are characterized by having both a convex and a concave end.

Mosasaurus (Photo 446; compare to Photo 445)

Upper Cretaceous, especially Taylor group. A rather large mosasaur, characterized by a long mid-section with about thirty-five vertebrae from shoulders to pelvis and teeth extending to the tip of the snout. A thirty-foot-long specimen is on display in the Texas Memorial Museum in Austin. *Clidastes* (Photo 447) a small, common, delicate mosasaur, is in the same subfamily. It has small centrums, often wider than high, and with an extra interlocking structure at the base of the vertebral spines. Its teeth are rather smooth-enameled and have a distinct front and back cutting edge. It is often found in the mid- to early Upper Cretaceous. Photo 452 shows an interesting mosasaur bone with shark tooth scratches. Shark teeth are common amid Upper Cretaceous fish and reptile skeletons.

Platycarpus

Upper Cretaceous. A medium-sized mosasaur with a stout build. Only about twenty-two vertebrae between the shoulders and the pelvis. Jaws fairly massive.

Tylosaurus (Photo 450; compare to Photos 445, Text illustration 23, Color Photo 47)

Upper Cretaceous, Austin and Taylor groups. This is the largest Texas mosasaur. Teeth conical, slightly recurved, with a hint of a keel front and back. Teeth on lower and upper jaw stop with a definite protruding "nose."

Globidens (Photo 451)

Upper Cretaceous, Taylor or Navarro groups. Most of what has been found of this mosasaur are its blunt teeth, shaped like a sharp-topped mushroom. These were supposedly for crushing shellfish.

Coniasaurus (Photos 453, 454)

Upper Cretaceous period. A seldom-reported small,

"mosasaur-like" creature, especially in the Eagle Ford group. It occurs in fossil crab localities and has both blunt and sharp teeth, perhaps adapted for seizing crabs and then grinding up their hard parts. Vertebrae are like small mosasaur vertebrae (convex on one end and concave on the other). Lloyd Hill of Dallas has been the most successful recent collector.

Order Crocodilia (Crocodilians) (Photo 455)
Triassic period to present. Fossils of crocodilians usually include the armored skin plates (scutes), Photo 455; conical, rather stumpy teeth and vertebrae that resemble those of plesiosaurs (both ends are rather flat); with generally more of a bump on the ventral (lower) side. Texas's largest crocodilian was *Phobosuchus* or *Deinosuchus,* found in Upper Cretaceous rocks in the Big Bend. Its jaws opened five feet wide.

Order Pterosauria (Flying Reptiles)
Quetzalcoatlus (Text Illustration 24)
Upper Cretaceous, Big Bend area. This is the giant flying reptile once rumored to have a wingspread as large as a jet airplane. Later study shows a spread closer to forty feet. Pterosaurs in general are often spotted by their hollow bones, which crush down during fossilization. Such bones, unidentifiable to genus, have been found in the Upper Cretaceous rocks of North Texas. They may remain rare because of the difficulty of their delicate skeletons being preserved, as is the case also with birds.

Orders Saurischia and Ornithischia (Dinosaurs)
(Text illustrations 25, 26, 27, 28 and Photos 441, 442. See also Tracks, Color Photo 45)
Triassic period through Cretaceous period. Small to large reptiles with a characteristically upright posture. Texas has more than a dozen major kinds of dinosaurs. One *Tyrannosaurus* bone is suspected from the Big Bend region. The horned dinosaurs are represented by *Chasmosaurus* and *Torosaurus.* The duck-billed dinosaurs are represented by *Edmontosaurus,* a hadrosaur. A *Tenontosaurus,* from Wise County, can now be seen in the Dallas Museum of Natural History. The well-known dinosaur tracks at Glen Rose, Texas (and on many Central Texas ranches), are mostly attributed to *Acrocanthosaurus,* a three-toed meat-

eater with rather thin, distinct toes (Color Photo 45), and to *Pleurocoelus*, a large brachiosaur-like creature with bathtub-sized footprints showing small, stubby toenail marks. Hadrosaur prints, with three stubby, fat toes, have been found in Upper Cretaceous rocks, especially near Lake Grapevine in North Texas. Texas's most recently discovered dinosaurs include *Postosuchus*, named after Post, Texas, where it was recently discovered by Dr. Sankar Chatterjee of Texas Tech University. It represents one of the few Triassic period dinosaur finds in Texas. Although very productive in other western states, the Jurassic period is extremely poorly exposed on the surface in Texas, consisting mostly of the Malone formation in far West Texas, and has produced no Texas dinosaurs.

Class Mammalia

Fossil Sloths (Photos 458, 459, 460, Text Illustration 29)

Pleistocene epoch. Bones will be in Pleistocene sediments and not heavily mineral-replaced, but are stocky and strange in shape compared to other mammals of that time. Teeth are simple enameled pegs.

Glyptotherium (Photos 461, 462, Color Photo 50, Text Illustration 30)

Pleistocene epoch. Large (often five feet tall) armadillo-like mammals with bony "shells" that were not pleated and flexible like true armadillos. Texas species lack the spiked tail mace of some of their more southern relatives. The old genus *Glyptodon* can only be used, if at all, for the South American forms. *Glyptodon petaliferus* Cope, once a catch-all Texas species, is out of use. *Glyptotherium floridanum* (Simpson) is a mid-Pleistocene species with shell scutes and central figures similar in size to the surrounding figures. *G. arizonae* Gidley is earlier Pleistocene with central figures a little larger than those surrounding. *G. texanum* Osborn is a Blancan Formation species of the late Pliocene epoch. Its central figures on the scutes are very large. One should also know that a true giant armadillo (with flexible, banded "shell") lived in Texas during the Pleistocene epoch. It was smaller than the *Glyptotherium* but much larger than a modern armadillo. It was *Dasypus bellus*.

Text illustration 23: *Tylosaurus*

Text illustration 24: *Quetzalcoatlus*

Text illustration 25: *Postosuchus*

Text illustration 26: *Tenontosaurus*

Text illustration 27: *Pleurocoelus*

Text illustration 28: *Acrocanthosaurus*

Text illustration 29: Sloth

Text illustration 30: *Glyptotherium*

Canis dirus (Dire Wolf) (Photos 463, 464, 465)

Pleistocene epoch. A very large wolf, often twice the size of modern wolves. Its fossils are often found in Texas caves, such as Innerspace Caverns near Georgetown, Texas. Unlike the cats, the jaw contains two molar teeth on each side, and the muzzle is longer. In front of the molars is a triangular cutting premolar called the *carnassial*. Wolf molars are not as elongate as are bear molars.

Ursus

Pleistocene epoch. The bears, of all the carnivores, tried to become more vegetarian. Their two molars are longer than other carnivores.

Smilodon (Saber-toothed Cat) (Photo 466, Color Photo 52)

Pleistocene epoch. Toothrow of few and all cutting teeth (one very small molar may remain in some cats); the well-known long, stabbing canine; face blunt. The lower jaw (mandible) is long and straight with only a small ramus. The saber-toothed cat of the famous La Brea Tar Pits of California, *S. californicus*, occurs in Texas; but there are two other species, *S. fatalis* and *S. floridanus*, found more often in Texas. *Homotherium* (Photos 467, 468, Text Illustration 31) is a somewhat smaller, perhaps more common Texas saber-toothed cat, often found in Texas cave deposits. The jaguar, *Felis onca*, is also a common fossil in late Pleistocene epoch cave deposits, more so than the saber-tooths.

Equidae (Photo 469, Text Illustrations 32, 33, 34)

Eocene epoch through recent. Teeth represent the most-encountered fossils. They are flat-topped with a complex enamel pattern. The teeth are small in Eocene forms and larger in later kinds. Overall size also increased over the sixty million years of horse evolution, as did the length of the ankle bone (cannon bone). The number of functional toes also decreased, such that modern species use only one for locomotion. Presumably this increased the stride and hence the speed of the animal.

Text illustration 31: *Homotherium*

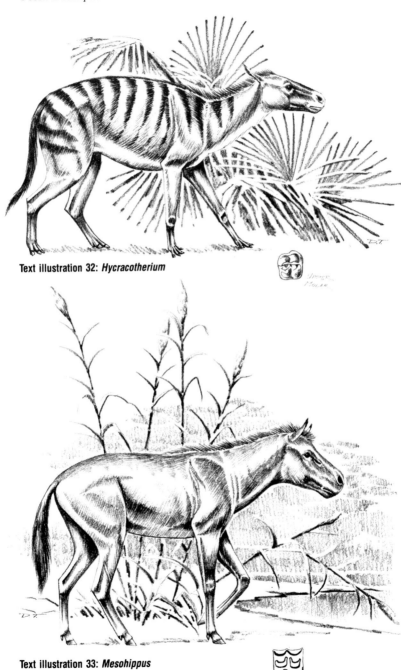

Text illustration 32: *Hycracotherium*

Text illustration 33: *Mesohippus*

Text illustration 34: *Equus*

Tapirus excelus (Photo 470)
. Pleistocene epoch. A tapir common to Texas during the late Quaternary period.

Rhinocerotidae (Photos 471, 472, Text Illustration 35)
Eocene epoch through recent. The earlier rhinos were small by modern standards and generally lacked horns. The distinctive W-shaped enamel pattern of the molar teeth is a common identifying mark.

Platygonus compressus (Photo 473, Text Illustration 36)
Pleistocene. A fossil pig with a flattened snout. Tusks fairly well-developed.

Tanupolama mirifica (Photo 474)
Pleistocene. A medium-sized fossil llama. Common 15,000 years ago in South Texas.

Text illustration 35: *Rhinocerotidae*

Text illustration 36: *Playtygonus compressus*

Camelops (Photos 475, 476, 477, 478, Text Illustration 37)

Pleistocene. Texas's most common fossil camel. Moderate in size and humpless. The metapodial (ankle) bone is distinctive because of its separated ends ("splayed"). Canine teeth are curved and fairly large. Other camels, some much larger than modern camels, lived in Texas.

Bison antiquus (Photo 480, Text Illustration 38)

Pleistocene. Bison teeth are the most-encountered fossils of these large grazing animals. The teeth are two to three inches long if root is intact and one inch across. Top of tooth is flat with enamel pattern featuring a loop bent almost horseshoe-shaped. *B. latifrons*, an early species, had huge horns, six feet from tip to tip. *B. antiquus* is a moderately wide-horned species often found with remains of earliest man in North America. *B. bison* comes out of fossil times to the recent and is the animal we still see alive today.

Text illustration 37: *Camelops*

Text illustration 38

Bison bison

Bison antiquus

Bison latifrons

Mammuthus americanus (American mastodon) (Color Photo 53, Text Illustration 39)

Pleistocene. An elephant relative, somewhat smaller and stockier than a mammoth. Mastodon teeth are distinctly different from mammoth teeth. Mastodon teeth have raised pointy cusps for chewing twigs and woody foods. Mammoth teeth, by contrast, are flat-topped.

Text illustration 39: *Mammuthus americanus* (American Mastodon)

OCCLUSAL VIEW OF THIRD
MOLAR

Elephas sp. cf. columbi (Texas Columbian mammoth) (Color Photos 54, 55, Text Illustration 40)

Pleistocene. A true and direct relative of modern elephants. Teeth are flat-topped with prominent cross ridges of enamel. Mammoths apparently ate more grass than did the pointy-toothed mastodons. It is customary to consider most Texas mammoths to be Columbian mammoths. The tooth-enamel folds on many Texas teeth, however, are more widely spaced (ten to twelve to the tooth) than the common formulas for Columbian mammoths would prescribe. Experts ascribe the difference to local variation. The term *imperial mammoth, Elephas imperator,* is reserved only for the outlandishly large specimens with large teeth having twenty or more enameled plates. The woolly mammoth, *E. primagenius,* has never been found in Texas. It was a northern species adapted to very cold climates.

Text illustration 40: *Elephas sp. cf. columbi* (Texas Columbian Mammoth)

Appendix:

Geological Area Maps of Texas

Chapter 2 provides an overall discussion of Texas' geologic past and a map relating to the various time periods. The following pages contain simple, yet detailed maps of the geological formations found in the distinct areas of Texas defined by the key map. Cities and major roads and rivers are included to aid in locating the area of your interest. Geologic symbols on the individual maps can be compared to the following chart to get an approximate idea of the name and age of each geological location. For more precise information, you can obtain very detailed maps from the Bureau of Economic Geology in Austin, Texas.

Era	Mill./Yrs.	Period	Epoch/Group	Symbol
Cenozoic	0	Quaternary	Recent	Qh
			Pleistocene	Qp
	5	Tertiary	Pliocene	Tp
	20		Miocene	Tm
	30		Oligocene	To
	40		Eocene	Te_4 (Jackson)
				Te_3 (Claiborne)
	60			Te_2 (Wilcox)
	65		Paleocene	Te_1 (Midway)
Mesozoic		Cretaceous (Upper)	Navarro	Kuu_2
	70		Taylor	Kuu_1
	85		Austin	Kul_c
	90		Bouquillas/	Kul in W. Texas/
			Eagle Ford	Kul_b or Kul_2
	95		Woodbine	Kul_a or Kul_1
	100	Cretaceous (Lower)	Washita	Kl_c
	110		Fredericksburg	Kl_b
	120		Trinity (Antlers)	Kl_a
	135	Jurassic*	Malone	J
	185	Triassic	Dockum	Tr
Paleozoic	225	Permian	Guadalupian	Pg_2 (Whitehorse)
				Pg_1 (El Reno)
			Leonardian	Pl_2
				Pl_1
	270		Wolfcampian	Pw
		Pennsylvanian	Cisco	IPv
			Canyon	IPmi
	300		Strawn	IPd
			Bend	IPa or IPm
	325	Mississippian		M
	350	Devonian		D
	440	Silurian		S
	475	Ordovician		O
	550	Cambrian	Upper	ε
Precambrian	1200		Van Horn	$pε_3$
			Packsaddle	$pε_2$
			Valley Spring	
			Allamoore	
	2000		Carrizo Mt.	$pε_1$

*Malone outcrops are now known to be Cretaceous.

Appendix Key Map

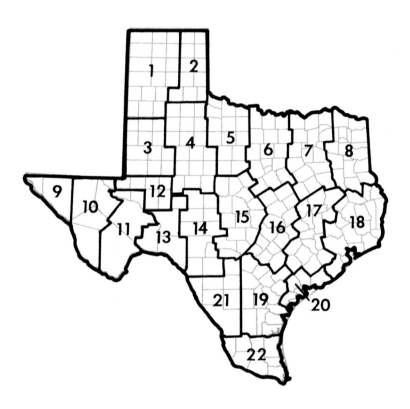

Area 1

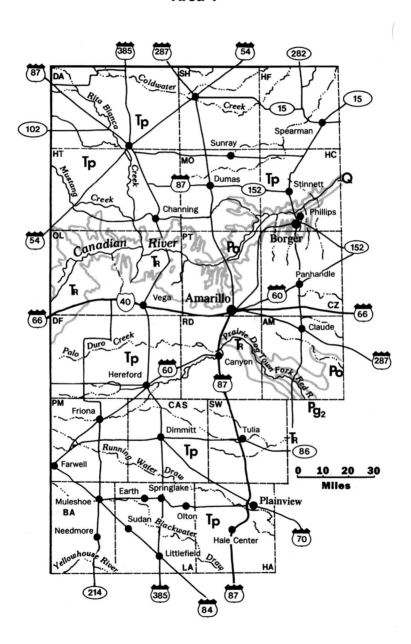

Area 2

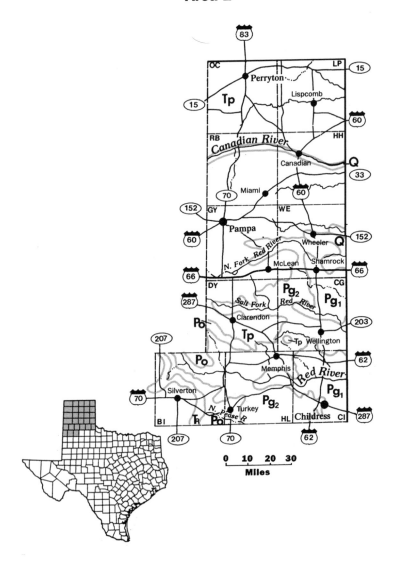

0   10   20   30
Miles

Area 3

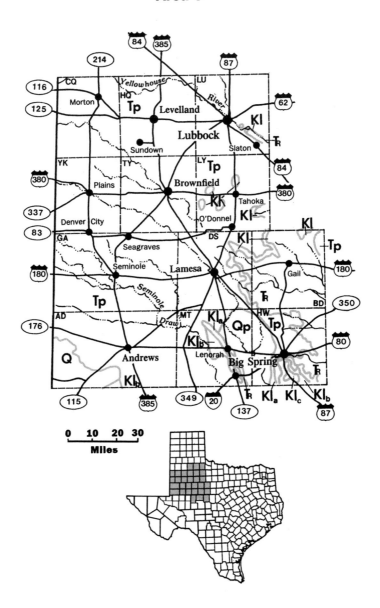

0 10 20 30
Miles

Area 4

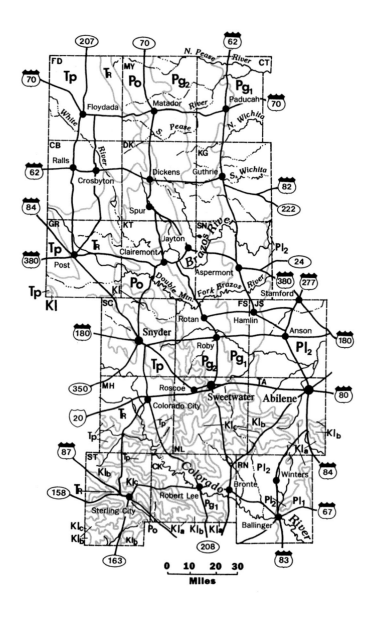

Area 5

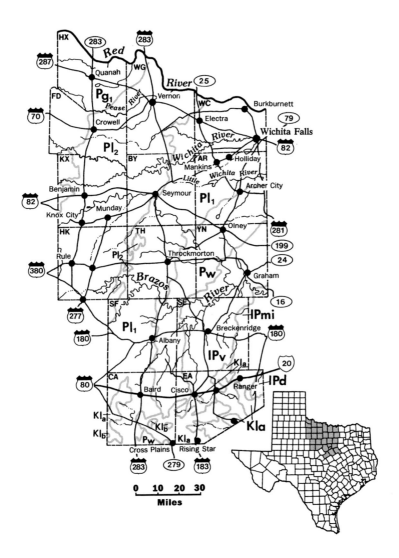

0   10   20   30
Miles

Area 6

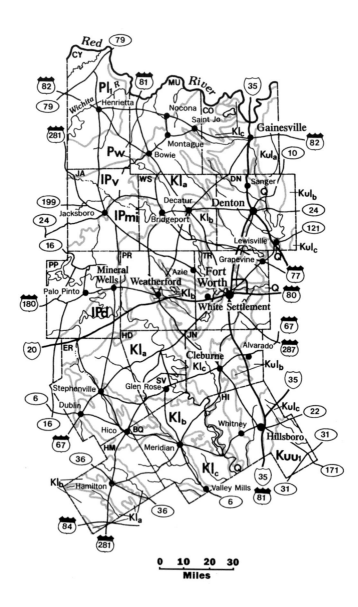

Area 7

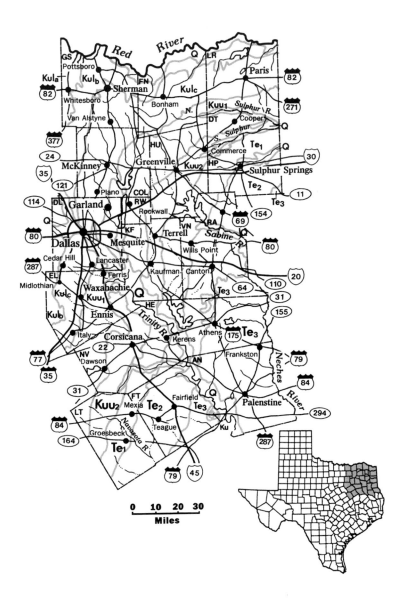

Area 8

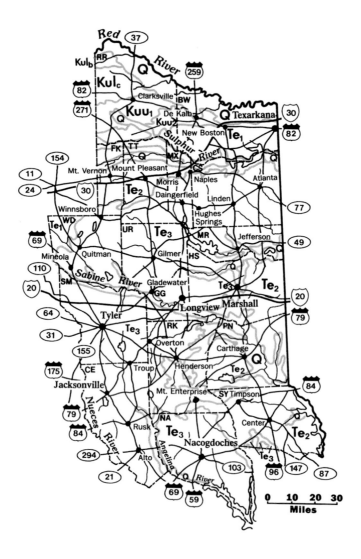

Area 9

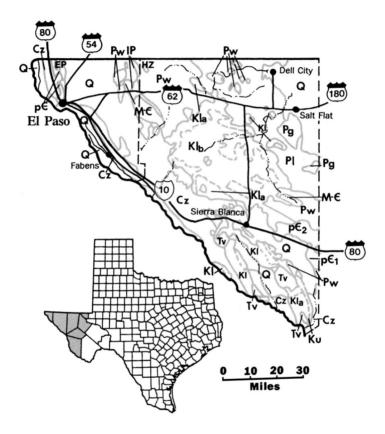

Area 10

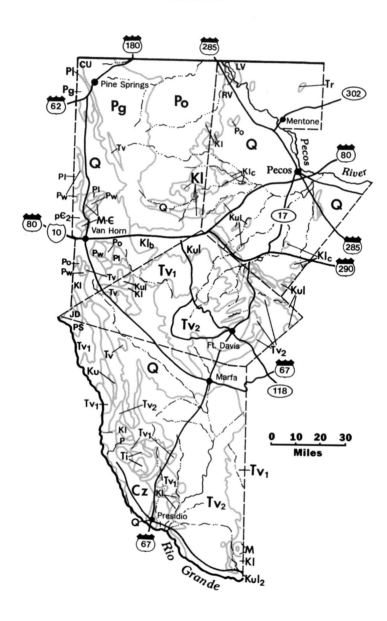

Area 11

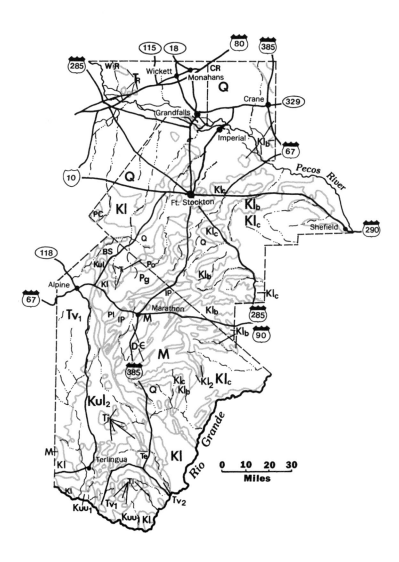

Area 12

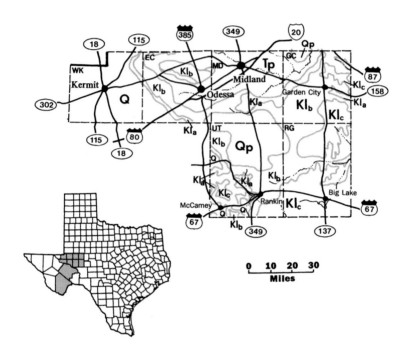

Area 13

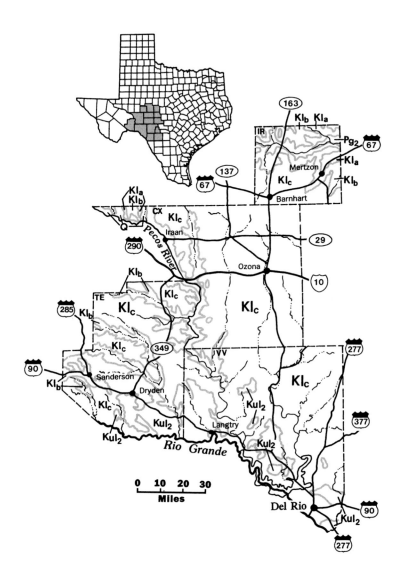

Area 14

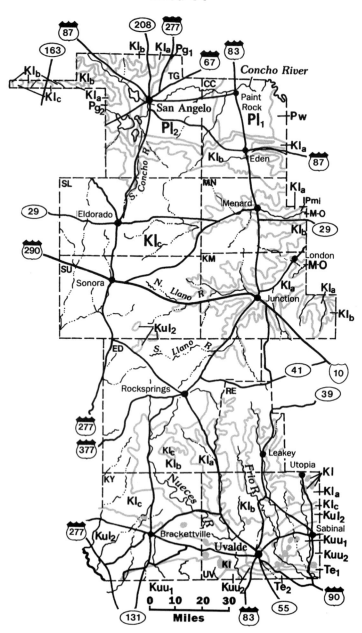

Area 15

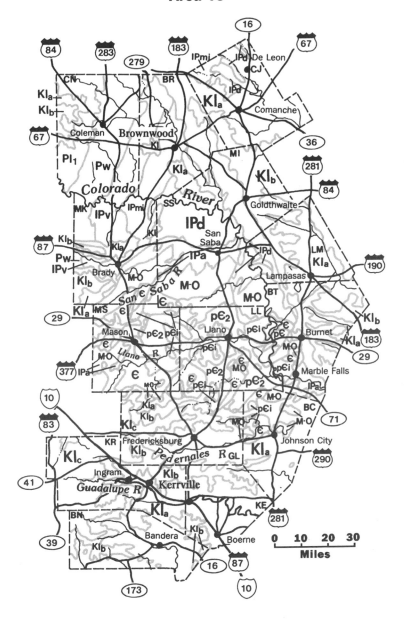

Area 16

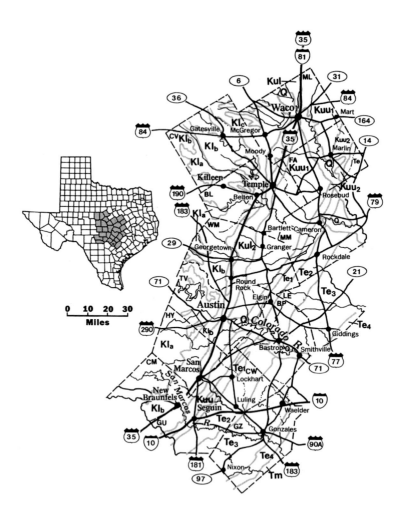

Area 17

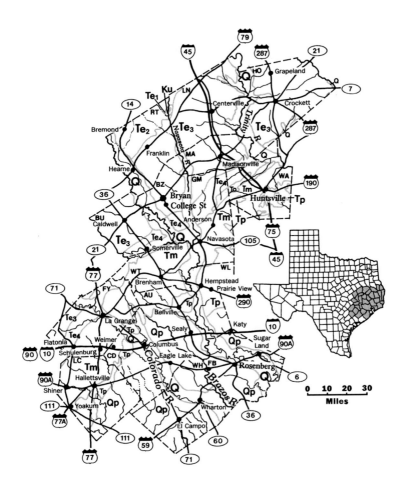

Area 18

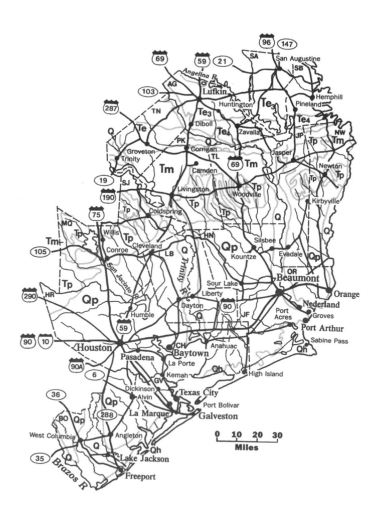

Area 19

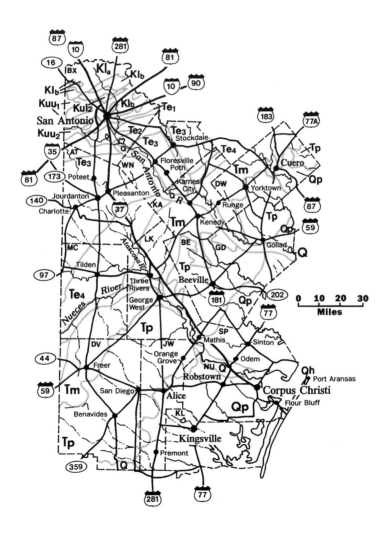

Area 20

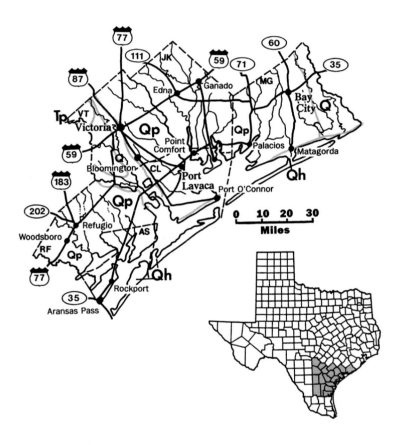

Area 21

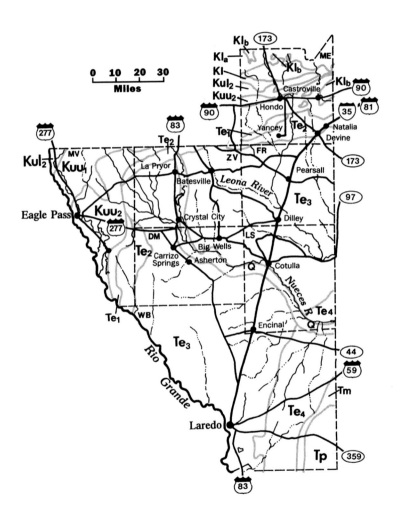

Area 22

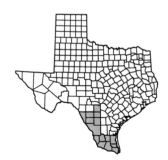

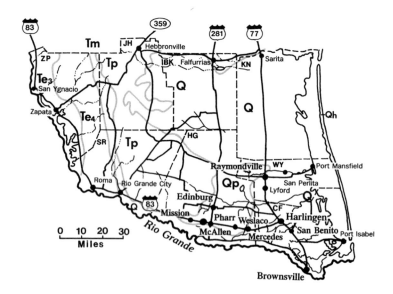

Glossary

Acute. Steep or very strongly shaped; not mild.

aff. Abbreviation for *affinis,* meaning "bears a resemblance to."

Alternating. Varying regularly, like "long-short-long," usually of only two changing elements.

Alternation of generations. In plants; two different growth forms, one producing spores and the next a sexual form. These occur alternately in the progressive reproductive history of the plant; first a spore stage and then a sexual stage.

Ambulacral area. On echinoids; one of five radiating areas of pores that form a five-rayed star on the test. See "interambulacral area."

Ambulacral grooves. On some echinoids the ambulacral areas are sunken in to form grooves.

Angular. Sharp angled; not smooth or even; jutting.

Anterior. To the front; "in front of."

Aperture. An opening; specifically, the main opening.

Apical. At the summit; on echinoids, where the five ambulacral areas meet.

Appendages. Leg or armlike structures.

Articulate. To fit together well; hinged.

Articulating faces. The ends of bones or other structures that in life hinge together or work next to each other in a hinging manner.

Asymmetrical. Not showing symmetry.

Attachment point. The flattened area or scar left by the fact that the fossil was once connected to something, for instance, another neighboring fossil.

Axis. A central portion; the middle of several parts.

Basal. At the base or bottom side.

Beak. Any curved, pointed structure; especially in brachiopod and bivalve descriptions.

Bilateral. Having two sides fairly much alike; often called "bilateral symmetry."

Bivalve. The group containing clams and oysters; an older term for the group is *pelecypoda*. Among similar creatures not included in *Bivalva* are brachiopods and snails.

Calcareous. Made up of calcium carbonate; see "calcified."

Calcified. Reinforced by addition of calcium carbonate, a common organically deposited mineral known as *calcite*.

Calcite. Mineral composed of calcium carbonate. It may be clear, yellowish, red, or brown (rarely other colors). It is harder than a fingernail scratch, but scratchable fairly easily by a copper penny. Fizzes in weak acid.

Callus. On snails (gastropods), an occasional covering over the operculum, an opening between whorls.

Calyx. (Pl. calices or calyxes.) The cuplike living compartment of one coral animal; cuplike part of a crinoid above the stem and below any arms.

Canal. A long, thin depression; in snails (gastropods) the slit in the siphon. See "siphon."

Cancellate. A pattern caused by intersecting lines forming a network of bumpy intersections.

Canine teeth. Usually very long, pointed grasping teeth; near, but not usually at, the front of the mouth.

Carnivorous. Adapted for meat-eating; grasping, tearing shapes.

Cartilage. A flexible tissue that is less firm than bone and that is usually formed instead of bone in situations needing flexibility in animals or in primitive structures such as the backbone of sharks.

Carapace. The covering on the back of a crab; the top part of a turtle shell.

Centrum. The rounded or bulky main portion of a vertebra, excluding any side, top, or bottom projections.

Cephalon. The head, or front, portion of a trilobite; see also "glabella." Other trilobite portions in this relationship are the thorax and pygidium.

cf. Abbreviation for *confer,* Latin for "compares favorably to."

Chevron. A V-shaped structure. In vertebrate tails, a V-shaped bone structure under the tail for channeling vessels.

Chitin. A plasticlike tissue composing the stiff parts of insects, crabs, and other arthropods.

Colonial. More than one animal living together, often forming one combined fossil structure.

Columella. A rising shaft in the middle of a coral calyx. In snails (gastropods) a shaft of dense shell at the center of the shell whorls.

Compressed. Pushed together; flattened over an area.

Concave. Sunken in; depressed.

Concentric. Shaped into rings that are around a common center.

Concretion. A limestone or reddish iron ore lump that forms around a fossil by percolation of ground water through other softer rock layers (eg., shales). Can falsely resemble a bone or other fossil. Septarian concretions are those that are cracked into small compartments separated by calcite veins.

Convex. The opposite of concave; bulged out.

Coprolite. Fossilized dung; it is fairly common as a fossil.

Coquina. Any rock made up largely of shell fragments, especially small clams.

Corallite. The structure built by one coral animal.

Corallum. The combined structure built by several coral animals living colonially together.

Costa(ae); costellate. Having a rather regular radiating pattern of ridges.

Cranium. The larger, upper mass of a skull, excluding the lower jaw (mandible).

Crenulate. Similar to saw-toothed, but with rounded teeth; scalloped.

Crown. The part of a tooth above the original gumline. In crinoids, the combined calyx cup and arms.

Crustacean. Of or like the crabs and shrimp.

Cusp. A raised portion of the enamel of a tooth.

Depressed. Sunken in.

Disseptiments. A bryozoan and coral term referring to cross-branches between arms of a lacey bryozoan colony or between septa of a coral.

Domed. High with broadly round shape.

Dorsal. On the upper side of the living animal; in vertebrates it is the spinal side. The opposite of ventral.

Elevated. Higher; raised.

Elliptical. Somewhat football shaped; an ellipse.

Elongate. Stretched out long.

Encrust. To grow on top of something, covering it over.

Fasiole. On echinoids; a weak, hard to see band of different texture running across or around some part of the test. Often mentioned in classification, fasioles are seldom well-preserved. The most common kind circles the ambulacral areas and is called a "peripetalous fasiole." Used little in this book.

Foramina. Pl. of foramen, meaning "an opening."

Form genus. A group of species that look superficially alike but are probably in need of new classifications. A useful term as a catch-all, practical category if one realizes that the apparent relationships are not likely to be biologically real. A traditional category.

Fossulae. Major divisions, or groups, of coral septa.

Genera. Plural of *genus*. A closest related grouping of different species.

Genus. A grouping of closely related species. In a Latin binomial name, it is the first and always capitalized of the two terms; eg., *Exogyra ponderosa,* the genus is *Exogyra.*

Glabella. Only the central lobe of a trilobite's head (cephalon); the portion to which the eyes attach.

Globose. Fat and rounded.

Granule. A small bump (pl. granular).

Holocene. "Biologically modern times." Time since the Pleistocene epoch.

Horizontal. Across the piece (like the horizon) when the piece is in its living position or a commonly viewed position.

Imperforate. Not perforated (punctured); not having a hole in it.

Inarticulate. A brachiopod term for the two valves being only loosely connected without a well-defined hinge.

Incisor teeth. In mammals, the frontmost nipping teeth; teeth in front of the canines. These form the tusks in elephants and some other mammals.

Inclined. Slanted.

Index fossil. A fossil that is distinctive of one geographic area or specific geologic time, so as to be useful as an indicator of that time or place.

Inflated. Roundly enlarged.

Infra-. A prefix meaning "in-between."

Interambulacral area. On echinoids; the portions of an echinoid test between the five rays of the ambulacral areas.

Involute. In coiled shells, meaning one whorl overlaps the earlier whorls.

Keel. A ridge resembling at least partly the keel of a sailboat (a ridge on its bottom). Often when the middle of something is ridged-up it is called "keeled."

Labial. The side of a tooth facing the lip; the outer side.

Lateral. Refering to the side; on the side.

Lingual. The side of a tooth facing the tongue; the inner surface.

Living chamber. In cephalopods, the outer chamber; the one in which the animal lived. It is always much larger than the other older chambers.

Lobe. A trilobite term; trilobites have a central (axial) lobe and, on each side of it, lateral lobes. These are the three lobes, running longwise of the trilobite, which give trilobites (tri#three) their name. In cephalopods, a bend in the suture line that curves away from the aperture (big end) of the shell.

Lobed. A wavy shape so deep as to almost cut off its deep undulations, making lobes.

Longitudinal. Generally refering to lines or long structures that run the long dimension of the fossil.

Madreporite. Usually the largest plate among several small plates at the apical system of echinoids; generally shows many very tiny perforations.

Mammillae. Small, narrow projections.

Mandible. The lower jaw; has two halves, left and right.

Margin. Edge; the rim of something.

Massive. Big; thick.

Matrix. The dirt or rock surrounding the fossil.

Maxilla. The bone holding the upper teeth; opposite the mandible.

Molar teeth. Somewhat flattened, grinding teeth; toward the back of the jaw when other kinds of teeth are present.

Muscle scar. A roughened area where a muscle once attached to a shell or bone.

Neural spine. The top spine on a living positioned vertebra.

Nodes. Points for the attachment of some structure or structures; in some cases only the appearance of such attachments as knobs or bulges.

Nutritive groove. An up-and-down groove on one face of a tooth root.

Operculum. The horny covering over the aperture (opening) of a snail (gastropod).

Ornament. Lines, tubercles, or other forms or textures that decorate the fossil's exterior.

Oval. Egg shaped.

Ovate. Much the same as oval.

Pelvis. The hip bone.

Perforate. Punctured; having a hole in it.

Periproct. The anal opening in an echinoid test. In "regular" urchins it is centrally located atop the test; in "irregular" urchins it has moved to the rear or to the underside of the test.

Peristome. The oral (mouth) opening in an echinoid test. In "regular" urchins it is centrally located on the underside of the test; in "irregular" urchins it often has moved slightly forward of center.

Pinnule. Small, leaflet-like division of a fern leaf (frond).

Pore. Small opening.

Posterior. To the rear.

Primary. Large; most important.

Pseudofossil. A false fossil; often just a tempting-looking rock.

Pygidium. (Pl. pygidia.) The tail portion of a trilobite.

Rachis. The midrib of a leaf or fern frond.

Radial plates. Plates in a crinoid cup at the base of each arm.

Radiating. Coming out in a star pattern from a central area or point.

Recurved. Curved first one way and then the opposite way.

Redeposited. A bed of rock or fossils that was originally deposited in one setting and then moved by erosion or other natural forces to be laid down elsewhere. Such a fossil may be much older than the bed in which it is redeposited.

Reticulated. A netlike pattern.

Reworked. Similar to redeposited, but may have been disturbed or eroded and put back down in the original beds; often shows wear suffered after death.

Rib. Obviously a bone in a vertebrate animal's chest area, but widely used on invertebrates to mean closely spaced parallel or evenly radiating raised lines or ridges.

Rostrum. A forward projection; a frontmost part.

Saddle. A down-curving feature. In cephalopod sutures, a curve toward the aperture (big end) of the shell.

Salicified. Fossilized by replacement with silica (quartz).

Secondary. The second level of some feature, usually slightly less in size or prominence.

Septa. (Pl. of septum.) The centrally radiating dividers that look like spokes of a wheel in the cups of most corals; or any similarly dividing wall in any fossil. That which marks off compartments or chambers.

Serrate. Saw-tooth textured; may be very fine or very large.

Siphon. In snails (gastropods), the extension of the end of the shell opposite the pointed spire.

Siphuncle. A tube leading back through old chambers in cephalopods.

Spire. Any very high area; on snails (gastropods) it means the pointed end of the shell.

Solitary. Occurring alone as opposed to colonial; free-standing.

Steinkern. A cast, usually being formed in a mold and lacking great detail. A German term meaning "stone core."

Striations. Fine lines, usually indented into a surface.

Strut. A long, thin structure, connected to something on both ends.

Sub-. A prefix meaning "lightly less than"; thus "subtriangular" means slightly less than triangular. In classification "subfamily" means a slightly smaller group than a whole family.

Sulcus. A brachiopod term for a deep furrow marking the middle of one shell-half (valve). A sulcus on one valve is usually matched by an upward fold in the other valve. In other fossils, any deep long depression.

Suture. A line showing the meeting place of two parts of a fossil. In cephalopods, the joining line between shell chambers. In vertebrates, the knitting point of various juvenile bones, eg., skull sutures.

Symmetry. (Adj., symmetrical.) "Matched shape," usually in reference to some point; eg., "radial symmetry" means "matching shape around a center point." "Bilateral symmetry" means "matching shape on two sides."

Synonymous. "Same as." When two species (or genera) are found to be actually the same, the more recent name is made a synonym of the older name.

Tabulae. (Pl.) In corals, the horizontal partitions of a corallite that divide it into ascending levels.

Terminating. Ending.

Test. Among Foraminifera and Echinoidea almost the same as "shell"; the exterior hard part of many animals.

Thoracic. Regarding the chest area; the area of greatest rib attachment.

Thorax. The middle portion of most creatures; on a trilobite it is the area from front to back, between the cephalon and pygidium.

Truncated. Cut off; as in a "truncated cone," which is a cone with the point cut off.

Truncation. That place which is cut off or flattened. See "truncated."

Tubercle. A small surface projection, often "wartlike."

Umbilicus. In snails (gastropods), a small opening left by the coils not completely touching. May be grown over by a callus. In cephalopods, a small depressed area right in the middle of the coiled whorls.

Undulating. Wavy.

Valve. One part of the two-part bivalve or brachiopods shell.

Varices. (Pl. of varix.) Bumpy lines on a snail, marking old aperture locations as growth progressed.

Venter. In cephalopods, the outer edge of the curve of the shell.

Ventral. The underside of the living animal; in vertebrates it is the rib cage side. The opposite of dorsal.

Vertical. Up and down when the piece was in its living position or is being viewed in its most ordinary position.

Whorled. Spiraling or arranged around some point. In plants: a group of leaves around the stem at one point. In shells: a spiral arrangement; the "body whorl" is the outer whorl.

Zoecium. (Pl. zoecia.) The small pits in which live the individual bryozoan animals of a colony.

Bibliography

Adkins, W[alter] S. 1918 (1920). *The Weno and Pawpaw Formations of the Texas Comanchean.* Univ. of Texas Bull., vol. 1856. Austin: University of Texas.

———. 1928. *Handbook of Texas Cretaceous Fossils.* Univ. of Texas Bull., vol. 2838. Austin: University of Texas.

———. 1930. Texas Comanchean echinoids of the genus *Macraster.* In *Contributions to Geology, 1930,* pp. 101-138. Univ. of Texas Bull., vol. 3001. Austin: University of Texas.

———. 1933. The Mesozoic systems of Texas. In *The Geology of Texas,* eds. E. H. Sellards, W. S. Adkins, and F. B. Plummer, pp. 239-518. Univ. of Texas Bull., vol. 3232. Austin: University of Texas

Adkins, W. S., and Arick, M. B. 1930. *The Geology of Bell County, Texas.* Univ. of Texas Bull., vol. 3016. Austin: University of Texas.

Akers, Rosemary E., and Akers, Thomas J. 1987. *Texas Cretaceous Echinoids.* Texas Paleo. Series, no. 3. Houston: Houston Gem and Mineral Society, Paleo. Section.

Akersten, William A. 1970. *Red Light Fauna (Blancan) of the Love Formation, Southeastern Hudspeth County, Texas.* Texas Memorial Muse. Bull., vol. 20. Austin: Texas Memorial Museum, University of Texas.

Albritton, C. C., Jr. 1938. Stratigraphy and structure of the Malone Mountains, Texas. *Geological Soc. of Amer. Bulletin* 49: 1747-1806.

Auffenberg, Walter. 1964. *A New Fossil Tortoise from the Texas Miocene, With Remarks on the Probable Geologic History of Tortoises in Eastern U. S.* Pearce-Sellards Series, no. 3. Austin: Texas Memorial Museum, University of Texas.

Austin Paleontological Society. N.d. [1980?] *Texas Fossil Localities.* Austin: Austin Paleontological Society.

Bardack, David. 1969. *Anatomy and Evolution of Chirocentrid Fishes.* Paleo. Contributions, vol. 40. Lawrence: University of Kansas.

Barnes, Virgil E., et al. 1972. *Geology of the Llano Region and Austin Area, Field Excursion.* Guidebook no. 13. Austin: Bureau of Economic Geology, University of Texas at Austin.

Berry, William B. N. 1960. *Graptolite Faunas of the Marathon Region, West Texas.* Univ. of Texas Pub. 6005. Austin: University of Texas.

Boese, Emil. 1928. *Cretaceous Ammonites from Texas and Northern Mexico.* Univ. of Texas Bull., vol. 2748. Austin: University of Texas.

Brand, John P. 1952. *Cretaceous of the Llano Estacado of Texas.* Report of Investigations, no. 20. Austin: Bureau of Economic Geology, University of Texas.

Bullard, Fred M. 1931. *The Geology of Grayson County, Texas.* Univ. of Texas Bull., vol. 3125. Austin: University of Texas.

Bybee, H. P., and Bullard, F. M. 1927. *The Geology of Cooke County, Texas.* Univ. of Texas Bull., vol. 2710. Austin: University of Texas.

Calahan, L. W. 1939. Diagnostic fossils of the Ark-La-Tex area. In *Shreveport Geological Society Guidebook, 14th Annual Fieldtrip,* pp. 36-56. Shreveport: Shreveport Geological Society.

Casanova, Richard, and Ratkevich, Ronald P. 1981. *An Illustrated Guide to Fossil Collecting.* 3d ed. Happy Camp, Ca.: Naturegraph Publishers.

Case, E. C. 1922. *New Reptiles and Stegocephalians from the Upper Triassic of Western Texas.* Washington, D. C.: Carnegie Institution.

Case, Gerard R. 1973. *Fossil Sharks: A Pictorial Review.* New York: Pioneer Litho Co., Inc.

Caster, K. E. 1945. A New Jellyfish (*Kirklandia texana* Caster) from the Lower Cretaceous of Texas. *Paleontographica Americana* 3: 168-220.

Chamberlain, C. Kent. 1970. Permian trilobite species from central Wyoming and west Texas. *Journal of Paleontology* 44: 1049-54.

Cloud, P. E., Barnes, V. E., and Hass, W. H. 1957. *Devonian-Mississippian Transition in Central Texas.* Report of Investigations, no. 31. Austin: Bureau of Economic Geology, University of Texas.

Cobban, W. A. 1953. Cenomanian ammonite fauna from the Mosby sandstone of central Montana. Professional Paper no. 243-D. Washington, D.C.: United States Geological Survey.

Conrad, Timothy A. 1857. Descriptions of Cretaceous and Tertiary fossils. In *Report of the United States and Mexican Boundary Survey,* ed. W. H. Emory, vol. 1, pt. 2, pp. 141-174. Washington, D.C.: U. S. Government Printing Office.

Coogan, Alan H. 1977. Early and middle Cretaceous *Hippuritacea* (rudists) of the Gulf Coast. In *Cretaceous Carbonates of Texas and Mexico,* pp. 32-68. Report of Investigations, no. 89. Austin: Bureau of Economic Geology, University of Texas.

Cooke, C. W. 1946. Comanche echinoids. *Journal of Paleontology* 20: 193-237.

Cragin, F. W. 1893. A contribution to the invertebrate paleontology of the Texas Cretaceous. *Geological Survey of Texas.* Annual Report, no. 4, pt. 2, pp. 141-294. Austin: State of Texas.

Damon, H. G., and McNutt, G. R. 1940. The Cretaceous formations in the vicinity of Austin. *Geological Society of America Guidebook,* 53rd Annual Meeting, pp. 3-15. Lawrence, Ks.: Geological Society of America.

Debrock, M. D., Hoare, R. D., and Mapes, R. H. 1984. Pennsylvanian (Desmoinesean) *Polyplacophora (Mollusca)* from Texas. *Journal of Paleontology* 58: 1117-35.

Decker, Charles E. 1944. *The Wilberns Upper Cambrian graptolites from Mason, Texas,* pp. 13-61. Univ. of Texas Pub. 4401. Austin: University of Texas.

Dunkle, D. H. 1958. Three North American Cretaceous fishes. *Proceedings of the U. S. National Museum.* 108: 269-77.

Echols, Joan. 1972. Biostratigraphy and reptile faunas of the upper Austin and Taylor groups (Upper Cretaceous) of Texas, with special reference to Hunt, Fannin, Lamar and Delta counties, Texas. Ph. D. dissertation, University of Oklahoma.

Emerson, Barbara and John, and Akers, Rosemary and Thomas. 1994. *Texas Cretaceous Ammonites and Nautiloids,* Texas Paleontology Series, Publication No. 5, Paleontology Section, Houston Gem and Mineral Society, 10805 Brooklet, Houston, Texas 77099.

Flatt, Carl D. 1976. *Origin and Significance of the Oyster Banks in the Walnut Clay Formation, Central Texas.* Baylor Geological Studies Bull., vol. 30. Waco: Baylor University.

Gardner, Julia. 1935. *The Midway Group of Texas.* Univ. of Texas Bull., vol. 3301. Austin: University of Texas.

Gries, Robbie R. 1970. Carboniferous stratigraphy, western San Saba County, Texas. Ph. D. dissertation, University of Texas at Austin.

Henderson, G. C. 1928. *The Geology of Tom Green County.* Univ. of Texas Bull., vol. 2807. Austin: University of Texas.

Hendricks, Leo. 1957. *The Geology of Parker County, Texas.* Univ. of Texas Bull., vol. 5724. Austin: University of Texas.

Herbert, John H. et al. 1990. *Texas Pennsylvanian Brachiopods,* Texas Paleontology Series, Publication No. 4, Paleontology Section, Houston Gem and Mineral Society, 10805 Brooklet, Houston, Texas 77099.

Hessler, Robert R. 1963. Lower Mississippian trilobites of the family Proetidae in the United States. pt. 1. *Journal of Paleontology* 37: 543-52.
– – –. 1965. Lower Mississippian trilobites of the family Proetidae in the United States. pt. 2. *Journal of Paleontology* 39: 37-40.

Hill, R. T., and Vaughan, T. W. 1898. *The Lower Cretaceous Gryphaeas of the Texas Region.* U. S. G. S. Bull., vol. 151. Washington, D.C.: United States Geological Survey.

Ikins, W. C. 1949. Stratigraphy and paleontology of the Walnut and Comanche Peak formations. Ph. D. dissertation, University of Texas.

Kauffman, Erle G. 1977. Illustrated guide to biostratigraphically important Cretaceous macrofossils, western interior basin, U.S.A. *Mountain Geologist* 14: 225-74.

Kelly, K. V., Jr. 1971. *Kelley's Guide to Fossil Sharks.* Gainesville, Fla.: K.V. Kelley, Jr.

Kier, R. S., Brown, L. F., and McBride, E. F. 1980. The Mississippian and Pennsylvanian (carboniferous) systems in the United States – Texas. Circular no. 80-14. Austin: Bureau of Economic Geology, University of Texas at Austin.

King, R. H. 1938. Pennsylvanian sponges of north-central Texas. *Journal of Paleontology* 12: 498-504.

Kniker, Hedwig T. 1918. *Comanchean and Cretaceous Pectinidae of Texas.* Univ. of Texas Bull., vol. 1817. Austin: University of Texas.

Laughbaum, Lloyd R. 1960. A paleoecologic study of the upper Denton formation, Tarrant, Denton and Cooke counties, Texas. *Journal of Paleontology* 34: 1183-97.

Lee, Wallace, Nickell, C. O., Williams, J. S., and Henbest, L. G. 1938. *Stratigraphic and Paleontologic Studies of the Pennsylvanian and Permian Rocks in North-Central Texas.* Univ. of Texas Pub. 3801. Austin: University of Texas.

Liddle, R. A. 1918. *The Geology and Mineral Resources of Medina County.* Univ. of Texas Bull., vol. 1860. Austin: University of Texas.

Lozo, F. E., et al. 1959. *Symposium on the Edwards Limestone in Central Texas.* Univ. of Texas Pub. 5905. Austin: University of Texas.

MacDonald, James Reid. 1983. *The Fossil Collector's Handbook: A Paleontology Field Guide.* Englewood Cliffs, N.J.: Prentice- Hall.

MacFall, Russell P., and Wollin, Jay C. 1972. *Fossils for Amateurs.* New York: Van Nostrand.

Matthews, William H., III. 1960. *Texas Fossils: An Amateur Collector's Handbook.* Guidebook no. 2. Austin: Bureau of Economic Geology, University of Texas.

McAnulty, Wm. N. 1955. *Geology of Cathedral Mt. Quadrangle, Brewster County, Texas.* Report of Investigations, no. 25. Austin: Bureau of Economic Geology, University of Texas.

Meade, Grayson E. 1944. *The Blanco Fauna,* pp. 509-557. Univ. of Texas Pub. 4401. Austin: University of Texas.

Meyer, Robert Lee. 1974. Late Cretaceous Elasmobranchs (sharks) from the Mississippian and east Texas embayments of the Gulf coastal plain. Ph.D. dissertation, Southern Methodist University.

Moon, C. G. 1953. *Geology of Agua Fria Quadrangle, Brewster County, Texas.* Report of Investigations, no. 15. Austin: Bureau of Economic Geology, University of Texas.

Moore, Clyde H., Jr. 1964. *Stratigraphy of the Fredericksburg Division, South-Central Texas.* Report of Investigations, no. 52. Austin: Bureau of Economic Geology, University of Texas.

Moore, Raymond C., ed. 1957 – . *Treatise on Invertebrate Paleontology..* Lawrence, Ks.: Geological Society of America.

Moore, Raymond C., and Plummer, F. B. 1939. Crinoids from the upper carboniferous and Permian strata in Texas. In *Contributions to Geology, 1939,* pp. 9-468. Univ. of Texas Pub. 3945. Austin: University of Texas.

Moreman, Walter L. 1942. Paleontology of the Eagle Ford group of north and central Texas. *Journal of Paleontology* 16: 192- 220.

Newell, Norman D., et al. 1953. *The Permian Reef Complex of the Guadalupe Mountains Region, Texas and New Mexico.* San Francisco: W. H. Freeman and Co.

Norton, George H. 1965. Surface geology of Dallas County, Texas. In *The Geology of Dallas County,* pp. 40-94. Dallas: Dallas Geological Society.

Offeman, Irene D., et al. 1982. *Texas Cretaceous Bivalves and Localities.* Texas Paleo. Series, no. 2. Houston: Houston Gem and Mineral Society, Paleo. Section.

Olson, Everett C., and Beerbower, James R. 1953. The San Angelo formation, Permian of Texas, and its vertebrates. *Journal of Geology* 61: 389-423.

Perkins, Bob F. 1960. *Biostratigraphic Studies in the Comanche (Cretaceous) Series of Northern Mexico and Texas.* Memoir no. 83. Lawrence, Ks.: Geological Society of America.

Plummer, F. B., and Hornberger, Joseph. 1935. *Geology of Palo Pinto County.* Univ. of Texas Bull., vol. 3534. Austin: University of Texas.
– – –. 1943. *The Carboniferous Rocks of the Llano Region of Central Texas.* Univ. of Texas Bull., vol. 4329. Austin: University of Texas.

Renick, B. Coleman. 1936. *The Jackson Group and the Cata-houla and Oakville Formations in a Part of the Texas Gulf Coastal Plain.* Univ. of Texas Bull., vol. 3619. Austin: University of Texas.

Rhodes, Frank H. T. 1962. *Fossils: A Guide to Prehistoric Life.* New York: Golden Press.

Roberts, J. R., and Nash, Wm. 1918. *The Geology of Val Verde County.* Univ. of Texas Bull., vol. 1803. Austin: University of Texas.

Roemer, Ferdinand. 1852. *Die Kreidebildungen von Texas, und ihre organischen Einschlusse* (The Chalk Formations of Texas and Their Organic Inclusions). Bonn: Adolph Marcus.

Romer, A. S. 1966. *Vertebrate Paleontology.* 3rd ed. Chicago: University of Chicago Press.

Russell, Dale A. 1967. *Systematics and Morphology of American Mosasaurs.* Bulletin no. 23. New Haven: Peabody Museum of Natural History, Yale University.

Scott, Gayle. 1939. Cephalopods from the Cretaceous Trinity group of the south-central United States. In *Contributions to Geology, 1939,* pp. 969-1097. Univ. of Texas Pub. 3945. Austin: University of Texas.

Scott, Gayle, and Armstrong, J. M. 1932. *The Geology of Wise County, Texas,* pp. 41-63. Univ. of Texas Bull., vol. 3224. Austin: University of Texas.

Sellards, E. H. 1920. *Geology and Mineral Resources of Bexar County.* Univ. of Texas Bull., vol. 1932. Austin: University of Texas.

Sellards, E. H., Adkins, W. S., and Plummer, F. B. 1933. *The Geology of Texas. vol. 1. Stratigraphy.* Univ. of Texas Bull., vol. 3232. Austin: University of Texas.

Shattuck, G. B. 1903. *Mollusca of the Buda Limestone.* U. S. G. S. Bull., vol. 205. Washington, D. C.: United States Geological Survey.

Sheldon, Robert A. 1979. *The Roadside Geology of Texas.* Missoula, Mont.: Mountain Press.

Shimer, H. W., and Shrock, R. R. 1944. *Index Fossils of North America.* New York: John Wiley and Sons.

Shumard, B. F. 1860. *Descriptions of New Cretaceous Fossils From Texas,* pp. 590-610. Academy of Sci. of St. Louis Transactions, vol. 1. St. Louis: Academy of Sci. of St. Louis.

— — —. 1861. *Descriptions of New Cretaceous Fossils From Texas,* pp. 188-205. Boston Society of Natural Hist. Proceedings, vol. 8. Boston: Boston Society of Natural History.

Smiser, Jerome S. 1936. Cretaceous echinoids from Trans-Pecos Texas. *Journal of Paleontology* 10: 449-80.

Stanton, T. W. 1947. Studies of some Comanche pelecypods and gastropods. Professional Paper no. 211. Washington, D. C.: United States Geological Survey.

Stenzel, H. B. 1939. Tertiary nautiloids from the Gulf coastal plain. In *Contributions to Geology, 1939,* pp. 731-96. Univ. of Texas Pub. 3945. Austin: University of Texas.

— — —. 1944. *Decapod Crustaceans from the Cretaceous of Texas,* pp. 401-477. Univ. of Texas Pub. 4401. Austin: University of Texas.

Stenzel, H. B., Krause, E. K., and Twining, J. T. 1957. *Pelecypoda from the Type Locality of the Stone City Beds (Middle Eocene) of Texas.* Univ. of Texas Pub. 5704. Austin: University of Texas.

Stephenson, Lloyd W. 1941. *The Larger Invertebrate Fossils of the Navarro Group (Exclusive of Corals and Crustaceans and Exclusive of the Fauna of the Escondido Formation).* Univ. of Texas Pub. 4101. Austin: University of Texas.

— — —. 1952. Larger invertebrate fossils of the Woodbine formation (Cenomanian) of Texas. Professional Paper no. 242. Washington, D. C.: United States Geological Survey.

Stevens, Margaret S. 1977. *Further Study of Castolon Local Fauna (Early Miocene), Big Bend National Park, Texas.* Pearce-Sellards Series, no. 28. Austin: Texas Memorial Museum, University of Texas.

Storrs, Glenn W. 1981. A review of occurrences of the Plesiosauria (Reptilia: Sauropterygia) in Texas with description of new material. Master's thesis, University of Texas at Austin.

Strimple, Harrell L., and Mapes, Royal H. 1977. A new Upper Pennsylvanian fissiculate blastoid from Texas. *Journal of Paleontology* 51: 357-62.

Student Geology Society. 1977. *Guidebook to the Geology of Travis County.* Austin: University of Texas.

Thomas, M. C. 1968. *Fossil Vertebrates — Beach and Bank Collecting for Amateurs.* Venice, Fla.: M. C. Thomas.

Thompson, Ida. 1984. *The Audubon Society Field Guide to the Fossils of North America.* New York: Alfred A. Knopf.

Walter, J. C., Jr. 1953. *Paleontology of the Rustler Formation, Culberson County, Texas.* Report of Investigations, no. 19. Austin: Bureau of Economic Geology, University of Texas.

Weller, J. Marvin. 1936. Carboniferous trilobite genera. *Journal of Paleontology* 10: 704-714.
– – –. 1944. Permian trilobite genera. *Journal of Paleontology* 18: 320-27.

Welton, Bruce J., Ph.D., and Farish, Roger F. 1993. *The Collector's Guide to Fossil Sharks and Rays from the Cretaceous of Texas,* Before Time Press, 5 Remington Dr., Lewisville, Texas 75067.

Whitney, F. L. 1911. *Fauna of the Buda Limestone.* Univ. of Texas Bull., vol. 184. Austin: University of Texas.
– – –. 1916. The Echinoidea of the Buda limestone. *Bulletin of Amer. Paleo. Soc.* 5: 85-120.

Whitney, Marion I. 1952. Some new pelecypoda from the Glen Rose formation of Texas. *Journal of Paleontology* 26: 697-707.
– – –. 1952. Some zone marker fossils of the Glen Rose formation of central Texas. *Journal of Paleontology* 26: 65-73.

Wilson, J. A. 1974. *Early Tertiary Vertebrate Faunas, Vieja Group and Buck Hill Group, Trans-Pecos Texas: Protoceratidae, Camelidae, Hypertragulidae.* Texas Memorial

Muse. Bull., no. 23. Austin: Texas Memorial Museum, University of Texas at Austin.

Winton, W. M. 1925. *The Geology of Denton County*, pp. 17-39, 47- 62. Univ. of Texas Bull., vol. 2544. Austin: University of Texas.

Winton, W. M., and Adkins, W. S. 1920. *The Geology of Tarrant County*. Univ. of Texas Bull., vol. 1931. Austin: University of Texas.

Winton, W. M., and Scott, Gayle. 1922. *The Geology of Johnson County*, pp. 27-32. Univ. of Texas Bull., vol. 2229. Austin: University of Texas.

Young, Keith. 1957. *Upper Albian (Cretaceous) Ammonoidea From Texas*. Report of Investigations, no. 28. Austin: Bureau of Economic Geology, University of Texas.

– – –. 1959. Techniques of mollusc zonation in Texas. *American Journal of Science* 257: 752-69.

– – –. 1963. *Upper Cretaceous Ammonites from the Gulf Coast of the United States*. Univ. of Texas Pub. 6304. Austin: University of Texas.

Index

Charles E. Finsley is curator emeritus of earth science at the Dallas Museum of Natural History, where he worked for more than 30 years. He received his B.S. degree from Wittenberg University and M.S. degree in secondary education and geology from the University of North Texas. He participated in excavations of the Trinity mammoth, several large Cretaceous fish, and the Heath mosasaur as well as the preparation of the Wise County tenontosaur dinosaur and the Fate, Texas, giant sea turtle. He is a charter member of the Dallas Paleontological Society and an associate member of the Society of Vertebrate Paleontology. He is also the author of *Discover Texas Dinosaurs*.